NO PLACE TO

HIDE

A BRAIN SURGEON'S LONG JOURNEY

HOME FROM THE IRAQ WAR

W. LEE WARREN, M.D.

US AIR FORCE (RET.)

ZONDERVAN®

ZONDERVAN

No Place to Hide
Copyright © 2014 by W. Lee Warren

This title is also available as a Zondervan ebook. Visit www.zondervan.com/ebooks.

Requests for information should be addressed to:

Zondervan, 3900 *Sparks Dr., Michigan 49546*

Library of Congress Cataloging-in-Publication Data

Warren, W. Lee, 1969–
        No place to hide : a brain surgeon's long journey home from the Iraq War /
Major W. Lee Warren, MD U.S. Air Force (Ret.).
            pages cm
        ISBN 978-0-310-33803-1 (hardcover)
            1. Warren, W. Lee, 1969– 2. Iraq War, 2003-2011—Medical care. 3. Iraq War, 2003-
2011—Personal narratives, American. 4. Joint Base Balad (Balad, Iraq) 5. Surgeons—
United States—Biography. I. Title.
        DS79.767.M43W37 2013
        956.7044'37092—dc23 [B]   2013033127

Any Internet addresses (websites, blogs, etc.) and telephone numbers in this book are
offered as a resource. They are not intended in any way to be or imply an endorsement
by Zondervan, nor does Zondervan vouch for the content of these sites and numbers
for the life of this book.

Cover design: Faceout Studio
Cover photography: Senior Airman Jeffrey Schultze, U.S. Air Force, www.afcent.af.mil
Interior design: David Conn

Printed in the United States of America

To Lisa

CONTENTS

FOREWORD

After the fall of Iraq in the spring of 2004, the Air Force Surgeon General determined Wilford Hall Medical Center would lead the 332nd Theater Hospital, Balad AB, Iraq. The base was the hub for logistics and air evacuation out of Iraq, and it was under fire (twenty-plus rocket attacks per week) when our medics arrived. Roughly three hundred medics, a mixture of Air Force, Army, and Australian physicians, nurses, allied professionals, and technicians required to save lives, were sent into harm's way to care for wounded warriors and Iraqi citizens injured in the war.

As Wilford Hall Commander, I handpicked the deploying commanders, and every medic knew their friends would follow and inherit their work. It was a harrowing time. We trained for this mission for years, honing skills and modernizing equipment sets, but now friends had to leave families for four to six months to risk life and limb. I will never forget the first two rotations' farewells in the auditorium—the dedication mixed with fear and excitement in the eyes of the medics, the tears of families, the concern of friends and supervisors seeing the deployers depart.

These medics were incredibly dedicated to saving lives. Their work with the city of San Antonio and surrounding twenty-two counties established a trauma network second to none. Before stepping into Iraq, nurses were added to the team to capture trauma data in a registry for continuous learning. An experienced trauma surgeon, the "trauma czar," was chosen to establish the flow for casualties that would optimize survival. In the first weeks these medics eradicated a new drug-resistant bacteria that was contaminating wounds. The survival rate for casualties rose from 90 to 98 percent, and the story began to circulate: "Why do Marines carry a twenty-dollar bill in their boot? So that, when wounded, they can tip the helicopter pilot to take them to Balad."

This book captures simply, eloquently, and passionately what it means to be a physician in time of war. Every person who goes to war is changed. My emotional response to these chapters made me pause to consider that our best efforts to support medics were inadequate. It captures the reality so many experienced and the difficulty of returning to everyday life. Over ten years of war, we safely air evacuated more than ninety thousand injured and ill from Iraq and Afghanistan—five thousand were the sickest of the sick. This very personal story captures the essence of what it takes to be a military physician and the challenge for our nation to reintegrate all who deploy to war.

Lt. Gen. (ret.) C. Bruce Green, MD
20th AF Surgeon General

PREFACE

The stories told in this book are all true, as experienced during my time in Iraq in 2004–2005. I obscured details in some of them, as well as the names of some doctors, nurses, and medics, to protect their anonymity. I also changed the names and identification numbers of all Iraqis and terrorists and all American soldiers with the exception of Paul Statzer, who gave me permission to use his name and story.

I changed some names for practical reasons. For example, there were three Todds with me in Iraq. To avoid having to say "Todd the neurosurgeon," or "Todd the therapist," or "Todd the heart surgeon," I simply renamed two of them.

Since there were so many different people on the worship team and so many different chaplains, I combined a lot of the people into two characters—John and Chaplain W.

I am sure that some of the events I discuss in the book would sound different if told from the perspective of other doctors at the base or the soldiers or terrorists or Iraqis who were part of my story. In the chaos of battlefield medicine, it was common for us to hear from a soldier that our patient was a terrorist, or that the injuries had been caused by an IED, only to find out later that the patient was actually a good guy or that the "IED" was actually a land mine. Chalk it up to the fog of war as well as to the differences in the accounts of any two witnesses describing the same event.

The dialog in this book was recreated from memory, and

since it has been eight years since I was in Iraq, I am sure that some of the dialog, while true to the spirit of the conversation it recreates, nevertheless expresses it in words that differ from those actually spoken.

Finally, I didn't include all 120 of my emails home in this book. I modified and combined some of them to make sense in the context of this book. They were also edited for grammar (somehow I managed to make a few grammatical errors while emailing from the combat zone), and names were changed where appropriate.

CHAPTER 1

MAINTAIN CONTROL, LEE

Sit on your body armor on the flight in."

"Excuse me?"

The C–130 pilot laughed. It was December 28, 2004, and we were in the Base Exchange, or BX, at Al Udeid Air Base in Qatar. He looked at his colleague and said, "The major here's never been in Iraq, sir."

The shorter one wore silver oak leaves on his flight suit — a lieutenant colonel. And like the pilot who'd just given me the advice, he also wore pilot's wings. He leaned closer and said, "He said you should sit on your Kevlar. As opposed to wearing it. The bullets come in from below."

They walked away chuckling, no doubt at the bewilderment on my face.

I checked my watch: 1600 hours. Four p.m. Eight hours to go.

I shrugged their advice off uneasily and continued checking off the last few items from the list of things that I'd been told — since arriving here two days before from San Antonio — I would need at my new deployment. Things that had not been on the official packing list but that others had found useful, such as earplugs for the plane ride I was waiting for.

The one that would deliver me to the war.

Earlier in the day I'd been told that my flight into Iraq would be delayed until tonight, due to a mortar attack on the runway at Balad Air Base, my destination.

Balad was also called Mortaritaville, because at that point in the war it was the most frequently mortared base in Iraq. An Army friend who'd been there had emailed me a couple of weeks before I left about dealing with mortars:

Dear Lee,

Don't worry too much about the mortars; that's like worrying about lightning. You can't control where they hit, and most of them don't blow up anyway. Worry more about the rockets.

His advice wasn't particularly comforting.

The two pilots I'd just spoken with in the BX delivered people like me to Balad and brought us out. I decided it would be wise to heed their advice about the body armor, although I didn't look forward to a four-hour flight sitting on the hard ceramic plates.

Later on at the DFAC—dining facility—I enjoyed enchiladas and tacos served by an Asian contractor in an Arab country. The jumble of out-of-place foods and faces struck me as funny, perhaps because I'd been traveling for two days and was filled with an equally jumbled mix of emotions. But as the time to report to the airfield approached, I stopped chuckling, regretting my decision to eat something spicy.

I wandered around Al Udeid, taking pictures of the strange sights—such as a Santa and snowman still on display from Christmas three days before. I spent a while in a lounge chair next to the Olympic-sized swimming pool, but since I couldn't swim in my DCU—desert camouflage uniform—I grew restless and moved on, my mind swirling with questions about what I was about to experience, what I'd just left behind, and what might be left of me in the end.

A chapel with an open front door seemed like a good place to sit awhile. I walked in and took off my shades, blinking in the dim light until my eyes adjusted. There in the front, shining like Excalibur in the stone, sat a guitar on a stand, with no one around to tell me no. I played and prayed and ordered my thoughts as I can do only when there are six strings under my fingers.

Far too soon, it was time to go. I stopped in the restroom to handle an acute case of nerves. Or Montezuma's revenge, more likely—a just repayment for my poor dining choice at such a stressful time. I washed my face in the sink and took a long look in the mirror.

My eyes held blood and tears, the result of sand in the Middle Eastern air and sorrow in my Midwestern heart. The man looking back at me didn't fit my self-image. I expected to see a two-hundred-five-pound blond brain surgeon. Instead, I saw a DCU-wearing Air Force major about to board a plane for the war in Iraq, wearing a leather holster and body armor and helmet like any soldier in the Army or Marines, looking ready for whatever may come. I knew better: The real me was a man driven nearly to his knees by life over the past few months, and he wasn't sure he could handle what he was about to face.

He was about to find out.

I gathered my things and myself and walked out into the surprisingly cold Qatari darkness to find the airport.

The military is infamous for its "hurry up and wait" bureaucratic inefficiencies, but I was surprised at how smoothly processing the orders of a hundred or so people and palletizing our duffel bags went. Maybe it was because I was distracted by filling out forms and helping pass bags around and checking gas masks and gear, but those were the fastest two hours I'd spent since I'd left the States the morning after Christmas. The last thing I did was sign my name on the wall of the hangar where we waited, a wall full of the signatures and call signs of hundreds of people who'd passed this way before. I found a little blank area and wrote:

Major W. Lee Warren, USAF, MC, 859 MSGS, Lackland AFB, TX. Combat Brain Surgeon.

And then it was time.

A master sergeant whose DCUs were far too starched and clean to have ever been in Iraq held a clipboard and shouted with a nasally New England accent, "Form a line, backs to the wall, wait for your name to be called." It sounded like, "FARMA LINE, BACKS TA THA WA, WATE FA YA NAYME TA BA CAA."

It must have been minutes, but it felt like years before I heard, "WARREN, WAYNE LEE JOONYA."

Like the others before me, I stepped forward, made a right face, and marched to the master sergeant.

He leaned close, squinted at my dog tags, and checked my name off his list. "Gaad bless ya, Maja."

"Thanks, Sergeant," I said, the last words I spoke in Qatar.

I stepped out of the hangar and followed the line of people to our waiting C–130. We filed in, followed instructions about how to fasten our belts, and were told not to use any flashlights until we were off the plane in Iraq. I sat on a hard metal bench shoulder-to-shoulder with the men next to me. No one spoke. About two feet in front of me was another bench, equally crowded with people facing us.

When we were all on board, a forklift drove on, carrying pallets of all of our gear. I watched as the loadmasters lashed down the pallets, fascinated with their skill and technique and wondering how many other people these guys had packed off to war—and how many of them had come home. When I realized that the pallets had now sealed off our only way off this airplane, I had another thought: *I'm really going to war.*

As soon as the door shut, the lights went out. The last thing I saw before darkness enveloped me was a stain on my DCU pants from the vanilla latte I'd spilled on my leg after I'd stopped at the coffee shop next to the DFAC on my way to the chapel. *Nice,* I thought, *I'm flying into battle smelling of Starbucks. Very GI Joe. No wonder the Army guys make fun of us—they call us the "Chair Force."*

I'd never been in the Middle East before landing at Al Udeid, and I wasn't impressed with its blowing sands, desert temperatures, ubiquitous brownness, and featureless terrain. But Al Udeid Air Base was the gateway to everything I would experience of war. I would land there again in four months, at the end of my deployment. By that time, my opinion of the base would have changed drastically. Al Udeid with its swimming pools, computer lounges, and coffee shops is a much nicer place the second time you land there because it's so much better than any place you've been since the first time.

The C–130's engines roared to life, and for the next few hours I heard nothing but those engines and my thoughts. Sleep was out of the question.

I thought about the things I was leaving behind: Three children who knew their dad was going to the war in Iraq but were blissfully unaware that their parents' sixteen-year-old marriage was essentially over. My only brother, struggling with a life-threatening stroke. And just three weeks before, my hero—my grandfather—had died.

Flying through the darkness, I realized that I was completely unknown on the airplane. Although my name tag said *Warren,* and one of the other passengers was the surgical tech Nate from my hospital back in the States, no one *knew* me. I was part of a bay full of cargo, implements of the war machine of the United States. I was *Warren, W, 45SF*—the Air Force code for neurological surgeon.

I can't adequately describe how lonely I felt then, one inventoried item in a plane full of war parts, each interchangeable when they were lost or broken or had served their appointed time. I thought about the bullets and missiles I was sure were about to blow us out of the sky, and for a few minutes I hyperventilated and thought I was having a panic attack. Then I heard an old voice in my head, telling me to get a grip.

The voice was a memory from Pittsburgh in 1996, from the operating room at Allegheny General Hospital. I was a second-year resident in neurosurgery, operating that day with Dr. Parviz Baghai, a Persian immigrant and brilliant surgeon who for some reason took me under his wing early in my training.

A man was brought to the emergency room after a car accident. His head scan showed a massive brain hemorrhage, so I called Dr. Baghai, who told me to take the patient to the OR and start draining the hemorrhage. Dr. Baghai arrived just as I was removing a large portion of the patient's skull. Then, using a scalpel, I began to open the dura, the brain's thick, leathery covering. The patient's brain rapidly swelled out of the confines of his skull, something I had read about but never seen. I didn't know what to do—the brain was squeezing out of the dural opening like toothpaste. I said, "This guy's going to die."

Dr. Baghai, just slipping his hand into his glove as the circulating nurse tied his gown, reached over and dipped his hand into a bowl of sterile saline solution on the instrument table. "Watch this," he said.

Dr. Baghai placed his wet hand on the protruding brain and firmly *pushed it back into the man's head.*

"Put your hand on mine, gently," he said.

I placed my hand over Dr. Baghai's, gauging the pressure he applied. He looked at me. His brown eyes, all I could see of his face, held a hint of anticipation.

With our hands still in place holding the brain, Dr. Baghai took a small catheter in his other hand, closed his eyes for a moment, and then slipped the catheter between our fingers, deep into the man's brain. He drained about 20 ccs of cerebrospinal fluid, which relaxed the brain enough for it to stay within the head. Dr. Baghai then calmly removed the hematoma, closed the wound, and stepped away from the table.

"Never let the brain roar out at you like that," he said. "Be prepared for swelling, and handle it immediately or prevent it. You have to maintain control, Lee."

The patient did not die. He eventually fully recovered. Every time I have seen Parviz Baghai in the fifteen years since, he says the same thing in his crisp British English: "Do you still think that guy's going to die?"

The plane's vibrations began to seriously challenge my wisdom in having both coffee and Mexican food before the flight. It was utterly dark, I was utterly miserable, and I couldn't stop hearing Parviz Baghai's advice, "You have to maintain control."

Control had been the biggest issue in my life for the past several years. During the one-hundred-twenty-hour work weeks of my residency, I had acknowledged to myself that any semblance of a loving relationship at home had become playacting, purely for the benefit of the kids. That was the only thing keeping our marriage together—that, and the teaching of my parents' church that the only thing more sure to send you straight to hell than outright blasphemy was divorce. I had no tools to deal with interpersonal conflict because I was raised to believe that if you were really a Christian you never fought, you were always happy, and you never had problems. So instead of trying to discuss my feelings, I just smiled. Psychiatrists call this incongruity, when you display one emotion and feel another. In retrospect, it would have been frustrating and painful to be married to me during those years.

I satisfied my need for control at work. But by learning to have a white-knuckled grip on every aspect of my life outside my home, I became a miserable person. Only nobody knew it. I kept my Happy Christian with a Perfect Marriage face in a jar by the door like Eleanor Rigby, wore it when anyone could see, and never talked about it.

And so as I heard the echoes of the advice of my mentor, Dr. Baghai, about maintaining control, I was hurtling through the air, strapped into an airplane on a nonstop flight into the unknown, and I was terrified.

I felt nauseated. I really regretted the coffee now, and we were only halfway through the flight. I reminded myself to breathe. I checked my pulse along with my faith: heart racing, faith plummeting. In fact, my faith had been on life support recently, and my prayers over the past few months had seemed weak and ineffective. I had not stopped believing in God, but I was almost convinced that he no longer believed in me.

The guy to my left was young, probably twenty or so, much taller than my five-foot-nine. He had huge arms; I figured he was a mechanic or something that required great strength. *He's a lot stronger than me*, I thought. *Why are they sending a couch potato like me off to war?*

To my right was a man about my size. I had noticed his rank before the lights went out: lieutenant colonel. He had the look of a professional, and even in the darkness his calm presence told me he was less scared than I was. *That makes no sense*, I thought. *How can I feel someone else's fear level in the dark?*

I realized what I was doing. My old insecurities were bubbling to the surface, and my thoughts were just a symptom. I've always secretly believed that everyone around me was smarter than me, better at the task at hand. I think this is one of the reasons I've been successful professionally—I've been so afraid that I would fail and that everyone would finally realize I wasn't really smart enough to be there. The joke would be on me. Now, on the C–130, I found myself doing it again.

A wild, erratic movement of the aircraft, followed by another, and then another in quick succession, shook me out of my thoughts. I had been told by other C–130 pilots that they frequently took ground fire when flying through Iraq, and that they made evasive maneuvers as they began to descend prior to landing. Even with the warning, I wasn't ready for this.

Were we being shot at? Was someone trying to kill me? I didn't know—but I do know that the pilot gave us a ride I've never experienced on any roller coaster. Several people vomited, and the smell of whatever they had eaten filled the cabin.

When we finally landed, we taxied for what seemed like hours. My heart was beating out of my chest as I imagined stepping off the plane into a hail of bullets as the base was over-run by screaming, bearded Al Qaeda terrorists on black horses, their scimitars and AK–47s flashing in the light of tracer and machine-gun fire. That was the first time I realized how long it had been since I'd slept, and I reminded myself that I was landing on a very secure American military installation and not in the middle of some movie about Ali Baba and the Forty Thieves.

The engines kept running as the C–130's rear door lowered, and I could see the headlights of a forklift driving on to remove the pallets of gear. Someone climbed on board and instructed us to stand and form two lines. We followed him out of the plane and into Iraq. I looked down in the darkness and saw my boots on the ground of a foreign nation at a time of war.

I was hungry, needed to use the bathroom, and felt terribly alone. But at the same time, I was fascinated that the Bible says God chose this very area—the zone between the Tigris and Euphrates Rivers—as the place to begin human history. The canopy of stars twinkling above me would have looked the same to Adam and Eve peering up from Eden.

My second thought was that Iraqis had built the concrete runway on which I stood. Americans had fought to capture this base at the start of the war last year.

Three buses waited on the Tarmac. I thought they were for us. They were not. As we approached, we were ordered to form two lines and wait. I could see the same forklift loading gear onto the plane from which we just exited, and as we got to the buses, I saw that they were filled with fully armored and armed troops. They looked so young and innocent, but their faces conveyed no emotion; they were robots with grenades and machine guns, their eyes clear and jaws set. The plane that had delivered me safely to the base was about to take these robot-soldiers off to some less-safe place, like a bus hauling one person home and another to work. The engines never even shut down.

Other buses arrived for us. We would be driven to a processing center and checked in to the war, as packages might be processed in customs before delivery to their final destinations. I looked back at the C–130, now filled with troops on their way to battle, and watched the ramp retract, sealing them in. It reminded me that I was now here, for better or for worse, my ride about to depart and the path I'd just walked getting farther away.

My bus drove into the coming dawn. I heard in my head: *You have to maintain control, Lee.*

Good luck with that, I thought.

CHAPTER 2

JUST A LITTLE BOMB; NOBODY DIED

The bus delivered us to a gravel parking lot in front of a cinder-block building sometime around five in the morning. In the light of the street lamps I could see a metal sign — *Welcome to Balad Air Base* — on a high chain-link fence topped with razor wire. We walked single file into the building, which turned out to be a classroom. A low grumble went through the crowd. I suspect we all had the same thought: *Are you kidding me? We travel for thirty-six hours and you're going to make us sit through a lecture?*

I smelled coffee and noticed a long table along one wall. Cold muffins in plastic wrappers, room-temperature bottled water, and lukewarm coffee from several pump-top containers made up our first meal in Iraq. I ate a lemon-and-poppy-seed muffin like it was manna and quail straight from the Lord.

After a few minutes, a tall, tired-looking senior master sergeant walked in and cleared her throat. She was holding a clipboard, her hair in a tight bun, and she yawned while she waited for us all to find seats. She clicked a key on her computer and a slide appeared on the wall behind her. She nodded to an airman in the corner, who turned off the overhead lights.

"Welcome to Balad. We have a few things to cover, and then you'll each meet someone from your duty station to take you to your quarters."

We learned that the Army had another name for Balad Air Base; they called it Logistical Support Area (LSA) Anaconda, and it was the largest US base in Iraq. We were but a few of the thirty-six thousand military and civilian personnel stationed there.

She continued, "Now let's talk about mortar attacks."

The lecture deteriorated from there. A room full of glassy-eyed, sleep-deprived people heard about Alarm Reds, bunkers, sand vipers and scorpions, the perils of camel spiders, and how to avoid starting international incidents by staying out of the base mosque. After filling our heads with visions of all the ways we might get ourselves killed here, we experienced the excitement of filling out forms. When the bureaucracy fest was finally complete, we were dismissed. We filed outside and saw representatives from each duty station. The man waiting on me was yet another sergeant—where were they getting all these sergeants? He threw my gear into a Humvee and drove me to the hospital—my duty station—to check in.

How much longer before I could go to my quarters and sack out?

We drove through a gate, the Humvee on the rough road bouncing my helmeted head against the door a couple of times. Everything smelled like dirt—although it probably smelled better than I did in my sweaty, three-days-without-a-shower DCUs. We stopped in a dark gravel parking lot in front of a group of tents. One had a red cross on the door and a sign, "Emergency Department."

"Here we are, Major," the sergeant said. He waved for me to follow, then walked through the door with the red cross on it. This "group of tents," I suddenly realized, was the hospital.

I stepped over a two-by-four plywood threshold and saw my first casualties of the Iraq War.

Wood-and-canvas stretchers on metal-frame tables were lined up along the tent walls, four on each side. The nearest bed held a naked brown man, his left arm wrapped in bloody gauze. Eyes open, he was staring at the ceiling, but he wasn't moving. A nurse, wearing a purple shirt, DCU bottoms, combat boots, body armor, and helmet, worked on him, her back to me. I stepped close enough to see around her. She was inserting a Foley catheter into his bladder. The patient's chest, belly, and left thigh were covered in small cuts and larger gashes, as if someone had swiped a weed eater over the left side of his body. His neck and face were covered with burns. When I looked where the nurse was working, I winced — and prayed that he'd already had all of his children, because he certainly wasn't going to have any more.

Someone had written on his forehead in black marker a number, 1856.

The nurse found her target, and bloody urine filled the catheter bag. She looked up at me from her work — but really, she was looking through me. Her green eyes blinked so slowly I wondered if she was falling asleep, and her shoulders sagged under the weight of the Kevlar. She was chewing gum.

"Somebody call the urologist," she said to no one in particular.

I looked around. The other beds were filled with equally bloody and burned brown people, but all medical personnel standing by the beds were busy attending their own patients. The sergeant with me said, "I'll go get him, ma'am."

He crossed the tent and disappeared through another door. I looked back at the nurse, who was now wiping blood from the man's face.

"What happened to him?" I asked.

She looked at me and chewed for a second, then answered

as if I had asked her about the weather. "Just a little bomb. Nobody died."

I pointed at the 1856 on his forehead. "What does that mean?"

She pushed her helmet up with the back of her gloved hand. "That's his name."

I leaned closer, thinking maybe it was written in Arabic and I'd misread it. Nope, definitely just a number. "His name?"

She snapped off her gloves and dropped them on the bed. She yawned and rubbed her eyes. "I'm sorry, I've been on duty for eighteen hours. You must be new. These terrorists never have any ID on them. We use the numbers to keep track of their care until we find out who they really are."

Terrorist? I looked down at the semiconscious man. He obviously had some type of head injury to go along with the burns, not to mention the nightmare in his groin and the bloody bandage over the stump of a wrist where a hand used to be. He looked to be maybe twenty or so, and he had a kind face. At least the right side looked kind; the left side was pretty torn up. I'm not sure what I thought the first terrorist I ever saw would look like, but I know I didn't expect him to be a skinny college-age kid. He looked like the guy who delivered pizza to my house in San Antonio. His blood looked like everybody else's I'd ever seen.

The sergeant returned, along with two other men wearing hospital scrubs. They stopped at the bedside and the sergeant pointed at me. "This is Major Warren, the new neurosurgeon."

The red-haired man on the left was pulling on latex gloves. He reached down to the patient's groin and explored the wounds there. "I'm Bob," he said without looking at me. He shook his head and grimaced. "Great, he blew them off. Debbie, tell surgery to get ready for an orchiectomy." He looked up at me, puffed out his cheeks, and shot his gloves into the trash can. "Nice to meet you," he said as he turned and walked back from where he'd come.

The other man was thin, about my height, with a shaved head. He extended a hand. "Hi, I'm Pete. I'm your partner. Welcome to Iraq."

I shook Pete's hand. His pale-blue eyes were bloodshot and looked as if they'd seen things they wished they could forget.

Pete pulled a penlight out of his pocket and looked at 1856's pupils. "Pupils aren't dilated. Probably just a concussion. Debbie, get him a head CT after Bob puts the boys back together." He beckoned to me as he turned to leave. "Come on, Lee, I was just about to make rounds."

The sergeant held up his hand. "Major, Doc here's been traveling for three days. Maybe hold off on the tour until tomorrow?"

Pete looked at his watch. "Give us fifteen minutes, Sarge. I'll just show him around a little."

I followed Pete down the hall and into another tent. This one had about twenty stretchers, and the people on them were different. The first patient was a large black man whose burned and blistered face was covered in Vaseline gauze to keep the bandages from sticking to his charred skin. "This is the ward where we keep the Americans before they medevac them out. Airman D here hurt his back trying to get out of his Humvee when they hit an IED. He's going to Walter Reed tomorrow."

Most of the patients were asleep; the few who were awake looked at me without speaking. All were bandaged in various ways, and some had casts or head dressings. I had seen the war wounded before, when the ones from home finally made it to Wilford Hall, the Air Force hospital in San Antonio where I worked. By the time they got home, they were clean, healing, and looked pretty much like any other patient.

Then, when I was deployed to Germany in early 2004, I'd seen them a little closer. Stable enough to fly out of Iraq but not enough to cross the Atlantic, some patients stopped at Landstuhl Regional Medical Center, an Army hospital. There they had a faraway look, smelled earthy, and didn't sleep well. Even in Germany, though, I'd only caught a whiff of what they would look like here. These were men who'd recently been boys but would never be again. They smelled like sorrow and fear and fire, and they all looked like they wanted to go home.

Pete checked a couple of charts, gave some orders to a nurse, and led me back to the sergeant. "Get some rest, Lee. You'll need it."

The sergeant drove me to a long row of ten-foot-square metal cubes, walked me to one of them, and handed me a set of keys, a broom, and a dustpan. In the gathering daylight I could see piles of sandbags stacked about four feet high lining the outside of the cubes. He pointed out the Porta-Potty just outside my room, and instructed me to report to the hospital commander at 0730 the following morning. I had about twenty-four hours to rest.

Beyond the departing sergeant, I saw the first rays of sunlight starting to probe the horizon. It was the dawn of my war.

I dropped my body armor to the floor and flopped onto the bed with its one-inch thick mattress, oblivious to the probing steel springs. On later nights I would try to find solutions to their merciless interruption of my sleep. But after three days of travel and the stress of the C–130 flight, they didn't bother me at all. I did not care that it was the beginning of my first day in Iraq; I had to close my eyes.

Several hours later, I woke to the sound of sirens, reminiscent of my Oklahoma hometown's tornado warning alarm. According to the lecture we'd been forced to sit through on arrival at Balad Air Base, this was an Alarm Red, which meant the base was under mortar or rocket attack. I remembered the sergeant's parting words as he left me in my trailer: "Major, tomorrow I'll give you a tour on our way to the hospital. Remind me to show you where the bunkers are." Not knowing exactly what to do, I covered myself with my body armor, donned my helmet, and fell back asleep. I woke up a few times during that day, ate power bars and snack crackers I'd brought in my duffel bags, organized my room, and finally went back to bed again.

Since none of the enemy's projectiles found their way onto my trailer that evening, I slept through the night. On my first morning as a participant in the Iraq War, sleep finally gave way to an acute awareness of how badly I smelled. Three days of travel without a shower, followed by a day of terror-filled, sweaty sleep, produced a body odor offensive enough to motivate me to head out into the unknown in search of a shower.

Still dressed in my dirty DCUs, I put on my boots and stepped outside to search for the nearest facilities. I walked down the sidewalk in a monochrome world. Everywhere I looked, I saw one hue — brown. Brown dirt, brown buildings, brown vehicles, and brown uniforms. The constant desert wind carried blinding sand, hiding the green of scattered trees and patches of grass and frustrating the dawn sky's attempt at blue. If this was the place God chose for the garden of Eden, why was the predominant color so boring?

Three blocks later I found the shower trailers. Two rectangular cubes sat on wooden decking, one marked "Males" and the other "Females." A huge plastic drum sat between them, connected to the trailers by pipes. Foot-high block letters warned us that this was "Non-Potable. Do not drink."

Signs inside the trailer reminded me I was in the desert, and water for showers was in short supply. I was to use the water for no more than sixty seconds at a time. This is known as a *combat shower*. I shaved at a sink with two faucets, one of which had a sign, "Do not use this water for brushing teeth." I wondered what types of bacteria were found in water deemed safe enough to wash with but not to have in my mouth.

A few minutes later I emerged from the trailer, shivering in the cool morning air and smelling more like myself. I managed to find my way back to my room, where I put on a fresh uniform, ate two candy bars I found in my backpack, and opened my laptop computer to write about my journey so far.

A knock on the door announced the arrival of the sergeant; it was time to formally check in at the hospital. When I asked about email, he said, "It'll take about three days to get your account set up—I'll take care of it."

We walked the one hundred yards to the parking lot and his Humvee. Along the way, he pointed out a long, rectangular row of concrete tubes, about five feet high and four feet across. "The bunkers," he said. "You'll find them all over the base. When you hear the Alarm Red sirens, put on your gear and head to the nearest bunker until they sound the All Clear."

Just past the bunkers were sand-covered blue Porta-Potties and a trailer marked *Laundry*. "Take your dirty clothes there. The Filipino contractors will do them for a couple of bucks."

I thought, *I have a laundry service in Iraq. I didn't have a laundry service in San Antonio.*

Since last night's Alarm Reds hadn't amounted to anything, as far as I could tell, I was about to ask the sergeant if the bunkers were really necessary. Before I could speak, he pointed to a trailer just past the laundry—still standing, but mostly destroyed. "A mortar hit there last week in the middle of the night. No one was killed, thank God." He continued, "Most of these mortars have about a thirty-foot kill radius."

We were about fifty yards from my room.

I looked at the laundry, where twenty or so people stood in line for their clothes. All of them were within thirty feet of the blown-up trailer, meaning that if the mortar had landed in the daytime, many people would likely have died. I checked the strap on my helmet, but it didn't make me feel any safer.

We climbed into a Humvee for the five-block drive to the hospital. As I looked out the window, the sergeant played tour guide, pointing out items of interest. Balad was a bustling, noisy military city of over thirty thousand people, ten times larger than my hometown of Broken Bow, Oklahoma. I saw defunct Iraqi tanks, rusted airplanes, concrete bunkers everywhere, and a huge airfield. The sergeant explained that Balad was Iraq's largest air base under Hussein's rule, and now LSA Anaconda was the Army's major supply and distribution center for the war. Convoys left here every day to carry the goods of warfare to the troops—convoys that would face IEDs and other perils along the way. I didn't know it yet, but the attacks on those convoys would supply me with many of the patients I would treat, and many of the nightmares I still have.

We pulled up to the hospital and I stepped out of the Humvee, excited about starting my new job as a combat brain surgeon—an excitement that was equal parts fear and anticipation. The morning sun cut through the sandy haze in the sky, slightly diminishing the monotony of the one-color world in which I now lived.

How could I feel so blue in such a brown place?

CHAPTER 3

EVERYWHERE I LOOKED, I SAW DIRT

Here you go, Major. Good luck."
The sergeant dropped me off at the gate to the 332nd Air Force Theater Hospital and drove away with a wave. A guard checked my ID and waved me through. I remembered how I felt when my mom left me at kindergarten on the first day—how I had watched her leave, wondering what would happen. I'd felt scared, excited, and a little tearful—just as I felt right now. But today I thought, *Shake it off, Lee. It's showtime.*

The walk from the gate to the hospital was about a hundred yards. I looked around the compound as I walked and felt like I'd stepped onto the set of the television series *M.A.S.H.*, complete with a jeep-turned-ambulance with a red cross on its sides and a canvas stretcher leaning on its hood. A couple of nurses stood around a trash barrel, smoking with a group of weary-looking soldiers. A signpost held markers labeled *Balad 3 Miles, San Antonio 7,400 Miles*. Another sign said *Days Since Last Mortar Attack—3*. The word *Days* had been scratched out and replaced with *Hours*.

A Humvee was parked inside the gate. A soldier stood on its roof, working on the machine gun mounted in a turret.

Another soldier was leaning on the open door with his head hanging down. A can of Coke sat on the roof above his head. As I approached, the private on the roof jumped down. He landed facing me. Our eyes met, but he looked right through me.

"Hello, Private," I said. "How's it going?"

He shook his head as if I'd startled him. He felt his chest and then his helmet with both hands.

"We hit an IED a few minutes ago."

I stepped closer to him and noticed for the first time that the side of the Humvee contained hundreds of little dents in its armor. There was blood on the turret where the private had been standing.

"Are you guys okay?" I asked.

He looked at the ground. "Our sergeant was in the turret. He's in surgery right now. We just got this new armor last week, or we'd all be dead."

I didn't know what to say, so I just stood there for a second as the reality of what he'd said penetrated my brain. It was the first time I truly understood that just a few hundred feet away was a gate that led out into the real war. These young men had been not far from the base when they were attacked.

"I'll go check on your sergeant," I said. The private thanked me and leaned back against the Humvee, digging in his pockets. He produced a cigarette and lit it. I noticed a little twitch in his right eye.

His partner was still leaning in the Humvee's open door, looking down. He never turned around.

I stepped around the Humvee and headed to the hospital.

The noise level increased, and it occurred to me that I hadn't heard silence since I'd arrived in Iraq. Wind, the distant *whump* of an approaching helicopter, the roar of a passing transport plane overhead, Humvees in the street—all these sounds jumbled together to provide a soundtrack to life in the war.

I studied the hospital as I approached it. It sat on a square concrete slab about two hundred feet on each side. The complex was composed of several tents arranged around a central, larger one. These were not little Boy Scout camping tents— they were about ten feet tall and built on wooden frames, like houses with canvas walls. The tents were connected by short walkways made in the same way, so you could go from one tent to another without going outside. At several points around the compound I could see short metal cubes that looked like my quarters, only sturdier. The tent hospital seemed to engulf the front end of each of the cubes, like someone had cut a doorway from the side of the tent and attached the cubes. I passed one on my way in and saw *CT SCANNER, FIELD, PORTABLE, US ARMY* written in black stencil on the side.

The emergency department was in the large central tent, and its double doors were marked with red crosses. It sat at the end of a wide concrete walkway connected to a helipad large enough for several helicopters to land at once. Two teenaged airmen played Frisbee on the sidewalk. I watched them for a moment, suddenly surprised at the ability of kids to relax in any situation. One of the airmen made a wild throw, and the Frisbee flew over his friend's head toward me. I bent to pick it up and noticed that the concrete was stained in several places. Dark red trails along the sidewalk told the tale of other days, when the pathway served a much more somber purpose. I flicked the Frisbee back to the airmen and walked into the hospital.

The six beds were empty. Clean white sheets gave no hint of the wins and losses those beds had seen before. I wondered what had happened to 1856.

"Good morning. You smell better."

I looked up and saw Pete. He shook my hand. "Glad you're here. The Australian you replaced left five days ago, and I've been on call ever since."

He looked like it. "Hey, do you know what happened to the sergeant they just brought in?" I asked.

"The IED attack?"

A surgeon walked toward us, blood on his scrubs, his mask hanging in front of his chest. Pete said, "Hey, Vic, how's that gunner doing?"

Vic stopped, pulled the cap off his head, and looked sideways. "Lost him. I'm going out to tell his squad now." He walked toward the door.

I wondered what I would say when it was my turn.

+

After breakfast and a brief introduction to the hospital commander, Pete took me on a tour.

The first stop was a dirty tent containing a desk with a computer, a couple of chairs, and a worn-out couch currently occupied by a snoring man wearing hospital scrubs.

"This is the surgeons' lounge. You can check email, hang out, crash on the sofa," Pete said.

"I could never sleep there," I said, thinking of the neck ache that poor guy would have when he awoke.

Pete laughed and punched my shoulder. "We'll see."

Next to the couch was a scraggly plastic Christmas tree, complete with blinking lights and tinsel. The walls were adorned with numerous crayon-drawn posters from elementary schools back home, thanking us for taking care of the troops and reminding us we were all heroes. A television set in the corner tuned to CNN was broadcasting a story about the developing problem of improvised explosive devices in Iraq. I thought of the dead sergeant and the shaken-up soldiers in the parking lot and wondered how Vic's conversation had gone.

Pete introduced me to several other members of the team

hanging out in the TV area, about to watch a college football bowl game. There were five general surgeons, two chest and vascular specialists, three orthopedists, an ear-nose-and-throat doctor, an ophthalmologist, and an oral surgeon. Overall, we had something like thirty doctors, fifty nurses, and another hundred or so technicians and support personnel.

The urologist I'd met over 1856's bed was there too.

"Hey, Bob. How'd it go with 1856?"

Bob looked away from the television and raised his left eyebrow. "Who? Oh, the guy from the other night. He's okay, going to Abu Ghraib soon." He turned back to the TV.

I nudged Pete and said, "Abu Ghraib? Isn't that the place where—"

"Yeah, the prison you heard about last year. When the bad guys are well enough to leave here they go to prison, usually Abu Ghraib."

The scandal at the prison had been world news in early 2004, less than a year ago. Horrible abuse of prisoners at the hands of poorly trained and undersupervised guards had led to several US soldiers going to prison themselves, and at least one general officer had been stripped of command and demoted. Ironic, I thought. Iraqi terrorists blow something up, get arrested, wind up in prison, are mistreated by their captors, and the story of their abuse becomes fuel for the recruitment of even more desperate insurgents from all over the world, some of whom end up in our hospital and eventually at Abu Ghraib. A cycle of sorrow that starts and ends with hate. I remembered Jesus' words: *Love your enemy.* If anybody in that cycle had tried that, maybe some of these guys wouldn't be here.

Pete sat at the computer to check his email. I sat on a chair and tried to strike up a conversation with the other surgeons. No one was very talkative. I felt like a replacement soldier in an old war movie: A few of the squad's veterans are killed in battle.

In the next scene, rookies arrive to replace the fallen men, and nobody talks to them. The seasoned troops are suspicious of the newbies, afraid to get close to them.

When the surgeons around the TV said something to each other, I felt their camaraderie and brotherhood. These guys had been through a lot together, saved and lost lives together, been there for each other. And they were going home in a few days. I was an outsider to them. They were the seniors about to graduate, and I was the pesky freshman who'd somehow made the team. Pete was different. Maybe it was his personality, or maybe it was because we shared a specialty, but he accepted me and took care of me.

From the surgeons' lounge, Pete walked me into the central area of the operating room. Plywood panels framed the thresholds between the lashed-together tents. I suspect that my jaw dropped when I saw the area in which I was supposed to perform lifesaving brain surgery. A forty-foot square contained several desks and computers, shelves full of surgical supplies, refrigerators storing IV fluids and medicines. In the corners were four simple foot-controlled washbasins. These were the scrub sinks where we would wash our hands before surgery.

Everywhere I looked, I saw dirt. Dirt on the walls, on the floors, on the desks. How could I possibly operate here without infecting all my patients?

Pete pointed out the heavy plastic sheets hanging like drapes in each doorway. Their purpose, he said, was to keep the dust and sand from blowing through the hospital, keeping the air cleaner. "You should have seen this place before we took it over from the Army," he said. "We've cleaned it up a lot."

The Army had run a combat support hospital (CSH) at Balad until the Air Force was assigned to take over the bulk of the medical mission for Iraq in the fall of 2004. The Air Force assigned the 332nd Expeditionary Medical Group (EMDG) to turn the CSH into the 332nd Air Force Theater Hospital, a small part of the 332nd Air Expeditionary Wing. The 332nd had a history dating back to World War II. The famous Tuskegee Airmen, the "Red Tail Fliers," were the first all African-American fighter units. They painted the tails of their P-51 Mustangs red, and had the best record in history of protecting bomber pilots on raids over Germany. We were now standing in Iraq, in a tent hospital bearing the same insignia, part of a legacy of people assigned to save others; we were the Red Tail Medics. Pete was the first Air Force neurosurgeon deployed to the war. I was the second.

"Come on, let me show you where the action happens," Pete said. I followed him through another threshold into a twenty-foot-square metal box that contained two surgery tables about five feet apart, with two anesthesia machines, two sets of surgery lights, X-ray boxes, and IV poles. Although most of the hospital was made of tents, the operating rooms were hardened, designed to withstand mortar attacks. With four of these ORs, we would be able to operate on as many as eight patients simultaneously.

Walking around the hospital with Pete, my inner camera lens began to zoom in a bit, and I noticed that this place was highly organized. Once I got past the austerity and un-hospital-likeness of the environment, I could see that everything here was carefully thought out.

In one low-ceilinged metal cube, I saw racks of neurosurgery supplies. We had to anticipate needs, Pete said, because it would take a week or more to receive new items after we placed an order. If we ran out of something, we would just have to make do until the next airplane arrived.

In San Antonio, I could *demand* a particular brand of gloves if I didn't like what was available, and someone would scurry around until they found what I thought I needed. A three-ring binder on the shelf at my hospital, labeled "Dr. Warren's

Preferences," contained detailed instructions and specifics on what I used for every type of surgery I performed.

I came by it honestly; neurosurgeons are famous for being prima donnas in the operating room. We throw fits if we don't have a particular instrument available right away. In fact, some of my colleagues have been known to toss instruments across the room if they don't work properly or aren't what the surgeon had in mind. At a hospital cafeteria in Pittsburgh, I once overheard a group of scrub technicians discussing the worst experiences they'd ever had in an operating room. One of them laughed and said, "Working for those perfectionist neurosurgeons, hands down."

When Pete showed me the instrument sets we would use in surgery, I realized that a prima donna, perfectionist attitude would not work in Iraq. There were only four sets of sterile brain surgery instruments available, the contents of which had been chosen by a surgeon years before and had been sitting in a warehouse waiting for a war ever since. It took three hours to clean, process, sterilize, and repackage the instruments for their next use, and we didn't have backups for most of the instruments. So if multiple patients arrived at once, so that several operations had to be done in rapid succession, we could run out of sterile brain-surgery-specific tools. I would have to learn to work with whatever was available.

In the middle of the hallway Pete led me down next, a low spot had standing water, and on either side of it were muddy footprints. There were water stains on the walls. We were in the Iraqi rainy season, Pete explained, and when it rained, as it had two days before, parts of the hospital flooded.

Just past the mud hole in the hall sat the intensive care unit. This tent featured parachute cords stretched along the walls. These cords replaced the fancy racks and poles found in more upscale ICUs, but held the same monitors and IV infusion pumps we'd had in the ICU back in San Antonio.

No sooner had we entered the room than we heard an explosion that seemed to come from somewhere close by. I dove to the floor—then looked up to see that the others had reacted only by calmly walking to the racks of body armor. The ICU nurses and techs put on their armor and helmets and resumed working.

Pete extended a hand and smiled. "Let's go to the locker room and get our armor. That was a mortar. You'll get used to it." A few seconds later, the Alarm Red siren began to wail, announcing to the rest of the base that someone had just tried to blow up the hospital. I realized that if I were to die from a mortar or rocket attack, the one that killed me would probably trigger the alarm to save someone else. The siren would be a clanging eulogy for the dead Lee Warren.

Protected by Kevlar, we returned to the ICU. The unit was full of patients, stratified by their degree of injury. Lying in one bed was a burned-up American soldier missing a leg and an eye. In the next bed over lay an Al Qaeda terrorist who'd been shot while detonating the bomb that had caused the American's injuries. No separation, no delivery of different care based on a patient's nationality or actions. The nurses and doctors and techs simply delivered care to the injured—injured who'd been brought here by medics willing to risk themselves to bring in the wounded, even the bad guys.

Pete pointed out the terrorist. "Mind changing his head dressing? I've got to get the transfer paperwork done so the American can fly to Landstuhl tonight."

I pulled on exam gloves and reached for the man's head. As I laid my hands on his blood-soaked bandage, he startled from his morphine-induced sleep. I don't know what I'd thought I would feel when I first touched a terrorist. Did I expect them to be slimy, reptilian, maybe have horns like the Devil? When

I looked down on the young man, I simply saw a person. His skin felt warm, his blood was sticky, and his carotid pulse felt just like the other thousands I'd felt. He had brown skin, brown eyes, and brown hair, with bandages on his head and arms and abdomen from the operations that had saved his life. Groggy from morphine and brain injury, he looked up at me with an unsteady gaze. He had 1841 written on his chest, a tube in his nose, and a catheter in his penis. How had he ended up here? I wasn't wondering about the bomb-to-Black Hawk-to-Balad pathway, but the philosophical one. What had led him to risk his own life to take someone else's?

Once I'd removed the man's bandage, I cleaned his wound and learned something about Pete. The man's scalp wound was jagged and complex, and had required hundreds of sutures to repair. The knots were all squared, the wound edges were precisely aligned, and the tissue was healing beautifully. It was perfect, the surgical equivalent of a well-played symphony.

I looked up at Pete, who was now standing across from me. "Nice work," I said. "I'm not sure I could have put that together as well."

Pete gave an aw-shucks grin and shoved his hands in his pockets. "We'll see."

In the tent next to the ICU was a makeshift nursing unit, with twenty or so cots holding mostly Iraqi and insurgent patients and very few Americans. Pete explained that the Americans rarely made it to this ward because as soon as they were stable enough to fly, they were transported to Landstuhl, Germany, before the flight to Walter Reed Army Hospital back in America. The Iraqis and other non-Coalition patients were stabilized in the ICU and then had to be cared for until they were well enough to be discharged home or to an Iraqi civilian medical facility (although there were very few of those left at the time) or, in the case of insurgents and terrorists, sent to a military prison.

One of the Iraqi patients in the ward was a man Pete had operated on the day before I arrived. His head was wrapped in white gauze, with a wire coming out the top. The wire was an intracranial pressure (ICP) monitor, which is used to track the pressure inside the brain. A sign on the wall above the patient read, "No bone on the left. Handle head carefully."

I pointed at the sign. "What happened, another IED?"

Pete shook his head. "He's not a war victim, just a bad driver. He wrecked his car. Lucky for him, a bunch of American Marines were nearby. They called for a Black Hawk, and the medics brought him in."

I thought about this while Pete looked at the chart. American soldiers in a war zone stopped what they were doing and put themselves at risk to help a civilian and get him to the military hospital where a military brain surgeon saved his life. Then they continued their real missions.

"I didn't know we were allowed to treat civilians," I said.

He smiled. "We treat everybody. We're Americans."

Pete showed me the patient's initial scan, which showed only mild swelling of the brain. Pete had opted for immediate surgery and had performed an operation known as a decompressive craniectomy. This procedure involves removing a huge piece of a person's skull, which allows the brain to swell outward under the soft scalp instead of swelling inside toward the brainstem. Neurosurgeons have performed this procedure for many years — usually on patients who have failed all other measures for controlling their intracranial pressure.

Once the brain swelling goes down, the bone can be safely reattached to the patient's skull to protect the brain. In America, we keep the skull flaps sterile and freeze-dry them for implantation later, but in the old days the standard technique was to make a small incision in the patient's abdomen and insert the skull flap there for safekeeping. I had read about that but had never performed it or seen it outside of a textbook.

I was about to ask Pete where we stored the bone flaps when I noticed a four-inch-long incision on the patient's right lower abdomen. I pointed it out. "Is that what I think it is?"

Pete laughed. "Yeah, bone flap. We don't have any way to store them here, and we don't know if we'll be here when the patient is ready for it to be reattached, so we just put them in the belly. Same for the Americans, so we know their bones won't get mixed up with someone else's or lost on the way home."

I cringed at the thought of putting in the wrong bone flap. "You'll have to show me how to do that," I said.

"Don't worry. There will be plenty of opportunities."

Pete turned to the nurse, and I studied the patient's scan again. To me, it didn't look bad enough to justify the early surgery. Why had Pete not simply treated him conservatively, giving medicines to control the brain swelling and waiting to see if he could keep the patient from having to have surgery at all? Most people with this patient's degree of brain swelling could be managed with medicine and several days in the ICU. For me, surgery should be the last resort in treating a patient. If you can keep all the brains God gave you inside your head, that's better for you. Our rule of thumb is to try to avoid surgery if we can, because the First Law of Neurosurgery is absolute: You're never the same once the air hits your brain.

Pete's patient was awake and doing very well, and his postoperative CT scan showed very little swelling and no visible brain damage.

"Why did you go straight to surgery?" I asked. "The first scan didn't look so bad."

Pete pointed at the first scan. "You see that little bit of

swelling there in the white matter, that mild edema in the temporal lobes? What happens to that in forty-eight hours?"

"It gets worse—unless you give him Mannitol, maybe barbiturates. You could always put him on a ventilator, reduce his cerebral blood-flow needs, control it medically. I doubt he'd ever need to be operated."

Pete chuckled. "You're right. In San Antonio or Dayton we'd have one nurse per patient. And that nurse could stand here for the hour it takes to deliver a dose of Mannitol. And he could watch the ICP monitor and call the neurosurgery resident every half hour for new orders when the ICP went up. How many patients do you see in here?"

"Twenty."

"And how many nurses?"

"Three."

"And how many neurosurgeons?"

I got the point. "Okay, you're saying we don't have enough time or people to manage these injuries conservatively."

Pete shrugged his shoulders. "Look, when it's your turn, you make the call. I'm just saying if you look at a scan right after an injury and you see something that you know is going to get worse for three or four days, you need to remember where you're standing. And that your luck is about to run out."

"What do you mean?"

Pete touched his watch. "You've been here a day and a half, and we haven't had a mass casualty situation. So I don't expect you to have this perspective yet. But probably, two days from now, every one of these beds will be filled with new people, and we won't have room for anybody who's only here because we didn't get them out fast enough. Unless you want to move some of them to your quarters and give them their Mannitol doses there."

A nurse approached the bedside to change the man's IV bag. She looked at me sideways with a tight grin, her forehead wrinkling. I felt scolded, like a student whose professor had pointed out how stupid he was in front of the whole class.

Pete tapped the monitor, his index finger pointed at the ICP tracing, which currently read 0. "What do you think that number would be if I'd chosen not to operate?"

I thought about the hundreds of these patients I'd seen over the years. Surgery was always the easy answer, because you could so reliably eliminate ICP issues. But conservative treatment works, if you're patient, and you can save people the risk of removing part of their brain. But Pete was right, because the ICP would still be higher even on Mannitol. "Fifteen or twenty," I said.

Pete nodded. "Still normal, but a lot of work for everybody. And he'd still be here three days from now. Let's go. Pretty soon you'll agree with me."

I nodded slowly as Pete walked away. I looked at the still-smiling nurse, who seemed to enjoy watching me be schooled by Pete. The ICP tracing bounced around from 0 to 1, and I thought, *We'll see.*

+

We finished the tour, passing the lab, the radiology department with its field CT scanner, and the physical therapy clinic where soldiers with minor injuries were evaluated to see whether they could stay in the fight or had purchased their tickets home with the price of some disability. I met three interpreters, Iraqis chosen for their strong command of English and their willingness to help us converse with patients who spoke only Arabic. These men were Muslims, but they understood capitalism. They had a commodity we needed, and they were willing to sell it to us. This attitude wasn't universally accepted among their neighbors and family members, and while I was in Iraq, more than one of them would pay dearly for their perceived collaboration with the enemy.

Back in the surgeons' lounge area, the Christmas tree still twinkled with tinsel and blinking lights. But someone had removed the angel from the top, replacing it with cardboard cutout numbers: "2005." It was now a New Year's tree, a couple of days early.

Pete had to meet with the squadron commander for a few minutes, so he left me in the lounge to watch TV, assuring me that he would return shortly to walk me to dinner.

The sleeping surgeon on the sofa was gone. In his place was a young soldier. His helmet and body armor sat at his feet. In his arms he cradled his M – 16 rifle, pointing toward the floor. His eyes were locked onto the opposite wall of the tent as if looking for something far away — the "thousand-yard stare" of shell-shocked World War II soldiers in old movies. His knuckles were scraped and bloody, and he had a small abrasion on his forehead, as if he had struck his face on something.

I sat next to him. "Are you okay, soldier?"

He turned and leaned closer to me, then shook his head and pointed to his ear. "I can't hear you, sir," he shouted. "What did you say? My ears are still ringing."

Now that he had turned, I could see that the other side of his face was burned slightly, and several small square pieces of skin were torn off. The pink-white squares against his dark complexion made a checkerboard pattern on his face. He smelled like a campfire.

I spoke louder. "What happened?"

His hands were shaking. He saw me looking at them and gripped the rifle tighter. "Land mine. My lieutenant's in there." He nodded toward the ER.

I squeezed his shoulder. He was the first American soldier I touched in Iraq.

"I'll check on him for you. Stay here."

I turned and walked into the ER, where four people stood

around a bed. A pile of clothing—bloody DCUs and under-wear—lay on the floor next to the bed. An anesthetist was trying to intubate the patient. I smelled a horrible combination of burned flesh and stool. Vic, the general surgeon I'd met earlier, was talking to an ER doctor who had his hands on the man's groin, putting pressure on the femoral artery. I looked over his shoulder and saw the jagged edge of the lieutenant's femur, stark white bone in a sea of red, muscles and arteries and flapping ligaments barely attached to the lower portion of his leg. The other leg, missing below the knee, was tied off with a tourniquet around his thigh. A long laceration curved up from his groin into his lower abdomen, and from the smell it was obvious that there was a bowel injury.

There was blood all over the bed and all over the ER doctor, but none seemed to be coming out of the patient now. I looked at the injured man's face. Pale, listless eyes stared at the ceiling. He had sandy hair and burns on his face and neck. I guessed he was in his early twenties.

The anesthetist managed to get the breathing tube in. I looked at the monitor—his blood pressure was low and his heart rate very high. He was in shock from blood loss and probably becoming septic from the bowel injury. The bacteria in his colon were in his bloodstream now, and would soon cause an overwhelming infection if Vic and the others couldn't stabilize him in time. But at this point blood loss and shock were bigger threats to him.

Vic bumped me out of the way. "Move it—we have to get him to the OR."

I watched as they rolled the stretcher through the lounge and into the operating room.

When they passed the private, he stood and watched his lieutenant go by. The private stood and reached his hands toward his officer, then dropped them to his side. "LT," he softly called the officer's name.

I put my arm around the private and guided him back onto the sofa. When he looked at me, his eyes trailed down to the caduceus symbol over my left pocket—the snake-and-staff icon that identified me as a doctor. He looked into my eyes, shaking in the aftermath of what no eighteen-year-old should ever have had to witness.

"He gonna make it, Doc?"

"They're doing everything they can for him."

He turned his head and leaned closer, raised his eyebrow.

I said it again, louder.

He put his face in his hands, sniffed hard, and began to sob.

"Where's the rest of your squad?"

The private straightened and blew out a long sigh. "They're dead. We were on a four-man patrol. We came to a little wall, LT told Juarez and me to go right, and he turned left with Sarge. I took about two steps before I heard the explosion. I woke up, Juarez was on top of me, LT was screaming at me to call the medics. Sarge was ... was just gone."

He put his face back in his hands and continued to cry.

I thought of all the things people say when someone dies. When I was growing up in a small town, funerals were places where church people shook the widow's hand and tried to say something encouraging. All of those phrases seemed wildly inappropriate at the moment. Somehow I didn't think that *Well, he's in a better place now* or *At least he didn't suffer* would comfort the private.

I looked at him, just a kid, probably with permanent hearing loss now and certainly with lifelong psychiatric issues, and I felt impotent. Most of the good things I've done in my life I've done with my hands while someone was anesthetized. I didn't have an instrument for this, couldn't cut this out of him or make it heal. Medicine was not what he needed.

I wrapped my arm around him and pulled him closer.

Vic walked out of the OR and stopped in front of the couch. He wore a look I'd seen in too many waiting rooms, had worn myself too many times, but with an extra layer of sadness that went beyond what a doctor feels after losing a patient. It would take me a few days to understand that look, but I think I was already feeling the beginnings of the difference between losing a patient to cancer or an aneurysm and losing a soldier because of someone else's hatred.

Vic knelt, put his hand on the private's shoulder, and looked him in the eyes. "We did our best, but your lieutenant's gone."

The private nodded and wrung his hands, which had begun to shake again.

Vic walked away, leaving me there with the private, and again I didn't know what to say.

Then the soldier in him took over. I saw it happen. He straightened, wiped his eyes, and gathered up his gear. The expression on his face tightened as if he had decided it was time to move on. When he turned to look at me, I saw resolve and strength mixing with the tears and pain.

He stood and slung his rifle over his shoulder. I squeezed his arm and said, "Hang in there, Private. It's gonna be okay."

I have no idea why I said that. In retrospect, it seems silly for me to have chosen those words, because at the moment it appeared that it was decidedly *not* going to be okay. But my words hung in the Iraqi air like one of those patronizing Christian metaphors I had just decided not to use.

The private squinted and slowly nodded, made a chewing motion like he was taste-testing the merit of my words.

"Roger that, Major," he said.

He stepped past me, put on his helmet, and walked away. I never saw him again.

CHAPTER 4

NO SKULL BONE ON LEFT, HANDLE CAREFULLY

I stepped into the hazy afternoon and strapped on my helmet. A blast of smoky wind brought the smell of burning chemicals, and the blowing sand stung my eyes. I squinted and dug in my pocket until I found my Wiley Xs, the dark wraparound sunglasses the Air Force issued to all of us to prevent eye injuries from IEDs.

It was dinnertime. Pete explained that there were three dining facilities, or DFACs, besides the small one in the hospital where I had suffered through breakfast and lunch. He offered to walk with me over to his favorite, DFAC II, which was close to the Post Exchange, or PX.

Halfway across the parking lot we passed a set of trailers marked *Hospital Personnel Only.* "Those are our showers," Pete said. "Plenty of hot water." Things were looking up; if I didn't mind walking half a mile in the cold morning air, I could shower without twelve naked teenage soldiers crowding me for their sixty-second cold showers. I smiled at the prospect—until it occurred to me that this didn't seem fair. Those guys spent their day outside the wire, taking great risks to protect all of us. Why should we have more creature comforts than they did?

"How come we get our own showers?" I asked.

Pete pointed back at the hospital. "Trust me, there will be days when you don't have time to walk to the other bathrooms. You might have five minutes in a whole day to clean yourself up, and things will happen to you that even a hot shower won't wash off." A look crossed his face I didn't understand—yet. His eyes fell and his voice softened. "But you'll still try."

We started to walk again, but we didn't talk much along the way. A flight of F–15 fighters took off and flew right over us, their twin engines drowning out any words we might have spoken. A bunch of clean-looking soldiers prepared their vehicles for a convoy outside the wire. Some of their Humvees had the new armor, but most of them hadn't yet received the upgrade. I wondered if I would meet any of these young people later.

A barrel of sand stood in front of the DFAC with a sign: "Clear all weapons before entering." Before they could enter, soldiers were required to aim their rifles into the barrel and work the slides to ensure that the weapons were unloaded. Just inside was an anteroom where we stood in line to wash our hands before we were allowed to eat. We stepped into the main room, made of plywood and tin. Five hundred people stood in line to select their food, all carrying weapons and wearing battle gear. The servers were mostly locals, Iraqis screened by someone who'd deemed it safe to have them work for us.

A vague queasiness worked through me as I watched a skinny, pimpled Iraqi teenager fill my plate with some unrecognizable meat-and-sauce dish. It wasn't the food, but a deep feeling of being unsafe. I wasn't judging the boy—but I *wondered*. My fear was reasonable; after all, a suicide bomber had blown up an American DFAC in Mosul, Iraq, on December 21, just nine days before. Twenty-two people had died in the attack, carried out by an Iraqi cafeteria worker.

We carried our trays to a long table. As we sat, I noticed a wedding ring on Pete's finger. I pointed at it. "Looks like you've got someone to go home to."

His smile said it all. "Wife and two boys. Well, it'll be three in about a month." His smile receded subtly. "I hope he doesn't come early."

I thought about the timing of my deployment and realized that there's never a good time to drop your life and fly off to war. Sacrifices come in many forms.

After dinner, we walked to the PX, which is like a miniature Walmart without the elderly greeters. Pete pointed out a flagpole in front, around which a small memorial was erected. A hole in the metal post had writing above it—RIP—with four sets of initials and ranks. A mortar had killed four people here, six months before.

On our long walk back to our rooms, Pete and I talked about our lives. He had the certainty I was missing—he knew that his wife and boys would be there when he got off the plane, knew the house would be just where he'd left it, knew that eventually they'd work their life back to normal. I didn't know what I was going back to.

"And here we are," Pete said when we arrived at my metal cube. I opened the door and Pete stuck his head in. He pointed to my fold-up electric guitar in the corner, designed for travel and much less expensive than the three "real" guitars I'd left with a friend back home. "Rock and roll," he said.

I shrugged. "Not these days. Before med school I was in a band, the Monster Tones. Even had the mullet to prove it. I played lead and sang backup."

Pete laughed. "So let's hear it."

"I didn't bring an amp," I said through a long yawn. The travel and the long walk in body armor hit me all at once.

"Another time, then. You need some sleep. This slow spell won't last long."

Pete walked off into the fading light of my second day in Iraq. I fell asleep in my DCUs.

+

At 2:00 a.m. I was startled awake by a tremendous, sustained roar. The trailer shook, and my metal-framed bed shimmied a few inches across the floor, knocking a picture off my bedside table. It sounded like an airplane was flying into my room. I rushed outside and saw the spectacular sight of six F – 15 fighter jets as they fired their afterburners and streaked into the night sky. Their twin engines looked like rockets in the darkness, shooting upward until they were out of sight. I didn't know the airfield was so close to my trailer, and that every morning at 0200 the fighters took off for their patrols.

I couldn't get back to sleep. Staring at the ceiling of my little metal prison, I felt so alone, so out of control. Everything about my life was out of sorts. My marriage was over, although we'd agreed not to tell the kids until I came home. I had done such a thorough job of pretending I was happy that they were unaware we'd had any problems at all. I had insisted that we maintain the charade, thinking that if I were to die in Iraq, they could hold on to their happy memories without the burden of knowing that what they believed about their parents' marriage was a lie. Their reality was like a movie set in which I'd built scenes that looked like a normal life while backstage I carefully orchestrated their perceptions. I knew that if I survived the war, I would pay — they would pay — for this deception.

I thought of my big brother Rob, then in a rehab facility after suffering a major stroke six months before. I had been in the hospital waiting room in Mississippi with my parents and sisters while Rob underwent emergency heart surgery. He'd had an infection that had caused his aortic valve to fail, then thrown debris into his brain, causing the stroke. During his surgery I'd gotten the phone call ordering me to Iraq.

I had sat in the ICU, talking to him quietly and crying the first tears I'd allowed myself in years, since I had always believed crying was for people who were unable to control their emotions. But there I was, a supposedly world-class neurosurgeon, powerless against a clump of bacteria that had destroyed half of my brother's brain. That day had begun the process of bringing together the two parts of my life I'd worked hard to keep separate for many years: my thinly veneered perfect-appearing home life in which I actually had no control, and my white-knuckled grip on the total control of every detail of my professional life. Despite many years of training and thousands of hours treating problems like my brother's, all I could do for Rob was cry, my tears running down my face and dropping like silent silver apologies onto his paralyzed left hand.

+

I walked in darkness to the hospital before 6:00 a.m. Since the base was blacked out at night and there were no city lights nearby, the sky displayed details I'd never seen before. I could appreciate individual differences in the sizes and colors of the stars and planets, and the moon seemed close enough to touch. Iraq sits at thirty-five degree north latitude, just like Oklahoma where I grew up, so the same stars and constellations had been there my whole life. But in Iraq, thousands more of the stars are visible since there is so little light pollution. Sometimes I could even see shadows on the ground from them.

Recent rains had turned the walk into a sloppy mess. By the time I arrived at the hospital gate, my boots and pants legs were covered in thick, brown Iraqi sludge. Pete was waiting for me.

He looked at my mud-covered legs and shook his head. "Now you know why they made you bring those galoshes."

I'd been issued three hundred pounds of gear, including a rain suit and knee-high rubber overboots, which were currently in a duffel bag under my bed.

During breakfast, an airman ran into the DFAC and stopped at our table, out of breath, her black hair in two pigtails high on the sides of her head. She grabbed Pete's arm. "Doc, they need you in the ER. Iraqi with a gunshot to the head."

We ran down the hall to the ER tent. Army medics stood around a wheeled gurney, helping an ER doctor and two nurses move a man onto a bed. The medics looked like EMTs you've seen before, with their medical bags and blue plastic gloves. The difference was that these two young men wore Kevlar and helmets and had M–16s slung over their shoulders with their kits.

Pete and I stepped past the medics. The man on the bed had his head wrapped in white gauze, which was mostly red now. He had a scraggly beard, a hooked nose, and a black number written on his chest, 1901. Pete began cutting the bandage off the man's head as he asked the medics what had happened.

"An Army patrol came upon a group of insurgents just as they shot this guy," one of the medics said. "Bystanders said he had refused to help the bad guys set off a bomb at our gate."

His left pupil was dilated, and there was brain oozing out of the hole in his forehead. There was no exit wound. The man was breathing on his own. While I was looking him over for other injuries, he reached his left hand up and smeared blood on the front of my shirt. The movement was not purposeful; he was flexing his arms in a movement called posturing. This meant his brain injury was severe and he would die if we didn't act quickly.

"Get him intubated and then to CT. We'll get the OR ready," Pete said to one of the nurses.

A few minutes later we were standing at one of the little washbasins outside the OR. We had changed into scrubs and were washing our hands for my first operation of the war. I felt the cold chill of doubt inching through my body. How would I do here?

A nurse had shaved and scrubbed the patient's head; the orange iodine prep solution mixed with blood ran down onto his chest, and I remember thinking that prepped skin looks the same no matter what color it is. Pete looked up at me and motioned toward the scrub tech, the airman named Nate I'd traveled here with from San Antonio.

"Airman, this is Dr. Warren's case," he said.

"Knife," I said, then felt the familiar pop of the steel scalpel in my left hand.

I was surprised to find that, once my scalpel touched skin, I was transported out of Iraq and into *my operating room*. The setting was irrelevant. In my career I had operated on many gunshot wounds — GSWs — to the head. The environment was different, but my hands were steady and my training sound. Maybe I could do this after all, I thought; it's the same as operating anywhere.

Pete and I worked together well, as if we could anticipate each other's next movement. We removed half of 1901's skull and all of his left frontal lobe, his left eyeball, and a mushroom-shaped bullet fragment. We placed an ICP monitor in his brain, and Pete tied the knots in the sutures I placed while sewing up the scalp. Then he showed me how to put the bone flap in the abdomen.

"We use the right side, far enough to the flank so that later in life no doctor would assume the scar was from a normal abdominal operation."

That made sense. If one of these patients came into an Iraqi hospital in future years sick from something like a ruptured appendix, the shape or location of the scar might mislead a surgeon into the wrong diagnosis if our scar was close to where an appendix or gallbladder surgery might normally be performed. The patients would be unlikely to understand or remember what we had done, given their condition at the time of surgery, and there would be no medical records for the doctors to use either. And since we used the left side for feeding tubes in patients with head injuries who can't eat for long periods of time, it wouldn't be wise to put the bone flap into the left side.

Pete made an incision in 1901's abdomen and had me sweep my finger through the fat down to the first layer of muscle.

"There, just above the rectus sheath. Run your finger around to make a pocket in the fat."

I placed the skull flap into the pocket I had created. Pete washed the wound out and closed it while I wrapped the man's head with gauze and wrote, "No skull bone on left. Handle carefully!"

Pete pulled off his gloves and patted me on the shoulder. "Congratulations, Doctor, you're now officially a battlefield brain surgeon."

+

That evening, we sat on the roof of a small building next to the hospital and looked over the fence into Iraq. I could see palm trees, the farmland, and dusty desert fields that bumped into each other here in the beginning of the Tigris Valley. In the distance, I could see Balad Village, the tiny town for which the base was named. A bunch of Iraqis walked around, looking at the fence.

"What are they doing?" I asked Pete.

"Beats me," he said. He took a long swallow of a nonalcoholic beer and handed me a bottle. "No alcohol allowed on base, General Order I-A," he said.

I remembered the lecture about the order. Basically, you could be court-martialed if you were caught with alcohol, pornography, or in the quarters of a member of the opposite sex while in the combat theater.

I thought about how thirty thousand mostly eighteen- to twenty-five-year-old soldiers might behave in this stressful environment during their deployments. I asked Pete, "Do you think the general order works?"

He shook his head slowly. "Well, in my time there have been several sexual assaults on base. And a few women have had to go home because of pregnancies. Plus, the ER docs see a few drunk soldiers every month."

"I guess putting on a uniform, taking an oath, and going off to war isn't enough to overcome some people's need for instant gratification," I said.

Pete clinked his bottle against mine. "To General Order I," he said.

The "near beer" tasted like grass to me, but at least it was cold.

Several of the Iraqis walked up close to the main gate to the base, approaching as a group until the guards raised their weapons and challenged them. They backed up a few steps and stood for a while, not moving. I saw a gunner up in the tower next to the gate, moving his rifle to follow the robed men through his scope. Finally they walked away, following the fence line closely. One of them ran his hand along the fence as he walked.

I wondered whether they were simply curious about the American military base, or whether some of them were enemies, looking for weaknesses, plotting attacks, and wishing us dead.

"You must have brought some luck with you. This has been the slowest time since I've been here," Pete said.

+

That night when the jets woke me up, I was in a cold sweat from a dream in which patient 1901 told me that the only reason he was shot was that we were here. "No Americans, no bullet in my head," he said. He wore an eye patch and held up the missing half of his skull, shaking it at me. "All your fault," he'd said right before the F – 15s saved me from whatever he would have gone on to say.

The dream left me with a feeling of impending doom, which still hung over me as I walked to the hospital the next morning. On the way, I saw a Black Hawk helicopter pass overhead. The pilot didn't circle into the wind like the others I'd seen land at the hospital. Instead, he flew straight over and did a very rapid descent onto the helipad. It was obvious that the patient they were bringing in needed help quickly. I ran the rest of the way to the helipad in time to see two medics unload an American soldier with his head wrapped in bloody gauze. I followed them as they ran his gurney into the ER.

"IED hit his convoy. Two others were KIA," one of the medics yelled to me over the roar of the rotors.

The patient was awake, probably nineteen or so, an Army private. I removed the gauze and saw that he had a tiny hole above his right ear and a larger one above his left. Whatever had entered had gone directly across his brain. That meant disaster. He was awake, his eyes staring at the roof of the tent, his pupils dilating rapidly. The helicopter crew had intubated him during the flight.

Pete wasn't there yet, and it took me a minute to realize that everyone was waiting on me to tell them what to do. "Get him to CT scan, now," I finally said, although I half expected someone to laugh and say, "Who are you to order us around? You just got here." No one did, thankfully.

The scan showed what I already knew it would. A piece of shrapnel had crossed his brain from right to left, directly across his brainstem. He was a dead man, but the rest of his body didn't know it yet. The injury was non-survivable, inoperable. I was filled with a feeling I'd felt many times before when faced with a patient I can't help. Powerless, impotent, stupid — and this time also angry since I knew that this kid had been murdered by some zealot too cowardly to wear a uniform and give the soldiers someone to shoot back at. After he'd set off his roadside bomb, the terrorist had probably just slunk back into the crowd and carried on with his life. Maybe he came to work at our base cafeteria; maybe he loitered around our gate.

"What do we do, Doc?"

I snapped out of my thoughts. They were waiting on me to decide what to do.

"Take him to ICU and keep him comfortable."

He lasted about two hours.

He was my first dead American, a type of innocence lost I still wish I could have back.

I walked back to my room that day unable to get the young soldier's dying eyes out of my mind. The flat world around me still seemed featureless, but now it felt sinister. In two days I'd already seen too many examples of the dangers lurking nearby. Filled with the uneasy feeling that whatever luck I might have brought with me to the war must be about to run out, I went to bed that night before darkness fell on my brown world. I didn't yet know that tomorrow the dominant color would change dramatically.

CHAPTER 5

FOR THE FIRST TIME IN MY CAREER, I DIDN'T KNOW WHAT TO DO

Just after sunrise the next day, I walked to the hospital to eat breakfast. The last bite of powdered eggs and sip of lukewarm coffee had just tumbled into my stomach when the "911" page summoned me to the ER.

Pete was already there, and I ran to the helipad with him and several other doctors and medics. Two choppers landed at the same time, and we helped medics offload six Iraqi National Guardsmen, all obviously burned and bleeding. All of them had bloody bandages on their heads. I remembered the tour Pete had given of our instrument room. I knew we didn't have enough sterile instruments to take care of these men quickly if they all needed brain surgery. Not to mention that there were six of them and only two neurosurgeons.

"What happened?" I yelled over the noise.

"Truck bomb. Twenty INGs were killed at the scene. These are the worst injured of the survivors. More are coming by ground," the pilot answered.

We pushed the gurneys into the ER, where several techs, nurses, and doctors were waiting. A colonel was in charge of the triage. He was called the Trauma Czar, and his job was to organize the process of deciding which patients needed the most urgent care during a mass casualty situation. I hadn't met him before, because he was only needed when more than one or two patients arrived at once.

The Czar moved from bed to bed, listening to reports about each patient's vital signs and extent of injuries. A nurse went around the room marking the men's chests or foreheads with their numbers.

I removed the bandage from my patient's head. He had a jagged laceration that was bleeding heavily. I pulled on a glove and felt inside the cut. My finger found a big hole in the skull and some type of metal in his brain. He needed surgery.

While I was probing the head wound, a heart surgeon took packing out of a gaping hole in the man's chest. The nurse came over and labeled him 1912. An orthopedic surgeon pulled a bloody blanket off and let out a stream of expletives. I looked down to see that both of 1912's legs were missing. One was gone above the knee; muscle and bone protruded from the stump, and blood sprayed from his still-open femoral artery. The other leg was gone about midway down the calf, but someone had tied a belt around it so it was not bleeding. There was one shoe in the bed with him, and it contained his left foot.

The Trauma Czar stepped to our table. "What's the story here?" he asked.

I was about to say what I'd found when the heart surgeon, who now had his gloved hand deep in the chest wound, spoke up. "He's cooked. There's a big hole in his heart, and he's bleeding out. I don't think we can save him."

The Czar looked at the orthopedist. He looked down at the young man's legs, then shook his head slowly.

"Major?" the Czar asked me. I reached down and opened the man's eyes, deeply recessed and darker than his brown skin.

"Pupils are blown, sir," I said.

"All right, let him go. Ted, Major, they need you at bed five anyway." He walked away, and as I watched I noticed Pete pushing his patient down the hall toward surgery. It dawned on me that the Czar had referred to me only by my rank. I was not one of his people.

On the way to bed five, I passed a man in bed four closely enough to smell his severely burned arm. All of his fingernails were missing. He was awake; we made eye contact. He had a pleading look, as if he were asking me to take the pain away. I kept walking.

The patient in bed five was young, probably nineteen or twenty, blown up by terrorists because he'd been brave enough to try to help his country by joining the Iraqi National Guard. His chest was labeled 1915.

One glance and I knew I would be taking him to surgery. His head dressing had fallen off, revealing that he had essentially been scalped by the blast. Most of his forehead was gone, and I could see brain oozing from the cracks in his skull. His neck and face were burned, and his left leg was bent so that his foot was folded forward onto his calf. He had dozens of shrapnel wounds.

An anesthetist was trying to insert a breathing tube. "There's too much blood in his airway. He's going to need a trach soon," he said, while using a sucker to clear the throat.

Ted the orthopedist tied tourniquets around the man's legs, then looked up at me. "That will hold him for a minute."

"Let's get him to CT scan," I said, still surprised when the techs began rolling 1915 down the hall at my command.

Four minutes later I was staring at the screen in the CT control room, watching the scan come across. "He's got a hematoma in his temporal lobe. He's got to go to surgery now."

"And that's not even the worst of it," I heard someone say.

I turned around. The ENT surgeon, a colonel named Joe, was right behind me. "He's also got half his blood volume in the bed with him and a hole in his trachea, not to mention the nightmare Ted's going to have to deal with. Let's go."

He walked out of CT, leaving me to help the techs get the patient out of the scanner. After we moved him to the stretcher, I saw a fist-sized glob of brain tissue on the Army-green blanket where he had been. Three minutes later we were in the OR.

"Ten blade," I said.

The scrub tech handed me a scalpel.

I stood at the head of the surgery table while Joe the ENT surgeon tried to perform a tracheostomy, a procedure to cut a hole in the trachea to use when the throat is injured and no air can get to the lungs. Ted the orthopedist and his assistant were working frantically to stop bleeding from shrapnel wounds and to amputate the man's left leg.

I could see the man's skull through twenty or so different scalp lacerations, each of them bleeding profusely. For the first time in my career, I did not know what to do. It was obvious that treating the brain injury would be useless if the patient died from blood loss while I did so. Every second I allowed his brain to swell, however, was costing him neurons; the already slim possibility that he would recover useful brain function was slipping away. I set down the scalpel, as the scalp was so open I didn't really need the knife anyway.

"Raineys."

The tech handed me a series of plastic scalp clips. Each one, when applied, can stop a quarter-inch-long strip of scalp from bleeding. I began placing them on every bleeding point. I used them all and sent for more.

Before that day, I had never lost a patient in the operating room, something I often bragged about to patients and colleagues. You do not get to die in my OR, plain and simple. If your disease or injury has mandated that this is your day to go, then do it in the ICU or before you get to the hospital. But if you make it to my surgery suite, you're going to survive at least long enough to die in the recovery room. I'm in charge, and you're not going to mess up my perfect record.

All those thoughts went through my head—along with the unwelcome realization that the rules were different here, that this patient had a different playbook, and that he's not listening to me. I thought, *Maybe I'm not in control here.*

Joe managed to get the trach in, then he tried to stop the bleeding from the man's jugular vein, carotid artery, broken mandible, crushed nose, and tongue lacerations.

Ted was fighting a losing battle also. The patient's pupils were dilating, meaning the brain swelling was worsening. We were running out of time. The anesthesiologist told us he had given the patient all of the available blood of his type, and the universal blood type, O negative, was very scarce. He said there were twenty US Marines en route to the hospital after a fire-fight, and some of them would probably need blood as well.

The anesthesiologist reached past me and squeezed a liter bag of saline with both hands, trying to improve the blood pressure. He looked over my shoulder and said to all of us, "Do you want me to give him the O neg?"

We looked at each other but no one spoke. There was no surgeon's bravado, just three men considering something we knew we wouldn't have to do back home. American hospitals rarely lose someone to blood loss, because we have more than enough of most any supply we need. Even if we run out of something, other hospitals can usually provide it quickly. Every patient gets whatever blood quantities they need, and we never give up on someone easily. In war, it's different. We knew that if we gave this patient the blood, then someone else, possibly an American, could die for lack of it. And our patient, even though a couple of hours ago he'd been young and strong, was unlikely to recover from these injuries no matter how much blood we gave him.

I knew what I had to do. I might have been the new guy, but I was at the head of the table. "That's it. Everybody stop. No more blood product."

Ted looked into my eyes and nodded slowly. Joe's face fell and he walked away from the table, snapping off his surgical gloves as he left the room.

I felt warmth on my right leg. I looked down — somehow my surgical gown had folded onto itself, and my leg was exposed. I was soaked in the man's blood. Even my sock and shoe were red, wet, and sticky.

My left glove was rolled down a little, and his blood had crept under the edge and onto my skin. His pulsating arteries had hit all three of us in the face and neck; we were all covered in the blood this Iraqi National Guardsman had shed as a result of a terrorist's hateful bomb. Trying to help his nation rise from tyranny into democracy, this man had bled to death.

The anesthesiologist spoke again. "He's gone. No pulse."

I looked up at the clock on the wall and replied, "Mark the time. 1915 is dead."

Ted looked at me and said, "Nice try."

I had no more words. We don't quit in America — not for lack of resources, not for lack of blood. We keep going, we win, we save lives. This was unacceptable, unprecedented, outrageous.

The floor was now totally red. So were the walls of the tent to my left; everybody's scrubs, every bit of formerly white sponge I could see, were now red, along with all the instruments and drapes.

To my right, three feet away, two general surgeons were operating on another patient, also bleeding everywhere. I was shocked that in my efforts to save my patient, I hadn't noticed them before this. Their patient survived the day only to die of shock and blood loss the next morning.

I walked into the surgeons' locker room, removed my blood-soaked scrubs, and sat on a bench to catch my breath. I was defeated, but the day was just getting started. More patients were coming in. My confidence was shattered, and doubt crawled up my spine into my brain and expanded like a gas until I was convinced I would be unable to survive here.

I changed into clean scrubs, but I didn't have another pair of socks, nor time to walk back to my trailer. I washed my socks in the sink, watching the red turn to pink and ultimately a not-quite-white again. I walked back into the ER, squishing a bit in my shoes, nauseated, scared, wishing the world wasn't red anymore.

CHAPTER 6

I'M NOT THE ONLY ONE GETTING SHOT AT HERE

By late afternoon on my bloody first Sunday in Iraq, I was emotionally spent, physically exhausted, and professionally vexed. I was allowed a fifteen-minute "morale call" home. After connecting through a switchboard operator in Bahrain, I waited five minutes on the line for another operator in San Antonio, who then connected me to the only number I had to reach my children, their mother's cell phone.

The call went to voicemail.

Dual feelings washed over me: a longing to hear my kids' voices and anger over the call not being answered. I swallowed my emotions and tried to sound normal after the beep.

I left a message: Daddy was safe and missed and loved them. I asked them to write. I hung up and dialed the operator again, hoping to call my parents instead. The operator said I'd already used my morale call for the week.

I hadn't spoken to my kids since Christmas Day, eight days before.

That evening, Pete invited me to church. We walked across

the base to a tent with a brown wooden steeple in front. Surrounded by sandbags to protect against a mortar or rocket attack, it looked nothing like a church. A line of soldiers waited to enter.

The man in front of me carried a squad automatic weapon, known as a SAW. His partner bore an M–16 with an attached grenade launcher. I saw a young man carrying a camouflage Bible, and I wondered, *In what scenario would you need your Bible to be camouflaged?*

The doors opened, and the Catholics began to exit from their service, which had just ended. A priest in brown DCUs but wearing a bright green robe blessed the exiting parishioners, who leaned forward to receive his encouraging words as they shouldered their weapons. Our line began to move.

Pete and I sat on folding chairs on the second row. A Marine lance corporal sat next to me. He didn't remove his armor or lay down his weapon. He stared at the cross on the wall and sat silently while the small band on the stage began to sing "Amazing Grace."

The service included quiet time for prayer and reflection. A few people walked to the front of the room, where they were met by chaplains to talk privately or pray together. Partway through the service, the lance corporal placed his rifle on the floor and released the strap on his body armor, allowing it to hang open like a man loosening his tie after a long day at the office. A very tall Army soldier in front of me was on one knee in prayer, and I noticed him sobbing into his hand.

I placed my hand on the kneeling man's shoulder. Without turning around, he took my hand, squeezing it into his giant palm.

As the prayer time continued, music softly playing in the background, I felt as if a weight were driving me into my chair. The day's events came to mind suddenly — not in a stream, but all at once. I felt the futility of watching someone die for lack of blood, heard the screams of burned men, heard the call go to voicemail, remembered I was *here*. Elbows on knees, I cradled my face in my hands and argued with God.

Why, God? Why am I here? Why are all these things happening? Why did my brother get sick, my grandfather die? Why did my marriage fail? Why couldn't I save that kid? What will happen to my kids if I die over here? Why are you doing this to me?

I was not crying; I was angry. Angry that my whole life seemed to parallel this mortar attack, even long before I arrived in Iraq. I wanted to know why, but instead of answers I heard explosions.

As the pastor was beginning to deliver his message, a powerful explosion drowned out his words. The subsonic thud caused by the mortar's detonation punched my chest and popped my ears. Everyone dropped to the floor, clutching at our body armor as an even louder second explosion shook the chapel.

The Alarm Red siren began to wail.

"Everyone stay here," the chaplain said. "There are no bunkers close by, so we might as well just pray."

He prayed for our safety, and for everyone on the base, everyone outside the wire, and for the souls of the men who were shooting at us. I remembered Jesus' words, *Love your enemies,* but I didn't much feel like praying for them at the moment.

I am not the type to say something like, "God sent those mortars to shake me up, get my attention." I believe God has more important things to do than putting thirty-five thousand people in harm's way to make a point to me. I'm comfortable blaming the attack on Muslim extremists who wanted to kill all of us, and to whom I was nothing more than a generic enemy. Nevertheless, in that moment the attack felt very personal, and my reaction to it still surprises me.

I looked around the room. A few chairs to my left sat an

Army Ranger with a square head and narrow eyes. He had grenades in a pouch on his chest, and his huge hairy hands wrapped tightly around some type of automatic weapon. He stared straight ahead, but I noticed a thin bead of sweat running down the right side of his face. It wasn't hot in the chapel.

Two teenaged Marine privates in gym shorts and T-shirts sat behind me. The girl had a peaceful look, her eyes closed, her lips moving silently in prayer. The boy had more pimples than any three average middle school kids, an M-16 at his feet, and a Bible in his lap. He hugged himself tightly and was rocking back and forth, staring at the ceiling.

Machine-gun fire answered the mortar attack. Another mortar exploded. In the silence after the mortar, I heard my dog tags rattle and remembered that my blood type was printed on them. I wondered how much B positive we had left at this point in the day.

A few moments before, I had been silently yelling at God, asking, *Why me?* But as I looked around the chapel I felt something new: *I'm not the only one getting shot at here.*

I was suddenly aware that every person in the room and everyone on the base had personal lives, live that were seriously affected by this deployment. Some of these people had struggling marriages, family illnesses, financial problems, or other issues that they'd been dealing with before the war and that would continue to trouble them after they returned home. Even those whose lives were in order were under the strain of separation and the peril of death. I wasn't alone; it wasn't all about me.

Over the next hour, there were thirteen explosions, each answered by bursts of machine-gun fire and the low thuds of our own mortars shooting back at the bad guys. Long before the attack ended, an Army major named Greg walked onto the stage, joined by a bony young lady in body armor who picked up a guitar. They sang a hymn as the chaplains asked us to take communion together.

As they passed around the trays containing unleavened bread and red wine, I felt something breaking loose inside of me, something shifting. I could not yet tell what it was, but I knew I was changing. For months, I had been focused on the events of my life that remained stubbornly out of my control, and I was angry and bitter about that lack of control. I was focused squarely on myself. Sitting in the chapel that day as mortars exploded all around me, holding broken bread and a plastic thimble of wine, I zoomed out of myself.

The attacks finally ended, the All Clear was sounded, and the service came to a close. The singer, Greg, announced that the entire church band was going home in a few days and the chapel would need new musicians. As I strapped on my helmet, I was vaguely aware of Pete disappearing up toward the stage. A moment later, he returned — with Greg. Greg had a thin smile, happy eyes, and a weary droop, like he'd been carrying a heavy load for a long time and was about to deliver it.

He shook my hand. "Pete here tells me you want to be in the praise band. That's great! We practice here on Wednesday nights."

I looked at Pete. He smiled and said, "Yeah, Lee can play guitar and sing, and he'd love to be involved."

Greg squeezed my shoulder. As he turned to walk away, he said, "I've been praying for a new praise band leader. See you Wednesday!"

"You've never heard me play or sing," I reminded Pete. "You've only seen my guitar propped up in the corner of my room."

Pete smiled and said, "It's good to have something to do. You'll thank me later."

During the walk back to our rooms, I received a "911" page

on my beeper. That meant, "Go to the ER." Since Pete had been up late the night before, he went to bed and I went to work.

Awaiting me in the ER was a civilian contractor. For some reason, this mental giant had decided to wander outside when he heard the Alarm Red sirens to "see what was going on." He hadn't thought a helmet was necessary. A mortar landed near him, detonated, and knocked him out.

His CT scan showed a small skull fracture and a minor bruise on his brain. His injuries didn't require surgery, so I wrote orders for the nurses to manage him overnight in the ICU, and then I walked to the surgeons' lounge to try once more to call my children. I got a different operator, who allowed the call.

During the five minutes it took to connect, my heart was aching to hear their voices. Kimberlyn — nicknamed Kimber — was twelve at the time, and I could picture her blonde hair and huge grin when she would answer the phone by exclaiming, as she always did, "Daddy!" Mitchell, then ten, would be the one to ask if I was safe. Even as a small child he needed to know things like that. Seven-year-old Kalyn had been my biggest fan since the day she was born. She would tell me to come home, still not able to comprehend why I had to go. The call finally connected and began to ring. My pulse quickened.

It went to voicemail for the second time that day.

I looked at the Christmas-turned-New-Year's tree, its glowing lights illuminating the back of some worn-out soldier sleeping on the couch, and I wondered if I would ever hear their voices again.

I passed through the physical therapy clinic on my way out of the lounge. I saw a digital scale on the floor and stepped on, curious about my weight — I wasn't eating much, and I was walking everywhere in all my gear. One ninety-seven; I had lost seven pounds in seven days. It didn't occur to me then, but I was wearing boots. I'd actually lost over ten pounds.

Leaving the hospital, I bumped into the sergeant who had been my chauffeur a few days before. "Been looking for you," he said. He had my email account set up. He gave me instructions on how to use it and reminded me that every email was screened. Any violation of security could result in a court-martial.

I went back to the surgeons' lounge, logged onto a computer, and kept a promise I'd made to my mom a month before. At the reception after my grandfather's funeral, Mom had passed a list around, and forty or so relatives and friends had written their email addresses down. Mom made me promise to send updates as often as I could. In exchange, the people on the list promised to send me care packages.

I'd been keeping a journal on my laptop whenever I had time, and I had the email list and the files on a thumb drive in my pocket. I made a group email list and sent the first three letters. I included my wife on the list, hoping she would share the reports with the kids, since they didn't have their own email addresses. The first two letters — I called them "Day 1" and "Day 2" — covered the trip from San Antonio to Iraq. "Day 3," which I had written earlier that day, recapped the events from December 30, 2004, through today, January 2, 2005. Now that I had email, I resolved that my reports from then on would be only one day behind. Even though no one in the States would see the emails I'd just sent for a few more hours, I now felt connected to them again. I hoped that when I checked email the next day I would hear from someone.

Soon I was sitting on the edge of my bed, taking off my bloody socks. I felt completely unsafe after the mortars and the gunfire, and I'd lost even the security of counting on my own skills. Unanchored, adrift in a sea of self-pity and fear, I thought of 1915. His charcoal eyes stared up at me, and I felt incompetent and guilty and utterly out of control. But something else was there, something hazy I couldn't yet grasp, but I knew I had to find it. I turned out the light and let the darkness envelop me.

Memories of the day washed through me. I remembered chapel: yelling at God and hearing the bombs. I thought of the Bible story of Job, who'd lost his kids and his fortune and finally his health. But when he questioned God, God put Job in his place: "Gird up your loins like a man; I will question you, and you answer me." Even though I did not then (and do not now) believe that God sent those mortars to get my attention, as I lay there in the darkness, I believed that questions were being asked of me—questions for which I did not yet have answers.

I thought about the communion service during the mortar attack, and regretted what I'd written in my email about the experience. I had described that communion as feeling *surreal*; in retrospect, that wasn't right. It had actually felt *very real*: a room full of people united in the purpose of giving themselves for the freedom of others, but sharing a ritual remembrance of another person's death two thousand years before. As the bombs fell and the tent walls shook, the group of strangers had been acknowledging the sacrifice of one for many, and it changed my perspective. Christian communion is a memorial to self-sacrifice, not self-satisfaction.

I tied something together in my mind then, something I'd missed before: That was 1915's blood on my socks, not mine. The little cup of wine represented blood shed on my behalf, not blood I had to give myself. And yet I could sit and yell at God with my skin intact and all four limbs attached and no number written on my chest. My wounds were internal, and no more important than anyone else's. My *why me?* questions suddenly seemed shallow and selfish.

Before I finally fell asleep, I had a vivid memory of a conversation during my neurosurgery training. Dr. Joe Maroon, my mentor and former chairman, taught me a principle used by sixteenth-century Italian sculptors called *disegno*. Dr. Maroon used the example to describe the way he sees a brain tumor or spine problem in his mind before an operation. He told me how Michelangelo could see David in the marble before he began to carve; all Michelangelo had to do was remove the marble to set David free. Before surgery, Dr. Maroon would envision the least invasive and most direct way to find the problem and repair it— like Michelangelo removing the perfect amount of stone.

I felt myself being carved, sculpted. Pieces of who I thought I was and how I thought of my life were being chipped away. I wondered what would be left when the Sculptor was finished.

CHAPTER 7

I CAN STILL SEE HIS FACE AND SMELL HIS BLOOD

The pressure wave from a powerful blast slammed into my chest like a linebacker and knocked me down just as I stepped into the common area outside the operating room. The scrub tech, Nate, who had been sitting on a nearby table, was blown onto the floor. Subsonic energy pulsed through my skull; my ears popped, and my head began to pound.

I didn't yet know what had happened, but I knew this: people had just died.

In less than a week of war, I had already become accustomed to the quiet thuds of distant mortars, the slightly louder and more intense sounds of rockets, and the whizzing you hear just before they detonate. I also knew by then that most things launched or lobbed onto the base didn't even explode — the people launching the mortars and rockets were poorly trained and using old Soviet, Chinese, and French munitions. I was grateful for the high failure rate, but the Alarm Red siren still scared me every time.

Explosive Ordinance Detail (EOD) soldiers would go out and gather up the undetonated projectiles and destroy them in controlled detonations. The EOD troops blew them up almost daily, and those explosions were very loud, very close, and fortunately usually announced ahead of time.

But whatever had just blown up was neither on base nor predisclosed. The fence separating us from them, outside from inside, *base* from *Iraq*, was two hundred fifty yards from me, known as *The Wire*. There was a gate, a guard tower, and young soldiers with guns and a tank. Their job was to protect us, and I realized that someone had just tried to kill them. Judging from the force of the pressure wave that had just knocked me down, I figured things were about to get busy.

I stood, noticing for the first time the fear that took a few seconds to register in my brain. I thought, *That was really close.*

The Alarm Red siren began. Nate was still on his hands and knees. He spoke first. "Doc, I better go get the OR ready."

"Roger that," I said.

+

EMAIL HOME
Tuesday, January 4, 2005

Good morning from Iraq, everyone.

Two hundred fifty yards from the hospital, outside the twelve-foot chain-link fence that surrounds our base, there are three checkpoints. These are designed to keep the bad guys out, and they consist of concrete barriers, guard towers, lots of men with powerful weapons, and three one-inch-thick steel cables, which serve as the gates. When the guards decide to let someone inside, they lower the cables.

The cables are called *wires*, and whenever someone inside the (relatively) safe base has to venture off base, we say that they are going *outside the wire*.

Trust me, you do not want to go outside the wire. But more

importantly, we definitely do not want the wrong people getting *inside* the wire.

They tried to yesterday.

Around seven in the morning, a taxi brought four INGs (Iraqi National Guardsmen) to the gate. The guards let the car through the first two checkpoints. When the driver let off the four INGs, he hit the gas and tried to run through the third checkpoint. The wire stopped him, and as our guys were firing on him he detonated the car.

Four ING guys and the driver were killed instantly, and many were injured. Praise God, though, even in this: if he had gotten past the wire, there were a hundred and fifty ING soldiers standing in formation just past the barrier beyond the wire. They would probably have all been killed or injured if he'd made it twenty yards more. Another hundred yards and he would have driven that taxi right into the hospital, and you wouldn't be getting this email.

+

Nate ran right toward the operating room, and I ran left down the hallway toward the emergency department. Others were heading there as well. As I entered the ER, the first group of patients was being brought in through the front entrance. In the midst of the chaos and with my ears still ringing, I had a passing thought: in this world, they are all patients. In the frantic moments of handling a mass casualty situation, the victims were assessed according to their medical needs; each and every one treated with the same skill and degree of effort. This had been drilled into our heads before deployment: it was not our job to judge who deserves our care. We were to treat whoever showed up, to the best of our abilities. In those minutes, they were not terrorists or insurgents or Iraqis or Marines. They were all our patients, wheeled on stretchers by medics who have to cross the wire and go out there when someone needs them. *At least I get to stay inside the wire where it's safe*, I told myself.

Casualties arrived almost immediately. Within minutes of the blast, stretchers filled the ER, the surgeons' lounge, the hallways—even into the area where we typically stored the dead.

On my way to the ER, I saw a nurse and a technician doing CPR on a teenage boy, 1954 written in black marker across his forehead. His gurney rested next to the Christmas-turned-New Year's tree. 1954 looked just a little older than my son, Mitchell.

Shaken, I paused for a few seconds. The scene seemed to slow down in time; it was as if I were watching a movie. When the perspective zoomed out, I saw utter chaos. People screaming, not all of whom were the patients. Human struggle writ large and real and *here*—death versus life, good versus evil, fear versus courage, twenty or more plays being acted out with their outcomes yet to be determined. Zoomed in, I saw *professionals* doing their jobs, excellently. Small kindnesses, hands patted, tears shed, people saved and people lost.

My brain reminded me to move. I had work to do. I snapped out of it.

In the hallway I had to step around a pile on the floor. When trauma surgeons cut clothing from the patients to identify their injuries, and orthopedists removed mangled and unsalvageable or already detached limbs, they were dropped on the floor to be dealt with later. I saw a man's hand resting on someone else's foot, neither still attached to their owners.

Medics had delivered to one corner of the room several people who seemed to have mainly head and neck issues. Our ophthalmologist worked on a man who had been looking directly at the car when it detonated, and the shrapnel had irreparably punctured his eyes. His operation would wait until the more seriously injured people cleared the operating rooms. The ophthalmologist taped the eyes shut for the moment.

Joe the ENT surgeon was working with an anesthetist and a tech to place a breathing tube into a bubbling redness that had once been someone's face. They failed, and he died two minutes later. They discovered in their efforts that his trachea was no longer connected to his lungs. His suffocation was merciful, as the rest of his body was burned terribly.

Two men in the first batch of patients were silent. In a world where most people enter our view screaming from the pain of missing limbs, ripped-open abdomens, or burned-off flesh, not talking means there is most likely a head injury. These two were mine.

The Trauma Czar strode through the room like a general might run the front line, encouraging his troops, shouting orders, forcing decisions. He stopped next to me. "Who goes first?" he asked.

The decision had to be made *now*. Time was of the essence, because our resources were limited and people were dying. I stood in the emergency department in the busiest hospital in the nation of Iraq, in trauma bay two, looking down on two badly injured men. Both had head injuries, both needed brain surgery. We had one CT scanner, and one brain surgeon because Pete had the day off. Someone had to go first, someone had to wait. I had to decide; the Czar demanded it of me.

I hesitated too long, so he repeated himself. "I said, 'Who goes first?'"

The question hung in the air, awaiting an answer only I could give. My profession does not allow indecision.

"Come on, Major. Make the call."

I was judge with gavel, executioner with axe, Roman Emperor giving thumbs-up-or-down. Someone would be given the chance to live, and someone would probably die.

I looked down at the two men whose lives rode on my choice, 1952 and 1956. In America, triage usually means, *Which not-so-sick ER patient gets to see the doctor first?* I'd never been forced to make a real life-or-death triage decision before, because I'd never been in a hospital where we had limited resources before. Here, the one I chose to treat first would have a significantly higher chance of survival than the other man.

"The guy on the left has a serious scalp wound," I said. "He's losing a lot of blood. Let's get him back to radiology first. The other guy's still awake; he can wait a while."

Orderlies wheeled 1956 off to the CT scanner. The scan would reveal the severity of his brain injuries and tell us whether he could be saved with an operation. During those minutes, the other man waited his turn; whatever was happening to the brain material trapped inside the confines of his skull would continue to happen until I finished treating 1956.

In San Antonio, while my patient was in radiology for a CT scan, I would likely be in my office, reading or returning phone calls, maybe watching *Sports Center*. Not in Iraq.

"Major, hold this guy's legs," I heard.

I turned to see who was calling. A general surgeon was working on a man's groin. Important parts of patient 1948 were missing; he would miss them if he survived. But he wouldn't survive the blood loss much longer, and the surgeon needed me to hold up the legs to help him see. 1948 was still awake.

In my new role as leg-holder, I headed to the end of the bed. The man had not been wearing shoes when the bomb went off. His legs were obviously broken; cuts and shrapnel wounds and multiple small burns covered them. I grabbed both ankles and lifted. "Alam! Alam!" he screamed. The morphine wasn't helping. His ankles and calves came up with my lift far too easily—his knees and thighs did not move. I heard and felt the crunching of his compound tibia fractures. The bleeding had stopped now; I carefully let the legs down and walked away, swallowing hard to keep from retching.

Keep it together, Lee, I thought.

Nate came in with a message: "Scan's done, Doc."

I ran to radiology past a sea of brokenness, wishing I could keep running, all the way home. A young airman, her blonde hair tightly braided atop her head, sat on a desk crying, her face in her hands.

1956's scan showed several skull fractures and a fairly minor bruise on his frontal lobe—straightforward stuff to repair in the operating room. I figured I could get this done while patient two was scanned and prepped for surgery, assuming he needed it.

A few minutes later I was in the operating room, trying to stop the bleeding from multiple lacerations in 1956's scalp. At the same time, 1952 finally had his turn in the CT scanner.

A few minutes later, another tech came into the room holding a mask up to her face. She hung the scan on a light box on the wall. "The Czar told me to bring you this scan, sir. And to tell you that the patient had a seizure and they put him on a ventilator."

I stepped away from the surgery table and examined 1952's CT scan. The scan showed an epidural hematoma, a true neurosurgical emergency. If you remove them quickly enough, the patient usually recovers fully. If you don't, they frequently die. And the difference in most cases between life and death is minutes.

1952 had been awake earlier only because the clot was not yet large enough to compress his brain and cause the coma. When I'd seen the two patients for triage, I had been more impressed with 1956's blood loss and his severe scalp wound, but his brain injury had turned out to be relatively minor.

I'd chosen the wrong patient to go first. And 1952 might die because of it.

I tried to quickly finish the repair of the skull fracture. Joe the ENT surgeon walked into the room, his hands held up in the air dripping water. He was scrubbing into my case. "Warren, I can close the scalp for you," he said. "The other guy needs your help right now. I told anesthesia to get him ready. He's in OR three."

I was shocked. A surgeon from a different specialty was going out of his way to help me. "You sure?" I asked.

"Yeah, go save that kid."

I scrubbed out and ran to OR three. Someone had already shaved and prepped 1952 for surgery. I washed my hands.

The anesthesiologist had on a lot of cologne. The smell made me realize that all I had smelled for two hours had been burned flesh, blood, and a variety of body fluids.

The procedure went well, and once I removed the blood clot, 1952's brain looked pretty normal. I found out later that he was one of the plotters of this day's attack, and he'd been standing a little too close to the action when the bomb went off. He ultimately recovered enough to be transferred to Abu Ghraib. I'd saved my patient's life, but he would not have done the same for me.

Later, when I had time to think about it, I would be thankful for the accuracy of the gunners at the gate. They'd killed the driver before he cleared the fence, so the bomb went off outside the base, killing over twenty innocent bystanders and injuring hundreds. Army medics had risked themselves to bring the most seriously injured people to us. The rest crawled or walked off to whatever medical care they could find in their villages.

The rest of the day was spent sorting through the remaining casualties, including a few US soldiers from another incident. The seeming chaos in the emergency department, although it never let up much, was never out of control. This was because the Trauma Czar managed it brilliantly. He was finishing his tour, so this was old hat for him by now. He and the rest of our medical crew had been here during the Battle of Fallujah and twenty other mass-casualty situations. They were seasoned; I was the new guy.

The Czar patted me on the shoulder. "Good job today, Major Warren."

"Thanks, Colonel. But I made the wrong call on those two head injury patients."

The Czar shook his head and offered a kindly smile. "No, you didn't. Triage requires you to go with your gut and with your eyes. Your first patient was bleeding a lot, and there was no possible way for you to know what the scans would show. Besides, you got his case done so fast the second patient was in surgery before his films even came off the printer. That was good work. Now go get some rest."

He walked away, leaving me for the first time in forty-eight hours with nothing to do. My sixth day in Iraq, and I'd spent it as the only neurosurgeon working a mass casualty with forty victims. Pete had been alone for over a week, so today he slept at the Czar's command. There is only so much one person can do, he said, and he insisted we take care of ourselves.

Only later did I realize that the Czar had called me by my name. I felt like I'd made the team, just in time for most of them to leave.

I was walking out of the hospital when I ran into Joe. "Thanks for your help today, sir," I said.

He smiled and said, "That's what we do here. If you set the right example, the next group will too. And cut out the *sir* stuff. It's just Joe."

I hadn't eaten in about fifteen hours, so I headed for the DFAC, thinking about what Joe had said. In a week or so, the new group would be here, and for a few days I would be the most experienced trauma surgeon in Iraq.

That evening in my ten-by-ten metal trailer with no windows, I prayed and cried and raged into my pillow, thinking of home and the incalculably horrible things I had seen that day. I knew that the past two days had begun to crack open the person I'd been when I arrived here, pouring something into me that would bind itself to my spirit. I was being changed but was not yet sure how. I was sure of one thing: I would never be the same.

I began to compose in my mind the email I would send to my family and friends back home the next morning. What I was experiencing here was important, and I knew that I had to find a way to do more than simply tell people what I was seeing and hearing. I wanted to allow them to *see* and *feel* and *taste* and *smell* the war and its effects on me. But I also knew that many of my letter's recipients would forward it to others I didn't know. So although I wanted to be very honest about what was happening in the war, I did not want to go into detail about my personal life. To be honest, I was afraid of being judged by some of my relatives and friends, since divorce is inextricably tied to failure and sinfulness for so many of those raised as I was. I couldn't stand the thought of having to deal with emails from relatives telling me I was going to hell—especially since I was half convinced of that anyway.

On the plane ride into Iraq I had wondered if perhaps God had given up on me. Now that I'd spent six days here, I felt like he was taking me somewhere. I just hoped to survive the trip.

When sleep finally came, I dreamt of cracking tibias, the bubbling faceless man, and the teenager's blank stare as the blinking Christmas tree lights cast their green and blue shadows across his eyes. Mostly, however, I dreamt of that day's second patient, the terrorist. He told me—showed me—how the attack had been planned and carried out. He said he would do it again—it was his duty. We assessed each other in my dream.

His duty was to destroy, mine to heal. He said it was my *job* to save him — to save him so he could kill me.

I would have this dream for many years. As I type this paragraph, separated by years and thousands of miles, I can still see his face and smell his blood. 1952.

CHAPTER 8

GLASGOW COMA SCORE OF SEVEN

I had been in Iraq almost a week, and the mass casualty situations of the past two days had rendered me weary and irritable and wondering what week two would hold. Pete led me down a hallway to a door I hadn't been through before. A sign said "Long-Term Care."

"Why haven't I seen this before?" I asked, stopping just outside.

"I haven't brought you here yet because none of these patients have head injuries," Pete said. "This is where we keep all the non-Americans until they're well enough to go home or to an Iraqi hospital, or to prison in the case of the terrorists. There's just one guy we need to see. I've been rounding on him every few days. We call him G. He lives near Balad Village, and he was working for the Army as an interpreter until the bombing."

"Bombing?"

Pete nodded his head. "Yeah, the bad guys apparently didn't appreciate him helping the Americans. They bombed his house. Broke his pelvis. His lower spinal column's in five or six pieces. We can't fix it here. His little daughter was badly injured also, burned. She'll survive it, though. She's in Baghdad at Ibn Sina."

A surge of anger rose through me at the thought of someone willing to blow up a family. The interpreter had just been trying to feed his wife and daughter, but in his society, working with the Americans in any capacity made him a target.

"Ibn Sina—that's the Army hospital where our other two neurosurgeons are, right?"

"Yep. Jeff and Don. Good guys, but they'll be going home soon. The Army is thinking of consolidating all the neurosurgery in the country here at Balad. One of us is supposed to go to Baghdad for a meeting soon, by the way. They want us to come to them. Baghdad is safer than here."

"One of us? That sounded predetermined," I said.

Pete laughed. "Well, here's the deal. There's a C-130 with my name on it headed for Al Udeid in about two weeks. Between now and then, the only way I'm leaving the ground is if a mortar blows me into the air. And besides, it wouldn't be fair for me to go and negotiate about the future of neurosurgery in Iraq when it's you and whoever replaces me who will be affected by the decisions made."

"True enough," I said, thinking of all the different ways a helicopter ride outside the wire could result in my death.

"And besides," Pete said as he flashed a huge grin, "I hear Baghdad is lovely this time of year."

I shrugged and laughed, reaching for the heavy plastic drapes that separated the hallway from the ward, but Pete grabbed my arm before I could step inside. He stepped in close—close enough I could smell the coffee on his breath—and spoke quietly. "I should warn you. Most of the patients in here are hard-core extremists waiting for a trip to Abu Ghraib or Guantanamo Bay. A couple of them have tried to escape in the past. They're not that sick anymore, and they can be nasty. One of them threw a bedpan full of urine on a nurse last week. We can't let them have metal silverware, either, because a few weeks ago one Iranian tried to kill himself. Be careful."

My skin tingled. I wasn't used to being around dangerous people.

I stepped into the ward and saw twenty or so men on green cots, all staring at the ceiling or sleeping. Unlike the regular wards, none of them had IVs or monitors. Most of them had on casts, bandages, eye patches, or other accoutrements of the injured. It could have passed for a convalescent ward in any VA hospital in America except for the canvas walls and the fact that most of the patients were chained to their beds. Not to mention that there was a skinny Army private with an M–16, a holstered 9mm Beretta, and full body armor guarding the room.

Pete pointed to the first bed on the left. "That's G, the interpreter we need to check on."

G lay on his left side, facing away from us. A nurse was behind him, changing a bandage on the man's back. He was so thin I could see the individual vertebrae in his tailbone. I thought about the story Pete had told me, how G's family was attacked because of his willingness to work with us. I tried to put myself in his place, wondering how I would feel.

We stepped around the bed and looked at G, whose eyes were closed. I could see the pain on his face while the nurse packed gauze into a wound in his pelvis. I wondered how bitter he would be, how angry that his little girl was harmed, his own life jeopardized for trying to make a living.

Pete smiled and placed his hand on G's arm. "Good morning."

G opened his eyes and looked up. The grimace he'd been wearing morphed into an enormous smile, and he spoke in perfect English.

"Peter! My friend."

"G, this is Lee. He's a neurosurgeon, like me."

"If you are like Peter, then you are my friend," G said.

I was amazed at the gentle spirit and positive energy that flowed from the kind eyes of this broken man. He had every right to be angry, even hostile. After all, our presence in his country had led to the attack on his family. But G showed only gratitude.

We talked to G for a while. Pete had to go to a meeting to begin the process of going home in a few more days, so I stayed behind to make rounds and handle anything that came up. I told G I would check on him later, then went off to the ICU.

As I walked around the hospital, I noticed that everyone seemed tense. Like Pete, all the other doctors and staff were almost finished with their deployments. Surgeons who had never bothered to wear their armor even when Alarm Reds happened suddenly sported their gear. No one wanted to get this far and then get blown up only a few weeks before heading home. I sensed that they were emotionally done with the war, that they'd soaked up all the terror and tragedy they could hold, and they were hanging on for dear life until the end.

I was walking to the hospital DFAC to get coffee when my pager went off. The screen said "911," so I headed for the ER.

"Twenty-year-old Army private," the medic said as he and his partner lifted the stretcher from the gurney onto the ER bed. "Tank gunner, hit in the head when they ran over an IED. He's GCS eight, breathing on his own but not talking."

GCS meant Glasgow Coma Score, a standardized assessment of someone's level of consciousness. The score is calculated by adding up points for the patient's eye opening, speech, and movement. A dead person gets one point for each, meaning the lowest score possible is three. Eight means you're almost in a coma. The soldier's brown eyes looked through but not at me.

"Private, I'm Dr. Warren. What's your name?"

No response.

His breathing was shallow, slow. I felt his pulse, also too slow.

I removed the bloody gauze from his head. He had a tiny, jagged laceration in front of his right ear, just below where his helmet would have covered. I put on a glove and felt inside the wound. There was a hole in his skull, and my finger slipped into it. Brain material covered my fingertip when I pulled my hand out of the hole.

He still didn't move. I reached into his armpit, grabbed a bit of flesh, and pinched him firmly, a standard examination technique to assess someone's level of consciousness. He extended his arms rigidly, bending his wrists toward the bed. I pulled a penlight from my pocket, flashed it in his eyes. His pupils did not constrict. I ran the GCS scoring system through my head: four points for his eyes being open, one for not talking, and two for extending his arms.

"He's not GCS eight anymore, Captain," I said to the ER doctor. "More like seven. He's getting worse. Better get him to the scanner."

We rolled through the waiting area on our way to radiology. Several filthy, haggard soldiers had wilted onto the couch. The smoky smell the injured private reeked of was magnified. These were his guys. I made eye contact with a staff sergeant, who raised his eyebrows at me. "You gotta save him, Doc," he said. "He's going home next month."

The CT scan was worse than the one of the other American I'd lost two days before. This private's brain was full of blood, and I could see a path of destruction across the screen ending at a chunk of metal lodged inside the left side of the private's skull.

"It's unsurvivable," I said, after mentally running through the criteria to diagnose brain injuries that never respond to surgery. "Take him to the ICU and let his buddies see him."

A few minutes later, I walked into the ICU and approached the private's bed. His sergeant and a couple of other soldiers had their hands on him, praying and talking quietly to him. I put my hand on the sergeant's shoulder. "I'm sorry," I said.

My words felt so inadequate.

The private stopped breathing a few seconds later. His

captain held his hands while he died. Tears flowed, and not just from the soldiers.

A chaplain entered the room and prayed with them. I excused myself and walked down the hall past the ward where wounded soldiers waited for their evacuation to the States. *The lucky ones*, I thought.

Then I silently chastised myself for thinking how lucky it was for someone to have only lost a limb or an eye.

Later that day, I saw an Iraqi man whose house had been accidentally hit by a mortar. He was brain dead on arrival, and all I could do was close his eyes. The man's house wasn't far from our base, and the mortar that killed him had most likely been aimed at us. I shook my head as I walked away, wondering what it would be like to grow up in a country where you had to worry about things like random bombs hitting your house.

Pete came to my room that night, bringing his friend Brian, a physical therapist who was also in his last few days in Iraq. We watched a movie on my laptop, and before they left I realized how for the hour and a half the movie played, I hadn't thought about the war at all. I had a new trick.

After Brian and Pete left, though, the war crashed back in. Every time I closed my eyes I saw the death and destruction I'd witnessed over the past few days. I tried to remind myself that I was a professional, that I'd seen plenty of people die before, some of them people whose injuries or disease exceeded my ability to save them. But this was different.

Although I'd seen many tragic deaths and many very broken people in my career, I had never made rounds in a hospital ward in which armed soldiers guarded the patients, lest they rise and attempt to kill the doctors. And I had never operated in a tent, in a desert, in a war in which bombs were falling, with dirt on the floor and dust in the air, where I couldn't trust the availability of the instruments and supplies I might need to finish a case. Most of all, although I had certainly had another person's blood on me before, I had never had *all* of it.

When I managed to force those thoughts out for a moment, sleep was no safe haven. Nor would it be for years to come. I'd only been in Iraq for a few days, and as terrifying as those days had been, I knew it was going to get worse.

+

EMAIL HOME
Thursday, January 6, 2005

Good morning, everyone, from LSA Anaconda!

I don't think I've explained this before, but Balad Air Base is a part of LSA (Logistical Support Area) Anaconda. It's a huge Army facility that serves as a hub for resupply to the FOBs (forward operating bases). The kids here go outside the wire every day in convoys to take stuff to the forward troops. They are in great danger.

IEDs are usually made from old artillery shells. The bad guys bury them in the road or hide them next to the road and detonate them remotely. Then when our guys crawl out of their burning vehicles the terrorists shoot at them. The guys here at LSA Anaconda deal with that every day.

Which brings me to our subject for today: Yesterday I witnessed an amazing act of kindness that really touched me.

We didn't have any serious casualties or mortar attacks yesterday, and we were all sitting around waiting for something to happen when someone ran in and said that there were tanks in the hospital parking lot.

I grabbed my helmet and armor and ran outside. Two enormous M1A1 Abrams tanks drove right into the lot. The crews got out and gave us all a tour of the machines, allowing us to take pictures and ask questions.

I asked one of the soldiers why they were here. He said that they were from the same unit as the private I told you about yesterday who was killed.

+

I looked at the tanker, a staff sergeant. His tight face and narrow eyes said he was one serious soldier. He took off his helmet, ran his gloved hand over his high-and-tight hair. "We just came to tell you all thanks," he said.

"Thanks for what?"

"Just for being here. None of us would be able to go out and do what we do if we didn't know you all were here for us."

After we spent a couple of hours playing with the tanks, posing for pictures, and talking to the crews, the soldiers climbed back into their machines and rumbled back into the war. We watched them drive away, all of us wearing the kind of smile that's only partly happy. The kind you find on your face when there's so much sadness you don't think you can bear it, but somehow something hopeful finds its way into your mind.

And that's what I felt. We'd lost that soldier, unable to use any of our fancy technology or skill to overcome the damage done by one projectile. But instead of being angry at us for our inability to save him, the tank soldiers wanted us to know they still believed in us. Even while they were hurting over their fallen comrade, they took the time to say thanks. Our collective morale, which had been plunging for the past few days, improved tremendously.

After they left, I found myself thinking that, first, you should never be so wrapped up in your own situation or problems that you fail to take the opportunity to help others. And second, the show must go on. The tankers knew they were still at war, still in Iraq, and still had jobs to do. They'd lost their friend, they'd grieved, and now they had to stay alive.

The war had taught me more about life in one week than I'd learned in thirty-five years before it.

CHAPTER 9

"DADDY, COME HOME RIGHT NOW!"

I began to change my behavior in the days following the visit by the tank soldiers. Pete and his colleagues were preparing to go home in a few days, and I would be the most experienced trauma surgeon in Balad for a while. This was laughable and also terrifying to me, since by the time they left I would have only about three weeks of combat surgery experience. The new people coming in would be scared, homesick, and worried—just as I had been. The last thing they would need would be an emotionally wrecked neurosurgeon, holed up in his room crying and yelling at God.

The injured translator named G had a lot to do with my attitude change. In spite of his injuries, his spirit and his smile were indefatigable. Every morning on rounds he greeted us in very pleasant English, the product of a British education. Amazingly, he never once complained about his wounds, his pain, or the heinous attack in which his daughter was also seriously injured. Instead, he focused on asking each of us how we were, smiling his frail smile, blessing and thanking us for taking care of him.

Other than bright spots like G, the days seemed to blend together into one long, repetitive scene. Someone said that life in a combat hospital could be summed up as "hours of boredom interrupted by moments of sheer terror," and he was right. Car bombs, IEDs, gunshots to the head, and mortars became routine parts of my life. I was no longer shocked to see someone's frontal lobe before I even picked up the scalpel, or to see empty eye sockets, missing limbs, burned-off scrotums; in our ER, these were the sore throats and bellyaches that could be triaged to wait a while longer than more urgent matters.

I was getting a great education. My rapid immersion into the practice of combat medicine had allowed me to weigh the medical evidence supporting Pete's early surgery ethos, which we'd argued about when I first arrived. One morning as we made rounds in the ICU, I noticed that the brain pressures of several of our craniectomy patients were reading very low. It dawned on me that in the twenty or so operations I'd done since I arrived, I'd never had to fight ICP after surgery, and we were almost always able to get people out of the ICU quickly.

I pointed at one of the monitors, a big green *2* displayed on the screen. "Look at that, Pete. I need to apologize to you."

Pete looked puzzled. "What for?"

"For doubting you. I thought you were way too aggressive with surgery when I first got here."

Pete waved me off and smiled. "That's what I thought at first too. The Army guy I took over from taught me what I taught you. He said he found a paper from Vietnam explaining that they learned the early surgery lesson there also. Hey, you hungry?"

"Starving," I said. Pete apparently didn't need the apology and wouldn't take any credit for the lessons he'd passed on to me. *More people should be like that*, I thought.

"Let's hit the DFAC before we finish rounds," Pete said.

"Sounds perfect."

We sat down to our usual breakfast of cereal with runny

powdered eggs. "I would kill for a banana or some fresh fruit," I said.

Later, while we were making rounds, we came to G's cot. There on his bedside table, shining yellow like twenty-four karat gold, was a perfect, unbruised Ecuadorian banana.

"Are you going to eat that, G?" Pete asked.

"No. Why do you ask?" said G.

"Because Lee here's been dying for one."

G smiled, rolled over onto his fractured hip, grimaced as he reached for the banana, and lifted it toward me. "I insist that you take it. You are my dear angel who saves me."

As I took the banana, he grabbed my head and pulled me into a hug.

I was very touched, surprised at how much this little gesture of grace moved me.

My perspective shift came in stages, starting with that first Sunday church service, then the loss of the young soldier and the visit by his brothers with their tanks, and then the way observing G helped me to see how small my troubles really were in relation to his.

The final piece came when I realized that I wasn't alone there in Iraq after all.

When I checked my email on day eight, something remarkable was waiting for me: dozens of messages, from at least ten states.

My initial emails had been retrospective, covering the first few days in small detail. Those emails took a few days to pass through the military screening system, and my family received several days' worth at the same time. The first replies came on day eight, and by then people had begun forwarding the messages around the country to their friends and families. I heard from my parents, my siblings, most all of my extended family, and many people I'd never even met. Some of them told me they had begun anticipating my daily "Warren Report," which due to the difference in time zones usually arrived after they'd gone to bed and was waiting for them when they arose each day. Since I was writing about the previous day's events, it felt to the readers like they were experiencing the war in real time, one day at a time.

Also on day eight, I received my first care package.

A cousin mailed a cardboard box full of cookies, candy, toiletries, and a card. I took it back to my room, squirreling away the goodies like a starving man. It felt so good to have something homemade and to know that someone out there was thinking about me, here in the war; I wasn't forgotten or discarded, as I'd begun to feel. I was connected.

Over the next few days, more packages arrived, filling my trailer. I started opening the packages in the hospital, allowing anyone passing by to take what they wanted. It became a daily ritual: around mail time people would wander into the surgeons' area to see what Major Warren's network had sent that day. Cookies seemed to work magic for people, and giving them away made me feel better about my personal troubles. None of the things I'd left in turmoil at home were different, but I didn't have to wallow in them.

Many of the care packages contained movies. Before long, I had quite a collection of DVDs, but only my laptop to watch them on. Pete and Brian became regulars in my trailer, crowding around the small screen for the short respite from the war. They would knock on the door and ask if it was movie night. The answer was always yes.

I was cleaning my room one night when I heard a knock on my door. On my doorstep was the captain from the next cube over. She was going home the next day, she said, and offered to let me purchase the television set she had in her room. I bought it from her, and Pete helped me to connect the computer to the television. Movie night was in business.

+

One morning, I used my morale call to try again to reach my children. I heard the clicks and connections of several thousand miles and numerous operators in three countries, and finally ringing, ringing, ringing, and then my wife answered. She put the kids on speakerphone.

"Daddy!"

The three voices in unison bandaged my wounded heart. The conversation went pretty much as I'd expected.

Kimberlyn, the twelve-year-old: "Daddy, I'm proud of you for helping in the war."

Mitch, almost eleven: "Where are you, Dad? Are you safe?"

Kalyn: "Daddy, come home right now. It's my birthday next week!"

We talked for what seemed like only seconds before another person nudged me, needing the phone. I said goodbye to the kids after saying I love you more times than I could count.

I hung up the phone, grabbed a Tupperware container full of homemade candy from my cousin's care package sitting on the desk, and walked across the surgeons' lounge to the old sofa. I felt a weight settling onto me, as if I were wearing two sets of body armor, but I wasn't wearing any. I sank into the couch and felt myself being pulled toward the edge of an abyss of depression and misery. I wanted to go to my room, hide under the bed, and wait for the war to be over.

"Mind if I sit here, Major?"

To my left stood a Marine Corps lieutenant colonel, in full battle gear.

"Of course not, sir."

The colonel sat next to me, leaned back into the sagging cushions, and dropped his helmet to the floor. He smelled like smoke, and had a few scratches on his face and hands. His skin had the leathery look of someone who'd spent too much time in the sun; I noticed a twitch in his eyes.

The colonel had a cut above his right knee that had bled through his uniform pants before clotting and stuck the fabric to his thigh; the stain was covered with dirt and debris.

"You should get that checked out, sir."

"I'm okay, Major. The lead vehicle in our convoy hit an IED about a mile outside base. One of my guys was killed, another is in surgery right now. I think both his feet are gone. The rest of us have cuts and scratches, but we're all right."

I didn't know what to say. Since none of his troops needed neurosurgery, I had nothing to offer this man professionally, which was the manner in which I typically was able to help people. Yet here he was, hurting, scared, smelly, dirty, and human; he wasn't a faceless United States Marine, he was a man same as me. I offered him a piece of candy.

When the colonel looked down at the praline-molasses candy my cousin calls "Aunt Bill's," his eyes widened slightly. He took one of the squares in his hand, then carefully brought it into his mouth. He closed his eyes as he chewed, then looked at me with a tight grin.

"My mom used to make that. Thank you, Major. I better go check on the rest of my guys."

The colonel walked away, shouldering his gear and the memories of what he'd just been through — standing, I thought, just a little taller. I sat for a few more minutes, thinking of how it seemed that every time I was about to bottom out emotionally, someone else would arrive whose problems were much more life-threatening. Here I was, watching as other people's kids came in with disabling or fatal injuries, shedding tears over only being able to talk to mine for a few minutes a week. Although after the war I was certainly going to have another battle on my hands, at least I was most likely going to get there alive and have a fighting chance to repair my relationship with my kids.

I stood and walked out of the hospital, lugging the unwieldy cardboard care package along with my backpack and body armor for the walk back to my room. A group of several Humvees and trucks was parked just outside the ER. The colonel I'd just met was standing in the middle of a circle of young, scared-looking Marines.

I adjusted my load and turned to walk around the group, but the colonel saw me and waved me over.

"Major, let me introduce you to my guys," he said.

I stepped into their circle, warriors being comforted by their chief. When I set down the box and my backpack, the colonel shook my hand and addressed his men.

"Marines, this is Dr. Warren. He's one of our protectors."

The Marines showed me their vehicles, pointing out several shrapnel holes, broken windows, and burnt paint from the IED and the fire it started as they passed through. I could smell the smoke on their uniforms, and several of them had cuts and bruises. It was easy to imagine the hell these boys had driven through.

One of the Marines, a lance corporal, showed me the armored door he'd been leaning on when the IED detonated. The door was dented in and had a quarter-sized hole in the window. He showed me a similar hole in the right shoulder of his uniform blouse where a piece of shrapnel had torn through, just missing his flesh.

I put my finger in the hole, thinking of the damage that burning piece of metal would have done to this man's arteries, muscles, and nerves had its trajectory been a half-degree lower.

"You're pretty lucky, Corporal," I said, in the understatement of the war.

"Aye, aye, sir," he replied. "The vehicle in front of ours was cut in half. When we got out, we started taking small arms fire from the buildings nearby. It was an ambush. My buddy was driving ..."

I squeezed his shoulder as his voice trailed off. He looked past me at the hospital, tears welling in his green eyes. In that moment his humanity broke past the hardened shell the Marine Corps provides its people. He seemed to shrink like a balloon with some of the air let out. I'd seen it a few times by then, how these troops wear their duty and their toughness like an alter ego. When they're in battle mode, Marines take on a persona that seems more machine than human. But in moments like this, the reality of losing a friend or coming close to death brings the human out for a while. I could almost hear his thoughts as he stood there in the desert: He was thinking about his friend, and realizing how close he had just come to being inside my hospital instead of standing in the parking lot.

Then, just as quickly, the Marine in him came back. His eyes narrowed, his height returned, and he looked very much like someone you would not want to have to fight.

"Colonel, we gonna go get those guys, right?"

"Roger that, LC," the colonel said. "Soon as I know about the rest of my Marines."

"I better be going, sir. Thanks for introducing me to your people," I said. "You think they would want this box of homemade cookies and brownies?"

The colonel reached into my box, took the rest of the Aunt Bill's candy, and put it into his pocket. Then he looked up at me and smiled. I could see the anticipation on the Marines' faces as they let their eyes fall into the box, but they held their positions, waiting for the command.

"Major, you're a good man. Marines, help yourselves."

The box was empty in about three seconds. Their smiles lasted a lot longer.

And so it went. From small acts of kindness performed by people in the throes of serious pain, unsolicited encouragement and confections from people thousands of miles away, and in the sharing of a two-thousand-year-old communion ritual, I began to see outside my own problems, outside myself. The kindnesses I was shown made me begin to seek to provide the same for others, and, as getting outside yourself is prone to do, I think it benefitted me the most.

+

One day, G's father arrived. It was easy to see where G got his attitude; the gregarious nature, huge smile, and loving heart were present in both men. G's father was a wealthy man who had connections in the old Saddam government. He told us that he had arranged for G to be treated in Jordan, at a hospital that specialized in complex spinal injuries but that it would take a while to work out the details of his transfer.

As I grew more accustomed to the constant noise, dust, and danger, as well as the frequent exposure to horrifically injured people, I also became much more aware of the beautiful things around me. Though they were harder to see, they preserved sanity and peace of mind when I remembered to notice them: a nurse tenderly changing the bandages of a severely burned man, a tiny flower somehow managing to grow through a crack in the sidewalk—and G's daily greeting.

One morning, when I stopped in to see G, another patient was in his bed. His dad had taken him in the middle of the night, the nurse told me, leaving unannounced in case any of the Iraqi hospital workers were connected to the terrorists who wished G dead. They didn't want to risk driving into an ambush. I understood — still, I wished I could have said good-bye. How had I grown so close to a bed-bound Muslim man I'd only known for three weeks that I missed him so acutely as soon as he was gone?

+

As January drew to a close, my newfound resolve to maintain a good attitude and be there for others was tested mightily. We had entered the rainy season, and there was mud everywhere. A several-hundred-yard section of my walk to work was covered by six inches of standing water. For ten days, the temperatures at night dipped into the thirties, and it rained almost every day. And I'd thought deserts were supposed to be hot and dry!

The enemy did not seem to mind the weather. Mortars and rockets landed around us almost every day, and as Iraq's first democratic elections approached, the intensity of those attacks increased. The incessant stream of brokenness in the hospital never slowed, but fortunately my skill level at handling the stress and chaos was growing, along with that of the team I'd been working with for a month.

One night I sat in my room, sorting through DVDs to fig-ure out what movie we would watch that evening. I looked at my watch; it was pretty late, and I hadn't yet heard from Pete. I sat on my bed to read as I waited for him, and before I knew it I was asleep.

Sometime later I heard a knocking on my door, and I star-tled awake.

"Lee, it's Pete."

I opened the door, flipped on the light, and rubbed my eyes. Pete stood on the doorstep, his back bent under the weight of three overstuffed duffel bags.

"What's up?" I asked, motioning him in.

Pete dropped his bags on my floor and clapped his hands on my shoulders. A smile split his face, and he reached into his pocket, retrieving a stack of papers. "I got my orders. I'm heading home tonight!"

His words punched me in the chest. I forced a smile, reminding myself that I should be glad Pete was going home.

As we talked, Pete dreamed out loud about his reunion with his wife and their boys. His excitement was palpable, visceral, and almost contagious. Almost. I knew that once he left, I would be on my own for a few days, and I had no idea who would be replacing him. Pete had become like a brother to me over the past weeks, and I didn't want to lose him. My emotions were in conflict—I dreaded losing him, and yet I was happy and excited for him that he would soon be home.

"I never thought I'd come to the war and find a friend," Pete said. "I'm going to miss you."

We spent an hour praying, crying, and promising to get together if I made it home alive. Finally, fatigue overcame him, and he pulled a blanket onto the floor and fell asleep in his DCUs. I was afraid I'd sleep through the alarm and be responsible for Pete missing his ride home, so I stretched out on my bed and stared into the darkness until it was time to go. I roused him, and we walked to the hospital, where I borrowed a truck to take Pete to the airfield.

I've never been very good at goodbyes, especially when I really don't want the person to leave. But this wasn't the time to say, "Why don't you stay a few more days?" Instead, I put my hand on Pete's shoulder and said, "Thanks for taking care of me here. I'll be praying for you."

Pete smiled and shook my hand, then pulled me into a hug. He looked in my eyes. "You'll do fine."

Over the next few days I sank into a mental funk, feeling

sorry for myself and worrying about everything. The news that Pete had made it home safely made me feel relieved and jealous and sad all at the same time. I resented that, because I'd had to come early, I didn't get to train with and integrate into the team that would arrive soon—and yet I'd arrived too late to ever fully be a part of Pete's group. I felt like I was in no-man's-land. But at least I felt that I'd carved out a place for myself.

As the replacements began to arrive, I worried: Would the new guys be competent and effective? Would I find a friend, someone to grow close to—a Pete? I felt as if I was losing a family I'd just been accepted into. We had been through mass casualties together, saved and lost lives together, been there for each other. I had overcome my inexperience and proved myself worthy of being one of them, been made welcome in their family.

After we finished working through the casualties on the last day we all worked together, the Trauma Czar stopped me in the hall and put his hand on my shoulder.

"Major," he said, and then leaned closer. "Lee, you've learned fast. The new group will be better because of your experience. Good job."

That was the only time he ever said my first name.

CHAPTER 10

THE IRAQI TODDLER

EMAIL HOME
Saturday, January 22, 2005

Good morning, everyone.

Yesterday I ran into a lot of new people. Most of the new surgeons are here now (except for my new partner, who is supposed to arrive tomorrow), and it's funny to see the same fear and excitement that must have filled my eyes twenty-three days ago when I got here. I feel like one of the old guys now, helping people find things and showing them around.

The people whose replacements haven't arrived yet seem like they're holding on for dear life. They don't smile; they shuffle around doing their jobs, but there's a pervasive sense of "let's get this thing done so we can go home."

We have letters and artwork from school kids all over America hanging throughout the hospital. It feels very strange the first time you open a letter and it's addressed to "Dear American Soldier." I always thought of myself as a doctor who sort of happened to work for the Air Force.

Now, though, I see clearly that first and foremost I am an American soldier (albeit a noncombatant per Geneva Convention rules). I am, for better or worse, one of the guys the mortars are aimed at. I am a GI, in a foreign country during a war. That's a far cry from my life as the little cotton-headed kid with the cowlick from Broken Bow, Oklahoma. And it's a far cry from my comfortable, Starbucks-visiting, BMW-driving, high-tech-surgery-performing life in San Antonio.

Here our suctions operate on a pump, and we have to turn them off during surgery because they are so loud we can't hear the anesthesia guys talking to us. I'm operating on guys who hate me, saving their lives so that we can send them home to the desert, and I'll never know if they get adequate follow-up care. This couldn't be more different from my life in the States. We're all adjusting, but this experience will definitely change my perspective on the things I thought were problems at home. None of them seem so important now.

I love you all and hope to hear from you.

Lee

EMAIL HOME
Sunday, January 23, 2005

Good morning from the frozen wetlands!

Yesterday's weather was absolutely atrocious. It rained all day and all night, and it's freezing and very windy. There is standing water in the hospital, and a huge lake out in front that I had to walk across to go back to my trailer last night. Everywhere that isn't covered in water is covered in mud—a very thick clay.

Yesterday started with a simulated multi-patient disaster. All hospital personnel were called in and had to pretend to examine, transport, operate on, and care for a huge group of fake patients that all arrived at once. It was chaotic, but it was also a great way to get all the new folks oriented to the process. It was actually a little worse than the real mass casualties I have worked since I've been here, but I think that's only because there were twice as many people as there would be in a real situation. All the last group of doctors are gone, but the techs and nurses stayed a few extra days to train their replacements, so hopefully the transition will go smoothly. I've been through a couple of real mass-casualty situations, and I feel confident that we can do it when it happens again. Unfortunately, it will.

Keep praying.

Lee

+

Just as I thought my day was about to end, my beeper went off.

I looked down at the pager. Its "911" message ended my plans to go to the gym. Back to the emergency room for me.

The tech manning the radio in the ER looked up from her desk as I ran in.

"Black Hawk's five minutes out. They've got a two-year-old Iraqi boy with a head injury from a car accident. He's not moving."

Perfect, I thought. *Pete's back in Ohio, and I've got a baby coming in with a brain injury.* My new partner was probably having a coffee at Al Udeid, and nobody else in the hospital had even scrubbed into a case here yet. I said a quick prayer that the new anesthesia people and nurses were good at their jobs and grabbed the phone to call the radiology tech.

A voice I'd never heard before answered. "X-ray, Airman Hernandez."

"It's Warren, the neurosurgeon. We may have a case. Get the CT scanner ready and tell the OR to stand by to do a craniotomy."

It was a cold, cloudy day, and the chopper came in hot, no turn into the wind and no easy flare like the pilots did when they knew we were watching. I've noticed over the years that even in civilian hospitals everyone seems to move a little faster when a child's life is in jeopardy. The medics jumped from the Black Hawk even before the skids completely hit the helipad. I sprinted across the Tarmac with a nurse and two techs pushing a gurney.

The gunner yelled over the noise: "Car wreck near Tikrit seven hours ago. Baby's not moving purposefully."

The medics set the litter onto the gurney, and I looked down at the smallest person I'd seen in the war. He was zipped into a body bag, with only his little face protruding. The medics had inserted a breathing tube during the flight, and one of them squeezed the tiny blue breathing bag every couple of seconds. Someone had figured out that putting people into body bags kept them warm during transport, improving people's outcomes after major trauma. I still wasn't used to seeing living people wrapped in the shrouds of the dead, but it worked. Seeing a two-year-old in a body bag, however, was another thing altogether.

We got him into the ER and unzipped the bag. Other than the bloody gauze on his head, he was a perfect, healthy-looking baby. I'd seen plenty of patients, even babies, with brain injuries from motor vehicle crashes, so I was expecting a big scalp laceration or maybe a depressed skull fracture. But when I removed the boy's head wrap, I saw that his injury had not come from a car wreck.

He'd been shot in the head.

His pupils were nonreactive, indicating that the pressure inside his head was far too high and his brain was not receiving enough blood flow. The CT scan showed a huge and expanding blood clot between the skull and the brain, known as a subdural hematoma. Without immediate surgery, he would die. He'd arrived for help so long after his injury because bad weather had delayed the flight. Because of his dilated and nonreactive pupils, and because so many hours had gone by since his injury, his chances of survival and recovery were slim.

Slimmer too, I thought, because I was alone. I'm not a pediatric neurosurgeon, and although all brain surgeons are trained to work on kids, there are major differences in how we care for babies as compared to adults. I hadn't operated on such a small person in a couple of years, and I was nervous. Especially since there was nobody there who could bail me out if I got into trouble during the surgery.

"Let's move, people. This little guy's out of time," I said.

Three minutes later, we were in the operating room, and I was shaving the baby's head. A nurse poured brownish-red iodine solution on the boy's scalp and scrubbed the skin. I watched as the fluid mixed with his blood and soap bubbles ran onto his chest, where I noticed that someone had written 2013.

"Knife!" I yelled over the roar of the suction pumps.

I was comforted by the familiar slap of metal on my palm, and I looked up into the only face I recognized. Nate was scrubbed in with me, the only other person in the entire hospital who had ever previously scrubbed into a case here.

I pulled the knife through the paper-thin scalp, making a question-mark-shaped incision that began just in front of his ear, curving backward and then upward, ending just behind the hairline in the middle of his forehead. I peeled back his scalp and the underlying muscle and saw the stark white of his temporal, parietal, and frontal bones.

The scalp was maybe four or five millimeters thick, less than a quarter inch. Every time I placed forceps on his skin, they left an imprint. I remembered my pediatric neurosurgery professor, Dr. John Myseros, teaching me how delicately the infant scalp must be handled, or the injured skin may fail to heal. I had to be extra careful, since all my instruments were designed for use on adults.

Every drop of blood counts in surgery. Adults have about six liters of blood in their bodies. Babies the size of 2013 have less than a liter, and he had already lost some. I tried to stop the scalp bleeding with Rainey clips, but they simply fell off. Again, no one had thought to include pediatric Raineys in the instrument sets. I used the cautery to cook a big scalp artery that was costing him a lot of blood, but worried about his little scalp healing if I compromised the blood flow.

"Pressure's pretty low, Doc," said the anesthetist, whose name I did not yet know.

"Give him more saline and type his blood."

I got control of the scalp, and it was time to open his skull. His blood pressure and my worries about his scalp would be irrelevant if I didn't get that clot out in time.

From the corner of my eye I saw movement. I turned to see a tall, extremely thin man being gowned by the scrub tech. Someone was scrubbing into my case.

He stepped up to the table and said, "I heard you had a baby in here. Mind if I help, Lee?"

I looked into his eyes, since the rest of his face was masked, and recognized Chris, a pediatric surgeon with an office a few doors down from mine at Wilford Hall. We had worked together on a few cases, but never operated together before. I hardly knew him. What was he doing here?

Chris must have seen the wonder in my eyes. "I got deployed as a general surgeon, just arrived today. I've never done a craniotomy before, but I can help you with the post-op care."

The kid's prospects for survival had just improved dramatically. "Glad to have you. Drill."

Nate handed me the drill, a one-hundred-thousand-rpm, nitrogen-powered, precision instrument with a bone-cutting bur 1.5 millimeters thick. I removed a large piece of his skull, revealing the thick, leathery covering over his brain known as the dura.

The dura bulged out of the head menacingly, red and angry and, worst of all, not pulsating. Normally the heartbeat is transmitted through the dura, and it pulses gently in and out of the edges of the skull. 2013's dura was rigid and still. Not a good sign.

Nate handed me a very small scalpel, and I sliced through the dura. Immediately, thick, clotted red blood began to squeeze through the opening. I thought of my mentor Dr. Baghai and his coolness in this situation. I thought, *Control this, Lee—do not let this kid die.* With scissors, I extended the dural opening, and a congealed, formed clot slid through and fell out of the baby's head. It looked like a piece of liver, and once it fell out I could see the swollen brain.

A large artery was pumping blood, and it squirted up into my face as I tried to gain control of it with cauterizing forceps. Once the bleeding was stopped, I pointed at the brain and said to Chris, "Pressure's off now. Say a prayer that the brain will start to pulsate. If it doesn't, we may have been too late."

We watched for what seemed like hours, and slowly the brain began to move. With every heartbeat, the brain turned less and less red, eventually achieving the healthier pink color of a normal brain.

I knew from the CT scan that the bullet had lodged just under the surface of the frontal lobe. Other than tearing the artery, which had caused the near-fatal subdural bleeding, the bullet itself hadn't done a whole lot of brain damage. I started to let myself believe that this kid could not only survive but maybe recover.

I dipped my little finger in sterile saline solution to make it slippery, then gently felt inside the hole in the frontal lobe. I could feel the metal bullet fragment there. Using the smallest forceps I could find, I pulled the bullet out and dropped it into a metal pan. When he heard the clinking sound you always hear on TV when doctors remove bullets, Nate laughed out loud. I turned to him to see what was funny.

"I've never heard that sound in real life before. The pans we use in America are plastic."

He was right; I'd never heard it either.

Chris nudged me and pointed at the brain. "What's that?"

I looked down and saw where he was pointing. A dark blue vein the size of a small sausage snaked across the surface of the boy's brain. It looked tense and swollen, as if it might burst.

"Vein of Labbé," I said. "It's the only way out for most of the blood in his brain. If it clots off, he'll die."

"What can we do to prevent that?"

I shook my head. "Keep his blood pressure up, keep him hydrated, and pray."

As I sewed the dura back together, I had a big decision to make. Should I put the bone back in, or leave it out? If I left it out, the baby would have to have another operation later, assuming he survived—a second chance for this dusty, make-shift operating room to expose him to infection, bleeding, and the general perils of brain surgery. But if I put it back in, he would be at risk for high intracranial pressure if his brain swelling worsened.

I looked at his brain, still pulsing nicely and now nearly as pink as a normal brain. When I was a resident and we were discussing theoretical surgical problems, we used to jokingly say, "WWJD"—meaning not "What Would Jesus Do?" but rather "What Would Jack Do?" Jack Wilberger was our department chairman, and he was (and still is) known for his sage wisdom and thoughtful solutions to difficult problems.

Dr. Wilberger and Dr. Baghai and the rest of my old professors weren't available to me for questions now, though. I remembered a piece of advice one of my fellow residents had given me: When there isn't a right answer, brain surgeons have to make a decision and "Just sell it, baby."

So I stood there for a few seconds, saying a prayer without hearing an answer, and made my decision. *JSIB*, I thought.

"Nate, hand me the bone flap."

I taught Chris how to attach the flap back to the rest of the skull, and he taught me a few things about sewing the thin, delicate scalp together. I put in an ICP monitor, and a comforting green 0 showed on the screen.

We rolled the baby down the hall to the ICU. I wondered who there would help us take care of him. Two soldiers stood in the hall, and one of them spoke as we passed by. "Doc, we heard that his parents tried to run a checkpoint. Marines had to shoot into the car. Both of them died."

I looked down at this precious Iraqi baby, 2013, and wondered how a brain-injured orphan would survive the war, and what would happen to him if he did.

CHAPTER 11

THIS KID'S GONNA DIE, AND IT'S MY FAULT

I was standing on the helipad, watching a huge, twin-rotor Chinook fly away from the hospital. Actually, I learned after the war that the helicopters everyone called Chinooks were really CH–46 Sea Knights, a slightly smaller Marine Corps version of the Army's CH–47 Chinooks.

I'd learned to recognize the difference in the sound of different types of aircraft, so that I could usually tell by the sound whether an approaching helicopter was likely to bring me business. Those we called Chinooks almost never flew in the daytime, probably because they offered such a slow and massive target. This one had landed at the hospital several hours before, after delivering a few banged-up Marines who needed minor care. I had a cup of coffee with the crew, and they let me look around inside the chopper before they took off to get back to their base before sunrise.

The gray ship eased into the misty sky and slipped off into the gathering dawn, back to the war.

I turned toward the hospital and saw Chris riding up on a bicycle, an odd sight, considering that he was wearing gym shorts, a T-shirt, body armor, and a Kevlar helmet. He wore a backpack over his armor, and I wondered how he managed to balance all that weight on the old Schwinn.

"What's up with the bike?"

Chris stopped, one foot on the pedal and one on the ground, and pushed his helmet out of his eyes. "I promised my wife I would never be outside without my protective gear on," he said, "but it gets really heavy walking around like that all day, so I found some wheels."

He dismounted and left the bike against the concrete barrier outside the ER. We stepped inside together, and he shed his gear. We were headed to the DFAC for breakfast when I heard someone yelling at me from the end of the hall. I turned—a nurse was running toward us. "Need you in the unit," he said. "The baby's ICP is really high."

The monitor read 70 where the 0 had been yesterday. An ICP of seventy is too high for the patient to survive for long. Normal pressure readings are under twenty, and most people have pressures less than ten most of the time. Seventy meant that the blood flow to the baby's brain was much reduced, and unless it was quickly restored, coma and death were imminent.

My first thought: Why did I put his bone back in?

I checked the monitor's connections, adjusted it, and turned it off and back on. The screen blinked while it reset, and the reading appeared: 73.

Then I remembered the first rule of patient care: examine the patient.

2013 was still on the breathing machine, since Chris had thought it best to let the boy's body rest on medications after the stress of his injury and surgery the day before. He was sedated with the drug Versed, which meant I couldn't really examine him thoroughly. I asked Chris to turn off the medicine drip, and asked how long it would take for the boy to wake up from the chemical sleep.

"Twenty or thirty minutes," he said.

If the ICP was really seventy, 2013 could die in that amount of time.

I looked at 2013's pupils. Normal.

Chris looked at the chart. "His vitals have all been normal, and his lab work is okay too."

"Maybe it's a bad box," I said. "Let's try another one."

I walked to the supply closet and grabbed another of the Codman ICP monitor boxes, the computers the monitor cables hook up to. The strain gauge monitor sends its information to the computer, where the data is interpreted and turned into a number we can use. We had three of the boxes in the hospital, and one of them was currently unused.

We waited the thirty seconds or so it took to boot up the machine, and I hooked the cable up and hit the button to tell the computer to give me a reading. The whole time we were waiting, I was thinking, *I hope my decision to replant the bone didn't kill this kid.*

The number flashed: 80.

I thought, *This kid's gonna die, and it's my fault.* "We better get him to CT. He must be bleeding into his head or swelling his brain."

We rushed the baby to the CT suite, where we waited ten minutes while the techs finished scanning a soldier's abdomen, full of shrapnel from an IED.

Then they rushed the soldier off to surgery—leaving no one to clean the blood and dirt from the scanner's table. In San Antonio, I would have sat at the desk while orderlies cleaned the machine and readied it for the next patient. But here, there was no orderly to do it, and I wasn't going to put that baby down in someone else's blood.

I found some paper towels and cleaning spray and wiped the scanner down. Then Chris lifted the baby from his stretcher and gently placed him on the table. The techs returned and set up the scan.

One by one the images crossed the screen. His brain scan was completely normal. There was no new bleeding or swelling. Yet the ICP was now 90.

"What could it be?" Chris asked.

I shook my head. "Venous thrombosis, maybe. If he clotted off the vein of Labbé, he's in serious trouble. I'll have to do a decompressive craniectomy, but that might not even be enough."

In America, we never have to wonder about things like that. I would have simply ordered an MRI, which would have shown definitively whether the baby needed surgery and what was causing the ICP problem. In that desert tent that day, however, I had few options to provide the information I needed to make my decision. WWJD? I wasn't sure what Jack would do, and I doubted that any of my professors had ever been in this situation.

The number kept climbing. It had been about fifteen minutes since Chris turned off the Versed drip. "Back to the ICU," I said to the techs. "I'm going to try something."

They wheeled 2013 down the hall while I ran ahead of them to the supply closet. I opened a new monitor kit, set up a sterile field in the ICU, and shaved a small patch of the baby's head.

"What are you doing?" Chris said.

"I'm going to put in a new monitor, just to make sure his pressure's really high. If it is, we'll go straight to surgery."

I knew I was taking a big risk. If the monitor was telling the truth, then I was wasting a few minutes of precious time — time 2013 really didn't have. But I also knew that I had never seen an ICP above thirty or forty in a patient with a normal CT and normal pupils. I couldn't believe the data, and I wasn't willing to take a baby back to surgery — especially not here — to find out that he had a bad monitor.

I made a small incision, then used a hand drill to make a pencil-eraser-sized hole in his head and inserted a brand-new monitor. I disconnected the old one from the box and connected the new one.

Thirty seconds felt like hours, but when the screen flashed, the ICP readout displayed: 2.

"It was just a bad monitor. He'll be fine."

Chris didn't restart the Versed drip, and in a few minutes the baby opened his eyes and began to move his arms and legs. Later that day we removed his breathing tube, and 2013 began to smile and interact with us.

I wondered afterward how many years of my life that broken monitor stole. I suppose I was the only person in the hospital who knew how scared I'd been of making the wrong decision, of costing that baby his life by my decision to put his bone back in or by waiting too long to take him back to surgery. Because when you're not sure what Jack would do, you just sell it, baby.

CHAPTER 12

A VERY ODD SKULL

I ran most of the way to the hospital from my room. The day had dawned cold and cloudy after the long rainstorm of the night before, and every step of the nearly mile-long route I took that morning led me through either standing water or an inch of mud. But the wet weather somehow hadn't kept the sandstorm from battering us that morning as well. If I'd thought about it, I would have found it curious to be wet and covered in mud and at the same moment having an asthma attack from breathing in the dirt-filled air.

The door to the emergency room lobby was a welcome sight, but I had to throw my weight to shut it behind me, the wind was blowing so hard. I'd wrapped a scarf around my head in a mostly futile attempt to filter out the sand, I had my dark black Wiley X sunglasses on, and I was wheezing like an old man with tuberculosis. I needed an inhaler.

"What's up, Lawrence of Arabia?"

I looked up and saw one of the new emergency room doctors staring at me. I realized how ridiculous I must have looked, so I unwound my scarf. I was covered in mud up to my knees, but there was sand sifting off my head and neck, and I felt like that kid in the old Peanuts cartoons, Pig-Pen, who always had a cloud of dirt around him.

"Sandstorm," I said between coughs. "I'm Lee, the neurosurgeon. You got any albuterol?"

He laughed. "Yeah, I wish I could sell the stuff. Everybody on base has asthma or bronchitis right now, between the sand and the stuff they're always burning. I'm Chuck, by the way."

He had a point about the burning material. Along with the constant noise, explosions, blowing sand, and mud, there was an ever-present smokiness in the air. Huge trash fires were burning almost all the time at several locations on base, and there were also frequent smoke clouds blowing by from distant oil field fires. It was like being in Los Angeles on a smoggy day, only a lot worse.

Chuck went into the pharmacy and returned a minute later with a couple of inhalers. I took a puff, inhaled deeply, and held the medicine in my lungs as long as I could stand it.

"Thanks. Sorry about getting your floor dirty."

"No problem," he said. His face got more serious. "I'm sure we'll be mopping it soon anyway. There are Black Hawks inbound with some US troops. IED blast. Could be our first mass casualty."

I felt two things at the same time: amazed that I was no longer afraid of those words, and amazed that even though I'd only been in Iraq for four weeks, I was at that moment the only doctor in the hospital who really knew what a mass casualty was.

I put my hand on his shoulder. "It'll be okay. You guys are well trained. We'll handle it."

I wondered whether, on my first day, I had looked as uncertain to Pete as this guy looked to me now. He stared off into the distance for a second, then turned back to me and said, "Hey, while we're waiting, could you look at a patient for me?"

He led me into the ER, where a skeleton-thin Iraqi man lay on one of the beds. He wore a robe and sandals and had a thick black beard and curly hair. A technician had the man's belly exposed and was performing an ultrasound. Two nurses and another doctor, one of the new general surgeons named Brian, were looking over the tech's shoulder, peering at the screen. They seemed to be arguing about what they were seeing.

"What's going on with this guy?" Chuck asked me. We approached the patient, who looked down disinterestedly at the circus-like atmosphere his own abdominal ultrasound was creating. There was a vague sadness in his eyes. I noticed now that he also had a major skull deformity—I had missed it at first, because the man's full head of hair camouflaged the shape of his head, but he clearly had a very odd skull shape. I probed the deformity gently, felt the concave lines of his skull and the softness underneath. He looked at me blankly, as if he had little interest in anything going on around him.

"He walked up to the gate and told the guards he had a stomachache, and that he was supposed to come here if he had any problems," Chuck said. "He had a letter with him, written in Arabic. We sent for one of the translators already. He's got some kind of mass in his abdomen, and that's why we called the surgeon. But we also noticed his head."

Still probing the patient's squishy scalp, I tried to remember all the types of cancer and infection that can cause the skull to erode. The patient was going to need a CT scan so that I could tell how extensive the damage was.

The more I thought about the combination of a collapsed skull and a painful abdomen, the more I felt that there was an obvious diagnosis, something that I should know but that was staying obscure in mind, dim, just out of my reach.

"Hello, Doctor. It is good to see you."

I looked up and saw Isam, one of the Iraqi translators. He was tall and muscular and looked like a young Omar Sharif.

He spoke to the patient, then shook his head at the man's

reply. "He's not making any sense, Doctor. The words he speak, they are, how you say? Like gibbering."

He was describing a neurological disorder called aphasia, which meant that the patient was unable to produce intelligible speech. Not too surprising, considering that the caved-in side of his skull was the left, and in most people the left side of the brain controls speech and language function. Either something was eroding the patient's skull and destroying his brain, or he had a brain injury. This also explained his apathy toward what was happening to him; people with left frontal lobe injuries frequently have something called *abulia*, where they seem to not care about anything.

This case was getting more and more interesting. The diagnosis now felt a little less remote. In my mind I could see the textbook on my shelf in San Antonio I would have normally reached for. I thumbed mentally through the chapters on disorders of speech and thought.

My subconscious library trip was interrupted by another comment from Isam. "Oh, this letter explains the problem," he said, holding the paper the patient had presented to the gate guards. "This man's name is Adnan, and he is an Iraqi from Balad Village. He was injured in a bombing last year, and was treated here by the Army doctors. It says his chart number was 1255."

A few minutes later, I had retrieved and was reading Adnan's chart. The diagnosis I'd been reaching for was completely wrong. "Guys, I think I know what your abdominal mass is," I said.

I spent the next thirty minutes giving the emergency room staff and all the new surgeons a lecture on decompressive craniectomy and letting all of them feel Adnan's belly, so they could learn what a piece of someone's skull feels like after it's been in their abdomen for eighteen months.

An Army neurosurgeon had saved 1255's life, buried the removed portion of his skull bone in his abdomen, and eventually Adnan/1255 had been discharged from the hospital into the care of his family. At that time, and still up to the point I arrived, the general consensus among military neurosurgeons was that replacing the bone flap in the tent hospital environment would lead to a high infection rate. Thus, once the patient was stable enough, he was discharged with his bone still in his belly, in the hope that after the war the Iraqi health care system would recover enough to take care of those patients.

An Iraqi physician had written the letter in Arabic and told Adnan to carry it with him at all times, because his brain injury kept him from being able to communicate his medical history—or much of anything else. The Army doctor had told the patient to come back to the hospital if he ever had any problems, so when he started having abdominal pain he just walked up to the gate.

Adnan's belly problem turned out to be nothing serious, but the case of the rock-hard abdominal tumor and sunken skull was definitely the most complex diagnosis the new team had yet faced. As doctors facing life-and-death situations constantly are prone to do, we saw the dark comedy in the situation and got a good laugh at our own expense, joking about discovering a new disease known as "Skull Belly."

The mass casualty we expected never materialized that day. Instead, we had a day of working up a medical mystery with an amusing and thankfully happy conclusion.

The next day would not prove to be as humorous.

CHAPTER 13

"GET THAT CAT OUTTA HERE!"

A thick black mix of smoke from oil field fires and burning trash, along with blowing sand, stung my eyes, burned my lungs, and obscured Tuesday morning's sunrise. Another day, another breathing treatment, another dose of whatever Iraq had to offer in my graduate course in trauma surgery, terrorism, and teamwork. *What's new?*

That mental question was answered as soon as I entered the ICU for rounds. Everything was new.

President Bush's Coalition of the Willing had received its major support from Great Britain and Australia. And some of those willing to help were Australian medics. Half of the new nurses and anesthesia staff were Aussies, along with an orthopedist and a general surgeon. The ICU nurses from Down Under had come in last night—and put their stamp on it. A huge Australian flag hung along one wall, and stuffed wallabies and kangaroos were positioned around the tent in strategic locations. One of the nurses had a rugby jersey on over her scrubs. No one actually said, "G'day, mate," but it wouldn't have surprised me.

It was our first day with only the new staff in the hospital, and the boss was going to make rounds with us. Someone at the Pentagon had decided that when they rotated medical staffs in their field hospitals, they needed to replace everyone at once, including the command staff. And so not only were we about to enter our first day of the war with an almost totally rookie team, we also had no leaders with combat experience. I thought, *This could be a disaster.*

I surveyed the room; people huddled into groups, staying close to the people from their own bases and specialties. It occurred to me again that my having to come early had robbed me of really belonging to either the old staff or the new one. At least I knew a few of the folks from San Antonio, like Colonel H, the new hospital commander. He was a plastic surgeon back home, and we had operated together a few times. I knew he was a good man, and I was glad he was here. But I've always hated when administrators make rounds. It's torture.

Colonel H insisted that the entire team — all the surgeons, ICU doctors, the therapists, a pharmacist, a dietitian, and several interpreters — round together on every patient in the hospital. The idea was good, making sure we all knew everything relevant about the care of every patient. But in practice, it was an inefficient traffic jam of differing philosophies, training biases, and egos vying for their own specialty-specific goals or pulling rank-over-experience power plays.

"Wow — whoever closed that belly was pretty sloppy," said one general surgeon.

I looked at the patient's wound, remembering the night Vic saved his life. An IED had gone off, and we had five INGs and a couple of Americans show up at once around two in the morning. I was operating on a young Marine, and Vic was working on this ING captain three feet away from me. Vic removed most of his large intestine and part of his liver in about thirty-five minutes.

Halfway through our operations, a loud explosion shook the operating room, and the lights went out.

"Everybody hold still," said Vic, his voice never cracking. "The backup generators will kick in in a minute."

I stood in the darkness, hearing the anesthetists scrambling for their hand ventilation bags so they could keep breathing for the patients while the power was out in the operating room.

Once during my residency, when I was about to clip an aneurysm, someone in the room tripped over the extension cord to the operating microscope and unplugged it. The scope went black, with my hands deep inside a girl's brain. Dr. Wilberger very calmly said, "Lee, hold your hands perfectly still, no matter what. If you move you'll either tear the aneurysm and kill her, or rip her optic nerves and blind her. This is what brain surgeons do—be still until you can see, and control your hands."

I stood there that night in Balad, waiting for the generator to restore the lights in the room and trying not to make the Marine's brain injury worse. Vic had his hands in the belly of his patient, and we both held still until we heard the roar of the machine, followed in a few seconds by the lights slowly coming back on.

I looked across the room at Vic, and he winked at me.

While he was closing his patient's wound, a tech ran in and said, "Dr. Vic, there are four more patients with abdominal wounds in the ER. They need you stat." Vic performed the fastest closure of an abdomen I'd ever seen.

Now, here we were five days later, and it wasn't infected, and the patient was eating and doing well. I thought, *It looks pretty good to me.*

The only advantage of rounding in such a huge group and with patients who didn't speak English was that most of the usual courtesies of rounding in America were absent; we didn't spend much time on the "And how are you today, Mrs. Johnson?" social interactions, at least when it came to the non-Americans. As we neared the end of the fourth hour of our first day rounding with all the veterans gone, I was close to finally having all of my new colleagues' names down, and to honing in on their personalities.

My new partner, Tim, had arrived the day before, smelling of the coffeehouses of Al Udeid and sporting a tan from a few days by the pool there while the war machine tried to find him a ride downrange, where I'd been waiting for him. Tim was about my size but had a dark complexion, dark hair, and dark eyes, almost like a negative of Pete. He'd had the same overwhelmed look I'd had when I gave him the tour, that look that said, "Wait—I'm supposed to be able to do *what* with all of this old equipment?"

This morning we were slogging through the last of the patients in the long-term care ward, and I'd heard just about every one of our new surgeons flex his philosophical muscles, each one crashing into the same ideological walls and ceilings I'd hit a few weeks before regarding just about all of the treatment decisions the now-departed other surgeons had made, since the new guys had yet to fully taste the realities of this environment.

We came to the bedside of a Syrian Al Qaeda terrorist whose right arm wounds were packed with gauze. He had been injured while trying to set off a car bomb, and later that day he would make his third trip to the operating room.

"I've never seen extremity wounds managed like this," said one young orthopedist through a nasally New England accent. "It's prehistoric. This guy's going to lose that arm."

A sniffing sound came from his partner, an Australian named Geoff. He had reading glasses on a chain around his neck, his head was polished marble bald, and he looked old enough to be the other guy's father.

"Look, mate, that's how it's done in a dirty environment. You're too young to have seen this work before. He'll be wiring bombs again in no time, if he ever gets out of Abu Ghraib."

"Well, it's unacceptable. That's not how it's going to be done here."

I hid a little smile, remembering similar statements most of the other surgeons had made that morning during rounds, including an almost verbatim reiteration of my original argument with Pete about how we managed head-injured patients. Except that today I had played the role of Pete, and Tim had played the naive and untested me.

We'll see about that, I thought.

Several beepers rang at once, a group mass-casualty page. Here's where we would see what these guys had in them.

We ran into the emergency department and saw Army medics and the new ER staff wheeling in ten stretchers filled with screaming, bleeding men. Colonel H erased any doubts I had about his ability to function as both administrator and surgeon. He ran up to one of the medics. "What happened, Specialist?"

"Ambush near Mosul, sir. Six Americans and four Iraqi policemen survived for us to pick up. Everybody else is dead on the ground. We got multiple gunshot wounds."

Colonel H pointed at one of the older general surgeons, a bald-headed colonel named Dave.

"Dave, you're the new Trauma Czar. Everybody, figure out what's going on with these patients and triage them. Nobody second-guesses Dave. Let's get to work."

Chris already had his hands on a young corporal's bleeding abdomen. Geoff and Bill, the orthopedists, started putting tourniquets on bloody limbs. The ophthalmologist, Augie, ran around the room shining a light into patients' eyes. Another general surgeon, Brian, took over CPR on an Iraqi man who was already in cardiac arrest.

One of the Iraqis had a bullet hole in the middle of his forehead, and I let Tim examine him while I watched. The man was maybe twenty-five, wore a wedding ring, and his lighter-than-normal complexion and clear green eyes made me think he had some European blood in his family line.

Tim performed a solid neurological exam, then looked up at me with his jaw clenched. He blinked hard, and I noticed a tiny tear on one of his eyelashes. "Brain dead," he said.

I repeated the exam. No pupillary response. No reaction to painful stimuli, no reflexes, his body temperature was normal, and he'd been given no medications to confuse the exam.

A nurse wrote 2037 across the man's chest while I double-checked Tim's findings.

Dave, the new Czar, appeared at 2037's bedside. Already his forehead was covered with sweat and he looked nauseated. But when he spoke, I knew he was fine. "Okay, you guys. A bunch of the other patients are going to need the CT scanner. What's your situation?"

I looked at Tim, his eyes now bloodshot with the rage you feel when you're too late to save someone. "Your call," I said.

Tim looked at Dave and shook his head. "He's brain dead, sir."

Dave sighed. "Then call it. As soon as you know you can't save a patient, move on to somebody else. If you're standing around a corpse, you're wasting someone else's chance to survive. Call it." He turned and walked off.

Tim looked at me, his eyes red and wide and no longer full of fear. He turned to the nurse. "2037 is DOA, mark the time as eleven twenty-three."

I spent the next couple of hours watching the new vascular surgeon, Todd, attempt to save the leg of an American. A lot of surgeons would have simply amputated the man's leg after seeing the mangled arteries and veins. Todd delicately picked out the bullet fragments, gently identified the ends of several blood vessels, and sewed in Gore-Tex patch grafts with hundreds of tiny sutures. His hands were steady, his focus laser-like, and he worked with a grace and efficiency I'd seen in only a handful of other surgeons in my career.

When Todd placed the last stitch, he took the clamps off the patient's arteries. I watched as the man's foot turned from a livid blue to a pinkish red. Todd reached for the foot, held his hand there for a moment, and casually said to no one in particular, "Good pulses. I think he'll keep his leg."

As I went from bed to bed that evening on rounds, I heard the stories of the patients and procedures involved in the day's work. Each of the surgeons had lost their mass-casualty virginity in different ways, but other than 2037, who died before he arrived, there were no deaths in our hospital that day. To a man, the surgeons' eyes were transformed from their clear idealism into the bloodshot realism of men who'd been measured and had passed the test.

We were going to be okay.

That night, Tim came over to my place and we chatted for a while, getting to know each other. I wondered how we would operate together, but I felt somewhat reassured by the training and sensitivity he'd shown at the Iraqi policeman's death.

There was a knock at the door, and I opened it to find three men, all captains, in DCUs.

"I'm Joel, this is Jeremiah and John," the tallest said. "Jeremiah and I replaced Brian. We're physical therapists. John is an occupational therapist. Brian said you guys watched movies here at night."

They came in, and John handed over a sack full of potato chips and dip. Movie night was still on, apparently.

We watched an old Steve Martin movie, *The Man with Two Brains*, which was hysterically funny to us because it's about a brain surgeon. Every time he's in surgery, a stray cat runs through the operating room and the surgeon yells, "Somebody get that cat outta here!"

When that movie finished, Joel mentioned that his wife had sent him the World War II miniseries *Band of Brothers*. We watched the first episode, and a vague heaviness settled over all of us. Watching a story about young men in another time and place go through the fight together, I wondered what the next episode of our own war would hold.

The next morning before rounds, Tim and I took Adnan/1255 to the operating room to repair his head and cure his case of skull belly. We'd decided the night before that since the infection rate in the hospital was so low since the Air Force had taken over, we would start putting the bone flaps back in earlier. Adnan would be the first patient to undergo the skull repair, called a *cranioplasty*, in the tent hospital environment.

It turned out that Tim and I were both left-handed, so we could work side by side and not bump elbows. Tim was efficient and had steady hands, but he didn't say much as we screwed the bone back onto Adnan's head with tiny titanium plates. I missed the easy rapport Pete and I had had, and wondered whether surgery with Tim would always be so remote and formal.

I remembered, though, that I'd been pretty nervous the first time I'd operated with Pete, wondering if I'd measure up to his standards and if I'd be accepted by the others as an equal. So I looked at Tim and said, "Hey, I like the way you operate. I think you're going to do great here."

Tim's masked face hid his expression, but I saw smile lines form in the corner of his eyes. He turned toward the anesthetist and said, "Somebody get that cat outta here!"

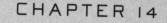

CHAPTER 14

THE NIGHT VANIA'S FAMILY WAS SHOT

EMAIL HOME
Wednesday, January 26, 2005

Good morning, America.

I awoke this morning feeling the full force of the fact that I am 7,000 miles from home, that I left one month ago today, that I have a steep road ahead of me when I get back to America. These realities crushed me down into the mattress, as if to convince me that I should just stay in bed.

But I prayed about it, and I remembered this: God is not surprised that I am here. All the days of my life were written in his book before one of them came to be (Psalm 139:16), and God determined the exact time and place where I would be in my life (Acts 17:26). That means that I am right where I am supposed to be.

Get out of bed, Lee. You're right where you're supposed to be. Carry on.

Thanks for listening. Since I don't have my normal folks here, all of you got to work through that with me. I appreciate it.

Many of you have written to ask about the baby who was shot in the head. Yesterday we learned a lot more about him, including his real name. You don't have to pray for 2013 anymore...

+

I walked into the ICU to check on 2013, the baby I'd operated on after he was shot in the head when his parents ran a checkpoint. A young Iraqi woman stood by his bedside, looking down at him.

In another time, another place, I would have thought she was a pretty young woman. But the person by the bedside, looking into my eyes, had an edge to her, steel in her spine. She said something in Arabic, and when I shrugged my shoulders and held up my hands, she turned away. She touched 2013's face gently and stroked his hair. Her eyes moistened, but when she looked at me again I saw not sadness but anger.

She might have been twenty, but I had learned that the rough environment and constant stress in Iraq made people look older than they really were. She wore a brown sweater over a khaki dress, had her hair pulled back in braids, and her head was not covered. I wondered if she was the baby's mother, but we'd heard from the soldiers that his parents were both killed in the shooting that night. She kept one hand on him and put her other hand on her heart, saying something softly over him that sounded like prayer.

I asked, "What is your name?"

She turned her head slightly, and I was glad that looks couldn't actually kill.

"Perhaps I can be helping," Isam said as he entered the ICU. "The guards sent for me."

I nodded. "Thanks. I need to know who she is, but she won't talk to me."

Isam cupped his hands in front of him and bowed slightly toward the girl. He spoke to her softly, and she replied. He pointed toward me and said something else. She wiped a tear from her eye and looked toward me again, her expression much softer now.

"Her name is Vania," Isam said. "She is his sister. I explain you are his doctor, who save his life. She thought you were soldier."

Vania's anger toward me was replaced by a grim gratitude. I never saw an expression resembling happiness cross her face, but at least there was a distant, hopeful look, as if she might be starting to believe that their life could return to some semblance of whatever normal was for them. With Isam's help, I learned that the baby's name was Mohamed, and that his parents were not dead after all. Instead, they were being treated in one of the few remaining civilian hospitals in Iraq, and were expected to fully recover from their wounds. This happy news was surprising but not shocking, since pretty much everything we heard about events outside the wire seemed to be subject to change. Information filtered unreliably through the fog of war.

I asked Isam whether Vania knew the details of the night her family was shot. When she heard his question, she sat down on the edge of Mohamed's bed. Her face hardened, and her eyes looked past Isam, through the tent walls, into a world where foreign armies shoot into cars full of babies and mommies and daddies.

Over the next few minutes, through interpreted words and looks that needed no translation, a tragic story emerged. As

I listened, as hard as this is to say, I couldn't find anyone to blame for what had happened.

Mohamed's parents had been driving along late at night. In a heavy rainfall, they came upon vehicles blocking the road and American soldiers yelling in English. A car was on fire beside the road. A few bloody bodies were strewn about, and the soldiers had several men lined up against one of their trucks, pointing their guns and screaming words Vania's father could not understand.

He did understand, though, that he and his wife and baby were in danger. He wanted only to get away, to get his family safely home. He wanted nothing of the war or the insurgency or the revolution Saddam had preached his entire lifetime. He just wanted his family to be safe.

Their world, Vania said, is one in which people are frequently ambushed, attacked, and senselessly murdered. It is a world where suicide bombers blow themselves up at weddings. Terrified, her father tried to accelerate past the burning car. That was all he remembered when he told this story to Vania days later, after the doctors had found her and brought her to her parents.

I thought about the Marines who had been there that night — probably just teens, perhaps in their twenties, trying to make sense of a chaotic and stressful situation. The part of the Sunni Triangle near Ramadi where the incident took place was at that time one of the most dangerous areas in Iraq, and we took care of Marines almost every day who had been shot or blown up because of insurgent activity there. Through the darkness and the rain, they would not have been able to see inside the car approaching them. They would have shouted at the driver to roll down the window and communicate.

I could feel the young Marine's heart racing as he decided what to do. Approach the car? Wait for it to stop and let the driver roll down the window? If the Marine made the wrong choice, the driver might detonate a bomb, and a lot of Americans would die. He hesitated — and in that moment, the driver accelerated rapidly, attempting to drive through the checkpoint. The Marine would have thought the driver was trying to attack, with either explosives or bullets. He and his colleague opened fire on the vehicle.

The car stopped. No explosions occurred. The Marines ran closer and looked inside — finding, to their horror, not a terrorist strapped to a bomb but a family of three, bleeding and moaning. The baby had a bullet hole in his forehead. Someone called for a medevac Black Hawk, and the medics loaded the baby on board. The parents were less severely injured, and the medics were able to arrange for them to be treated locally by civilian doctors.

It was a terrible situation, the kind of tragedy war forces on people. No one was wrong. No one was right.

Vania trembled as she finished her story. I told her through Isam that Mohamed had come through his surgery well and was ready to go home. I took the stitches out of his head while she held her little brother. I asked if I could hold him one more time, and she handed him to me.

As I had done every night since operating on him, I took Mohamed in my arms and pulled him close. He was one of those babies who burrows into your arms and lays his head on your shoulder as if he's going to melt into you. For me, the moment expanded: I felt the arms of each of my children, I felt all the love in the world flowing into me through this Iraqi baby I would never see again, and I quietly prayed a prayer of protection for him into his ear.

I had tears in my eyes when I gave Mohamed back to his big sister, a girl forced to face grown-up realities because of decisions made by two world leaders she'd never met. She said thank you to me and to the nurses and Isam, but her tone and the look in her eyes said more than her words. The uniform I wore represented the people who had put her family through this hell, and despite the fact that I had saved Mohamed's life, Vania no doubt felt the double cut of having to be grateful to the same people who had created their problem.

I watched the gate guards lift the wire and let Vania and Mohamed through. I didn't know whether to be thankful that I'd been there to help, or ashamed that Mohamed had needed that help.

CHAPTER 15

PLUGGED ROCKETS AND HOMEMADE BIOLOGICAL WEAPONS

EMAIL HOME

Thursday, January 27, 2005

Hello, friends.

Yesterday was frightening, even as we saw clearly God's hand of protection on us.

After rounds, about forty people from the hospital gathered in front of the Porta-Potties to wait for a bus to take them to a briefing on the other side of the base. Tim and I decided that he would go this time and that I would stay in case anyone came in needing our help.

Around 10 a.m., I was sitting at a desk by the ER when I heard a loud sound that reminded me of a bottle rocket. It was so loud and close that everyone noticed it. Then people ran into the ER saying that a large object had landed in the parking lot and made a crater.

It was a rocket. A ground-to-ground missile had landed on the exact spot where those folks had waited an hour before. It made a twelve-foot-deep crater, but it didn't detonate. At the same moment, at least six other rockets had landed on base—the first coordinated attack since I've been here. Somehow, not a single rocket blew up. The EOD troops said that the recent rain had made the ground so soft that the rockets just plugged into the mud. That's the last time I'll complain about the weather.

One of the rockets landed in the housing area where our trailers are, and another outside the gym where we work out. I don't know about the rest.

The path of the rocket that landed just outside the hospital would have put it about thirty feet over my head when I heard it. That's when you realize that the tent isn't going to help you much if something huge blows up one hundred feet away. Praise God for the non-detonation.

The Alarm Red sounded, and we spent the rest of the day in body armor and helmets as the EOD team tried to dig up the rocket so that they could move it somewhere else to detonate it. They spent hours digging, but finally decided to blow it up in the crater. First they put big concrete barriers around the hole to keep us safe.

Some people in the hospital joked nervously, some went about their business as usual, and some were clearly very afraid. One technician hid under her desk, crying quietly. It was the first time we've had that close a call or an attack directly on the hospital, and it made us all remember that we are at war. At one point they lined us all up in a hallway and told us to sit against the wall. I got pretty nervous, thinking that if the rocket exploded and caught the hospital on fire, there was no way out. I had a little pocketknife with me, and thought about how I'd never be able to cut my way through the canvas in time. I decided that if I survived the day, I was going to buy a bigger knife, like the ones the Army guys were issued. The Air Force didn't give us knives, but at least they gave us malaria pills.

During the Alarm Red, we received a helicopter full of US soldiers from right outside the gate, victims of an IED that blew up right around the time of the rocket attacks. I can't say much about them yet, but we were all busy for a while. Suffice it to say that I'm now convinced my new partners are at least as good as the guys who recently left.

When the EOD squad finally detonated the rocket, it shook the whole hospital and threw mud and gravel over a hundred yards away. I can't imagine what would have happened if that thing had blown up on impact, but I probably wouldn't be sending this email.

About an hour later, the All Clear sounded, and we were allowed to leave the building. I was too tired to eat, so I went to my trailer and slept for several hours, worn out from a full day of surgery and wearing body armor for twelve hours.

Around midnight, I had to go back to the ER because a patient came in complaining of headaches. His CT scan showed a large brain tumor. Even here, illness lurks. We sent him straight to Germany.

They installed a new gate at the hospital yesterday evening that looks a lot sturdier than the little wire gate there before. They stationed a tank out there too. I feel a little safer, I guess.

Have a great day, everyone, and give thanks for the fact that most likely no one will try to blow you up today. Your friends in Iraq can't say that.

I love you all, and miss you much. Gotta run for now, though. Patients are coming in.

Lee

+

"Wake up, Lee! I need to check my email while there's still time."

I looked up. Tim was standing behind me, patting my shoulder. It took me a few seconds to realize that I'd fallen asleep in front of the computer in the surgeons' lounge after I sent out my letter. I'd never left the hospital after I came back in to see the guy with the brain tumor, because an IED attack immediately afterward had produced twenty patients for us, six Americans and some Iraqi civilians, plus a bunch of insurgents who looked like they should be on an FBI Most Wanted List poster. Tim and I had operated all night, and when we'd finally finished the last case, I'd sat down at the computer desk.

I lifted my head and wiped a pile of drool off of the desk as I slid out of Tim's way. "What a night," I said.

Tim nodded as he logged on. "I think the enemy changed the rules yesterday."

I plopped onto the couch, trying to decide between going back to sleep or going to the ICU to check on our patients. We weren't going to do group rounds today because all the other surgeons were still in the operating room. All night long, in case after case, we'd seen that whoever had made this particular bomb had not been a very nice person, even by terrorist standards. We were used to finding ball bearings and metal shards in our patients after IEDs blew up. But this one had been full of razor blades and pieces of steel wire and rocks, coated with brown goo that the infectious disease specialist identified as human stool. I guess the bomb maker figured that if someone survived the blast, they might die later of infection — it was a homemade biological weapon. As disgusting and sinister as this was, it had occurred to me while I was removing a goo-coated rock from an Army private's frontal lobe that militaries have used bacteria as a weapon for centuries. War brings out the worst in people.

"Hey, check this out," Tim said.

I dragged myself off the couch and slumped over the desk. Tim pointed to the screen, which showed a photo of a pretty-girl-next-door type with a bright smile standing sideways, resting her hands on her protruding belly. "Your wife?" I said.

"Yep. And our daughter. First kid."

"Congrats. When's she due?"

Tim's face darkened. "About a month. We're going to try to set up a webcam so I can see her deliver."

I wondered how, with twelve other neurosurgeons in the Air Force, someone had chosen to send both Pete and Tim off to war when their wives were having babies. As much as I missed my kids, and as heartbroken as I was that my family had crumbled, I couldn't imagine being seven thousand miles away when your child is born.

"I'm sorry, man," I said.

A tech from the ER ran into the room. "Two more Black Hawks coming in. Another IED. They're about twenty minutes out."

"Perfect," Tim said, typing his reply to his wife's message. He leaned back in the chair and rubbed his eyes, yawning. He looked awful, I thought, but at least he didn't have to wipe his own spit off the desk. I probably looked worse.

"Hey," he said, "we just finished our fourth crani an hour ago. If there are any heads coming in, I hope we have enough instruments."

"Sit tight and relax," I said. "I'll check on the instruments and make rounds in the ICU before the choppers get here."

I checked my watch as I walked to the instrument-processing area. Techs brought dirty instruments there for cleaning and sterilization. Every instrument had to be removed from its tray, washed and replaced, and then steam-sterilized in an autoclave. We had two autoclaves, and it took about three hours to sterilize a tray.

Sergeant McDonald was washing instruments. He had on hospital scrubs, size small, I was sure; he was easily three or four inches shorter than my 5'9". I watched as he nimbly cleaned Iraqi and Syrian and American blood off forceps, scissors, and clamps. When he looked up, I saw in his red eyes and distant look the same crushing fatigue and general sadness I felt.

"What can I do ya for, Major?" he asked.

"Just checking on craniotomy instruments, Sarge. We have more patients coming in."

McDonald looked to his right, and I saw a stack of eight or nine dirty instrument trays waiting to be cleaned. Both autoclaves were hissing, and the room smelled like soap and steam.

"One of your sets is cooling off, ready to go, and one is about thirty minutes from being done. The other two, 'bout four hours. I gave my other two techs an order to get some sleep, so it's just me for a while."

I shook my head. "That's not going to work. If we have more than two patients who need brain surgery on those choppers, we're in trouble."

McDonald huffed and seemed to grow taller. He squinted at me, jaw muscles bunched. Pushing up his glasses with the back of a gloved hand dripping soapy water and holding a surgical clamp, he said, "You think I can snap my fingers and make these things clean, sir? I bump your stuff to the front of the line, I'll have ortho docs and general surgeons down my throat.

Everybody's all hot to have their stuff ready first. You guys seem to forget that when you're busy, we are too. I'm no surgeon, but I'm busting my hump same as you. So unless you got another autoclave somewhere I don't know about, it's gonna be four hours." He tossed the clean clamp onto the pile of instruments to his left, stared me down for a second, picked up a bloody retractor, and went back to work.

I turned and left, feeling like I'd just been dismissed after a visit to the principal's office. Until now, I hadn't thought about the fact that dozens of people were working hard to make sure I had what I needed to save someone's life. People like McDonald who never got to see the patients and would never be in the spotlight. But we couldn't function without them, and they were getting mortared and missing their kids, same as me. And he was right—when we operated all night long, somebody in the instrument room was in there sweating away, washing little bits of the war down the drain to give us back the tools we needed, knowing we'd soon get them bloody all over again.

In the ICU I saw Brad, one of the critical-care doctors, standing next to an Iraqi man I'd operated on a few hours before. The patient had a huge skull fracture from the IED blast, and when I'd removed his broken frontal bone and his destroyed frontal lobe, I had found a D-sized Energizer battery buried in his brain.

"How's he doing?"

"ICP is normal. Pupils aren't working, though. Augie thinks he's going to be blind in both eyes from the blast effect. His labs are all out of whack too. I've been having a hard time getting his blood sugar under control."

I wondered: Why would a healthy-appearing thirty-something-year-old Iraqi have a high sugar level? "Did someone give him steroids?" I asked.

Brad shook his head. "I think he's diabetic. The problem

we have with a lot of these patients is that they haven't had any health care for most of their lives. Our troops are all in good shape, have their shots, go to the dentist. When one of our boys has an injury, that's usually all that's wrong with him. These guys, not so much. They have high blood pressure, diabetes, heart disease, abscessed teeth. We have a pretty hard time taking care of them after surgery sometimes. Check out the Godfather over there." He pointed to the patient in the next bed.

I looked over and saw a middle-aged man, 2115, who looked remarkably like a young, tanned Marlon Brando. He had an open belly wound and an eye patch.

"Look at his hands," Brad said. His knuckles were enlarged, and his fingers were twisted sideways. "I think he has rheumatoid arthritis. I can't give him prednisone to help with that, though, because it will keep his abdominal wound from healing."

I remembered the US soldier from the night before, the one who had come to our ER with a headache, where I had diagnosed a brain tumor after viewing his CT scan. That soldier was on his way back to America, where whatever the diagnosis turned out to be, he would have access to every available medical technology and the best doctors in the world. He would have the highest possible chance of survival. But as I looked around the ICU, I realized that none of the non-American patients were likely to see even a family doctor again in their lifetimes.

"That's hard," I said. "It's one thing for us to save someone's life in the OR, but trying to keep them healthy for the long term must be frustrating for you."

Brad nodded.

With the Iraqi health care system in shambles, the doctor in me was frustrated along with Brad. But the "911" on my pager meant that the surgeon in me had to get back to work.

"Showtime," I said. "You should try to move some of these guys out, because we're about to have more."

I ran to the ER, hunger pangs reminding me that I hadn't eaten in almost twenty-four hours, and I'd been working for fifteen hours straight. More importantly, we still had about three hours before our other instruments would be ready.

I had a bad feeling about that.

CONCRETE BARRIERS AND RAZOR WIRE GUARDING THE ENTRANCE TO THE 332ND AIR FORCE THEATER HOSPITAL

ME AFTER FIRST HAIRCUT

SCRUB SINKS OUTSIDE OPERATING ROOMS

Me with tank shell

Chapel at Balad Air Base. Note sandbags for protection against mortar and rocket attacks.

Me leading worship at Balad Chapel

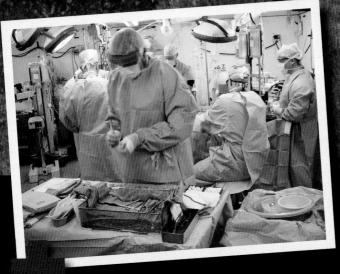

TYPICAL OPERATING ROOM SCENE, WITH
SEVERAL TYPES OF SURGERY HAPPENING
ON THE SAME PATIENT SIMULTANEOUSLY

ELECTION DAY, 2005. ME SCRUBBING
INTO SURGERY WITH MY PISTOL AFTER
WE WERE ORDERED TO REMAIN ARMED
AT ALL TIMES IN CASE OF ATTACK.

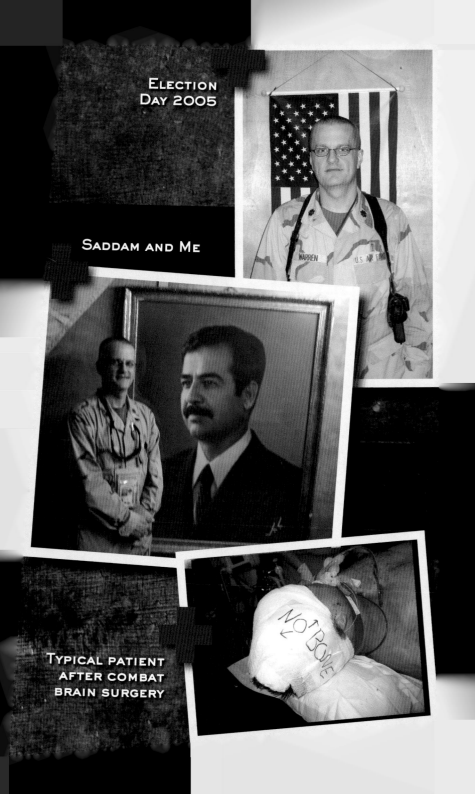

Election Day 2005

Saddam and Me

Typical patient after combat brain surgery

ME PLAYING MY GUITAR
OUTSIDE MY TRAILER.
NOTE THE SANDBAGS.

HUMVEES BORE SIGNS TO WARN IRAQIS
NOT TO APPROACH

MY HANDS IN SURGERY, USING A DRILL
TO REMOVE SKULL BONE

IN FRONT OF SADDAM'S
RESIDENTIAL PALACE, 2005

MEDICS UNLOADING SGT. PAUL STATZER FOR
EMERGENCY BRAIN SURGERY, MARCH 2005

MY WIFE, LISA, AND ME
WITH SGT. PAUL STAZER
IN PITTSBURGH, 2010

CHAPTER 16

THEY WERE STILL SCREAMING WHEN THE CHOPPERS LANDED

While Brad and I were talking, an American convoy outside the wire was passing through a narrow street, on their way to deliver supplies to soldiers at a forward operating base. Insurgents had planted bombs in cars on either side of the street; they hid while the vehicles funneled through. At the right time to inflict maximum damage, one of them triggered the bombs with a cell-phone signal, and the world exploded into fire and flying shrapnel.

After the explosion, while the dust settled and the shock faded, those who were conscious cried out in pain, terror, and anger, trying to find their missing buddies, children, or body parts. US medics, despite the danger, managed to rescue all the Americans and any other injured people still breathing.

The victims were still screaming when the choppers landed at Balad. A multilingual cacophony filled the air as I ran down the hall to the ER.

I heard their cries before I got there.

All eight beds were full, but medics were carrying more

burned, broken men into the overflow room and the surgeons'
lounge. Dave the Trauma Czar ran from bed to bed, trying to
manage the chaos; nurses started IVs and wrote numbers on
chests; and a couple of the surgeons were assessing patients. The
timing was bad—the ICU was nearly full, and half of the ORs
were still being used after last night's chaos.

The first man on my right was a Marine private, missing
a leg. Whoever had reached him first after the bomb went off
had removed the private's DCU belt and used it as a tourniquet
around the thigh just above where his knee would have been.
That had saved his life; I could see his femoral artery sticking
out next to his stark white femur, but no more blood was coming out. I put my hand on his chest and, leaning close, looked
in his eyes. Dozens of little wounds covered his arms, neck, and
face, and he smelled like gasoline.

He was staring at the ceiling, eyes pale and clear blue, and I
could see the tan line on his face from the sunglasses he'd been
wearing that had saved his vision. I shined my penlight in his
eyes. His pupils were normal. Then he startled me by reaching
up with his right hand, grabbing my collar, and pulling me
down almost on top of him. "My foot hurts," he said.

As I straightened, my right hand fell to his left side. My
brain knew what I felt there before I saw it.

I moved the sheet off his left side and saw that his left hand
was resting on the amputated portion of his right leg. His foot
and lower leg were still in his boot; someone at the scene had
scooped them up along with the private. His knee, I guessed,
was still on the battlefield.

I turned to the nurse. "He needs ortho. Grab one of them
when they get out of surgery. Get him some blood and a head
CT."

I patted the private's chest, thankful that his concussion
had taken the clarity of the situation from him for now. His

phantom limb pain would go home with him, along with his Purple Heart medal, but at least he was alive.

I moved to the next bed, where an Iraqi policeman was screaming something in Arabic and struggling against two orderlies, who were trying to keep him on the bed.

The policeman had a bloody bandage over his right eye and forehead, a long laceration on his face, and burns on his chest and arms. He was also missing several fingers. As I gave him a quick assessment, I noticed a piece of steel wire sticking out of his right thumb. I looked at it more closely—it was precisely placed *surgical* hardware, not the type of wire that would have come from a bomb blast. There was also a wound on the palm of his hand that looked a few weeks old, and a smaller one on the back of his hand. This puzzled me. The man had had some type of surgery in the recent past, but I was sure it had not been at our hospital.

An interpreter named Raul arrived at the bedside to help calm the man who was now fighting three of us. As I tried to take the bandage off his head, I had to lean on his chest.

Raul spoke to him in Arabic, and the man quieted. His eyes held both tears and rage, and his words hissed between clenched teeth as he answered Raul. The policeman gestured toward the patient directly across from him, currently being assessed by Tim.

Raul shook his head. "This man is Jafar," he told me. "He is policeman from Tikrit. He say the man in next bed is jihadist who set off the bomb today. Jafar also say he was off duty and in the market with his daughter when bomb go off, and Jafar watch her die from burns while he hold her hand. He ask if he can spend some time with that man."

Ice and fire flowed through me at the same time. Jafar's daughter had died only minutes before, right in front of him, and the man responsible was five feet away. In Jafar's place, I would want to have time alone with that man too. But for the moment, I had to be Jafar's doctor.

"Raul, ask him about the wire in his thumb."

After a conversation I couldn't understand, Raul said, "Jafar say he was in Baghdad two weeks ago. Terrorist shot him in hand, then Jafar shoot terrorist in head. Army doctor fix Jafar's hand. He has appointment tomorrow to take out wire. He ask if this can be done here instead."

With Raul's help, I informed Jafar that our orthopedists would be happy to remove the wire in his thumb. Under his bandages, I found several small lacerations and burns on Jafar's scalp and face, and a very red eye that Augie would need to see.

"Tell him I'm sorry about his daughter, and that he's going to be okay," I said to Raul. I squeezed Jafar's hand, gave the nurse a few orders, and moved on to the next bed.

Tim yelled, "I'm going to the OR with this one, the bomber. He's got a depressed skull fracture and he blew out both his eyes."

I watched as the orderlies rolled Tim's patient out of the ER. He couldn't have been over twenty years old, and he now had a serious brain injury and would be blind for life. His religion and his hatred had led him to kill and injure a lot of people, and if he had enough brain function left to realize it, his memory would forever hold the last thing he'd ever seen with his eyes: his own hands, just as they crossed the wrong wires. What would the future hold for this young man? A head-injured, blind zealot stuck in an Iraqi hospital or an American military prison, destined to remember the pain and the screams and the death he'd caused, but with no one around to praise him for anything he'd done. Everyone he would hear from for the rest of his life would tell him how wrong he was, how evil. And the men who'd sent him to do their work wouldn't miss him; they would just replace him with some other kid willing to fight for their ideals. There was no shortage of them.

I said a little prayer for Tim's patient, now known to me as 2137 — that he would somehow find peace if he survived his wounds and the operation he was about to undergo.

"Good luck, Tim," I yelled down the hall. Then I thought, *Only one set of instruments left.*

The next two beds held Americans, but Chris and his partner, Brian, were working on them. There was a lot of blood. Anesthetists started IVs, and Brian yelled to the Czar that his patient needed an OR, immediately.

Someone shouted, "This one's for you, Lee."

Mitch, an Australian general surgeon, had assessed an American Marine sergeant whose head dressing was soaked in very dark blood. That caught my eye even before I reached the bed. Head wounds usually cause bright red bleeding from scalp arteries, or else the blood clots on the bandage and mixes with dirt from where the patient falls, making a dark brown, almost rust-colored stain. This man's gauze, instead, looked as if it had been dipped in red wine.

Mitch was doing chest compressions on the sergeant, whose heart had stopped beating a few seconds before. A nurse was squeezing two bags of saline into a high-pressure infusion pump, a machine designed to refill someone's circulation quickly when they are losing blood too fast for normal IV lines to drip in the fluid. Mitch yelled for someone to give the man some lidocaine, and to get the blood bank working on some whole blood for him. An anesthetist was squeezing oxygen into the man's lungs through a breathing tube someone had inserted during the helicopter ride.

"I ran the whole body survey, and there are no other injuries," Mitch said while he pumped on the sergeant's chest. Every time Mitch compressed, the Marine's dog tags bounced a few inches off his chest, and the sound of his rib cage crunching and the metal tags clinking sounded like a snare drummer hitting rim shots between beats. The tags told me that the sergeant was a Protestant, his blood type was B negative, and his name was Yeager.

A tech held her hand on Yeager's groin, feeling the femoral artery to verify that Mitch's CPR was strong enough to move blood through the man's body. Mitch stopped after the two bags of fluid went in and looked at the tech.

"I have a pulse, Doctor," she said.

I looked up at the monitor. Yeager's twenty-nine-year-old, healthy heart had done its job. Hearts are amazing machines, programmed to serve a lifetime as long as you give them enough blood to fill them up. Once the fluid filled his tank again, and with the help of David's compression and the lidocaine, Yeager's heart kicked right back into motion. But with every beat, the stain on his head wrap was spreading.

I unwrapped his head and drew a sharp breath. Most of his scalp was missing. Between tangles of burned hair, through the voids where flesh had once been, were shards of stark white bone, and I could see that the bomb blast and whatever it had slammed Yeager's head into had fractured his skull in at least five places. I noticed that the blood coming out seemed mostly to seep from under the bone in the middle of his head, and that it was beginning to look lighter. That meant that the fluid in his veins was now composed more of saline than blood. I had to stop that bleeding, or Yeager was a dead man. But I didn't know yet how bad his brain injury was—whether there was any of what made Yeager Yeager left to save.

I lifted his right eyelid and looked at his pupil, a dark hole in a sea of clear green. I didn't have to lift his left lid, because it was burned off, along with most of that side of his face.

"His pupils are working," I said. "Let's get him to CT and see if he's salvageable."

The scan showed that Yeager's brain was very swollen. Even though this was one of the worst skull fractures I'd ever seen, the brain itself was whole. The bleeding seemed to be coming from a fracture across the sagittal sinus, the large vein that runs from front to back at the top of the brain and is responsible for draining all the blood out of the brain and into the jugular veins.

"I think we can save him if we get the bleeding under control," I said.

By the time I finished scrubbing my hands, Nate had shaved what was left of Yeager's scalp and prepped his skin. Nate and I draped out the head while the anesthesiologist hung four bags of blood and began to squeeze them into Yeager's IV. Tim was on the other side of the room, struggling to save the life of the terrorist responsible for Yeager's injury.

"Knife," I said.

Nate handed me the steel scalpel, and I traced an arc over Yeager's scalp from just in front of his left ear all the way across the top of his head to his right ear. I placed Rainey clips to control bleeding and peeled Yeager's scalp forward all the way down to his eyes. There were three holes in the skin big enough to put my hand through, and I knew that if I managed to save Yeager's life I would then have to try to figure out how to repair his scalp. But holes in his scalp wouldn't matter if he was dead, so I dismissed the thought.

"Drill."

Nate handed me the gold-colored Midas Rex drill, its green rubber hose attached to a tank of compressed air. My plan was to cut around all the skull fractures and remove most of Yeager's skull in a big chunk, stop the bleeding, then use metal plates to repair the broken bone before I replaced it.

I stepped on the drill pedal, expecting to hear the familiar whir and then drill my first bur hole. Instead, I heard a pop, then a burst of air hit my hand. I almost dropped the drill onto Yeager's head.

I turned the drill over and examined it. The coupling had exploded at the junction of the hand piece and the hose. The drill was destroyed.

"Somebody get McDonald. Tell him I need another drill immediately," I said. A tech ran out to deliver my order, but I could see the clock on the wall, and I knew what McDonald was probably going to say.

Sixty seconds later, the tech came back in. "Doc, McDonald says it'll be at least two more hours. The drills are still being processed with your other instruments."

I looked down at Yeager's head, at the pink-tinged blood, mostly saline, still pouring out from under his broken skull, and tried to figure out what to do next.

"Nate, hand me a mallet and a Langenbeck."

Yeager was bleeding out, and with no drill available, I decided to take advantage of his skull fractures. Nate passed me a small metal mallet and a fan-blade-shaped instrument called a Langenbeck elevator, and I began to chisel around the edges of the fractures, freeing each of them from the little bits of bone that still held them to Yeager's skull. One by one, I removed the fragments, saving the big one in the middle for last. I knew that the fracture in the middle, the one most of the blood was coming out of, crossed the sagittal sinus and was likely to tear the huge vein even more when I removed the bone fragment.

A tech ran into the room and handed the anesthetist working with Tim two units of O negative blood from a universal donor, the most coveted blood type because any patient can receive it safely. "Sir, the blood bank says this is the last of the blood. They're starting a blood drive now, but it will take about an hour to get more."

I looked at the blood seeping out of Yeager's head; it was red again. Everything we were putting into Yeager was coming back out as soon as it reached his brain. There was no more blood to give him, and no more time.

"Two more liters of saline. Watch his pressure, because he's probably about to lose a lot of volume," I said.

I picked up the Langenbeck and cracked through the bone from Yeager's left side, then carefully began to lift the fragment toward his right side. I looked under the bone as I lifted and tried to gently separate it from the covering of the brain so that it would not tear the sagittal sinus. Despite my care, as soon as I lifted the fragment, a huge gush of blood shot out of the sinus. I pushed the bone back down, and the bleeding slowed again.

"His sinus was torn in half by the fracture," I said. "I have to pull this piece of bone off to repair the sinus, but when I do he's going to bleed a lot."

"I'll push some neo—that should help," the anesthetist said. Neosynephrine is a drug called a *pressor*, which causes arteries to constrict and raises the blood pressure.

"Adson elevator," I said. I felt the pop of the bone-lifting instrument when Nate handed it to me.

I lifted the bone fragment and slid the Adson underneath to separate the bone from the covering of the brain. When the piece came off, a gush of blood shot out of Yeager's head, hit me in the neck, and poured down the front of my chest, underneath my gown and onto my skin.

"Sponge," I said, taking a cotton sponge from Nate and covering the hole in Yeager's sagittal sinus to stop the bleeding.

"Pressure's sixty over palp."

Yeager had lost so much blood in the three seconds it took me to remove the fragment and compress the sinus with a sponge that his diastolic pressure was unreadable, too low for the machine to detect.

"I'm going to try to sew it up. Give him more saline and neo."

I took a suture from Nate, planning to throw a stitch in the sinus and then replace the sponge until anesthesia could catch up with the blood loss. I would repeat this move until the sinus was repaired.

I lifted the sponge. Another splash of fluid from Yeager. Only now it looked about the same color as the saline we were giving him.

I went back and forth several times between placing sutures in the paper-thin sinus and ordering more fluid into Yeager. Blood was coming, but not fast enough. Every time I moved the sponges, blood-tinged saline squirted all over me.

But the worst news was that the sutures weren't going to hold. His sinus was so thin that the stitches were pulling through. In order to save him, I would have to put in a shunt. I ordered the tech to go get a vascular shunt, a Gore-Tex tube used to replace an artery or vein.

Just as she left the room, the anesthetist yelled at me, "Doc, he's gone into V-fib. Pressure's dropping."

This meant that Yeager's heart had developed an unstable rhythm, when the muscle in the ventricle quivers instead of contracting. Whatever fluid was in his heart was just getting jiggled around, rather than pumped into the rest of his body. He was going to require CPR again.

"Look at his pupils," I said.

The anesthetist pulled up the drapes and looked into Yeager's eyes.

"Blown," he said.

Yeager was gone. His pupillary dilation meant that his brain was shutting down for lack of oxygen, and his heart was refusing to pump. I tried one more time to close the sinus with another type of stitch, but when I moved the sponge, one last spurt of fluid shot me in the face again — and then it stopped. His tank was empty.

The tech ran in with the shunt in her hand.

"Don't open it," I said. "Someone else might need it. Yeager's dead, KIA. Mark the time."

I stepped away from the table, and for the first time in my surgical career I felt like I would vomit. I sat on the edge of the anesthesia machine as the anesthetist flipped the switch to stop monitoring Yeager's vital signs. I reached down and felt his wrist just to make sure: no pulse.

"I'm going back to the ER," Tim said from behind me.

I turned to see him finishing up the head dressing on his patient's head. 2137 — the terrorist who had killed Yeager, Jafar's daughter, and so many others — was still anesthetized. I knew that he was about to receive a couple of hours of state-of-the-art ophthalmological surgery by Augie, who would do what he could to remove the man's destroyed eyes and repair the holes, prevent infection, and improve his appearance. And I saw the red tubing running into his arm, the last two units of universal donor blood in our hospital.

It wasn't fair, and in that moment I wanted to hate this guy, 2137. But we had all spent years of our lives training to help and heal, and when someone is in front of you needing both of those things, you can't just walk away. I suppose this is the biggest difference between trained hospital personnel and teenage guards at a place like Abu Ghraib — attitude reflects leadership and training. Stick us in a prison and tell us to guard a bunch of bad guys who'd been shooting at us and blowing us up, killing our friends, and then undertrain us and leave us to our own devices, and some of those same behaviors may have come out in a herd mentality — the first time someone mistreated an inmate, everyone else would feel a little permission to do the same. But in a medical facility full of professionals who have dedicated their careers to caring for others, and led by someone who preached every day it was not our job to discriminate between our patients, the peer pressure of everyone else doing it right kept us all in line. Right then, watching the precious O negative blood drip into 2137, I wanted it to be different. I felt worse than when I treated drunk drivers in San Antonio, who always seemed to survive the car wreck they caused that killed someone's wife or daughter. At least those drunk drivers didn't wake up the next morning glad for what they had done. I knew that 2137 would feel remorse only that he'd been caught, and that given the chance he would do it again.

I remembered reading in the Bible that in Jesus' eyes, there is no difference between Jew and Greek, slave and free, man and woman. I supposed that extended to there being no difference in God's eyes between American Marine and Islamic terrorist, but at that moment I asked God *why*. Why Yeager and not the terrorist? Why Jafar's daughter and not this merchant of death?

God did not answer my question, so I went to the locker room and sat on the bench, soaked to my underwear in Yeager's blood and twelve liters of saline that had poured out of his head onto me. I cried, prayed, and slammed my fist into the locker.

Then my beeper went off, reminding me that we still had patients to take care of.

I changed scrubs, threw away my socks, and went back to the ER.

CHAPTER 17

I SAW IN 2137 EVERYTHING I HATED IN THE WORLD

EMAIL HOME
Friday, January 28, 2005

Good morning, everyone.

Please pray for the Iraqi people. This weekend they will hold their first free elections as they attempt to become a self-governed, elected democracy. Pray that these brave people won't cave in to the terrorists and their tyranny. From what I can see, the Iraqis are a smart and proud people, and they deserve better than they've had.

We are getting a little nervous about this weekend, but not as nervous as we would be outside the wire. We're making appropriate changes around the base for security, and our guys are prepared for anything. It's still weird to see the big freshly covered ditch where the rocket landed just outside the hospital. Scary.

This experience is making me realize what a privilege it is

to just have a routine—to get up every morning knowing basically what will happen in your life that day. Of course there are surprises, but for the most part you know. You are sure that if you want a vanilla latte from Starbuck's, you'll be able to get it. Here, we can't count on having milk tomorrow, or even electricity, Internet access, telephone service, or safety.

I can't even imagine what it would be like to live your whole life in a place where such uncertainty was constant. I think about these Iraqi folks I see every day. They can't stand on a street corner without fear. They can't go to Walmart and buy toilet paper or milk. They take what they can get.

And to think that I get upset in the OR at home if somebody changes brands of a sponge without asking me; here, I use every corner of every sponge until it's absolutely soaked because there's not enough to allow us to be wasteful. If we drop an instrument in the OR, it takes three hours to resterilize it—so we don't drop them. At home, surgeons get mad about something and refuse to use it, or they throw it across the room if it doesn't function properly. Here, if you threw something you'd just have to do without.

To my fellow surgeons out there: you really can get these cases done without all your preferences being exactly met. I can do a trauma case here in the same amount of time as at home, without any of my fancy instruments. We are very spoiled in America.

Last night I was called to the ER to see an Iraqi policeman who was shot in the face at point-blank range. Amazingly, the bullet went through his sinuses and completely missed both eyes and his brain. He's going to be okay. It's sort of like he had sinus surgery done. He must be living right.

Well, you all know from the news that a lot of bad things

have been happening over here. Just know that we're all doing okay today, and that God has extended his shelter over us so far. Thanks for all your support.

I love you all and continue to ask you for your prayers.

Lee

EMAIL HOME
Saturday, January 29, 2005

Good morning, friends.

Yesterday was the beginning of what we expect to be a very bad weekend. Several mass casualty situations occurred around Iraq, and we were steadily busy here at the 332nd.

I can't say too much about the guys I took care of yesterday; they're the guys you aren't supposed to know about, and they are doing amazing things. I did get to operate on a guy who would have otherwise died, and we got him out to Germany last night. I think he will survive, and he could actually do okay if he's blessed with a few breaks. The other patients weren't so blessed.

The mood in the hospital has been tense since that rocket landed so close, especially after all the mangled people we've seen in recent days. We've been ordered to full arms, and body armor/helmets everywhere you go. Also, tomorrow (and possibly Monday) we are not allowed to email or use the telephones at all, so all of you who assume I've been blown up every time you don't get my letter, please just relax until Tuesday. If there's no letter then, start worrying.

Please keep us in your prayers, remember that we're doing good over here no matter what the media may tell you every night, and that for the most part the Iraqis are glad we're here. Pray for success tomorrow, and don't worry when you don't hear from me. I'll be okay — God's got things for me to do when I get back.

I love you all,

Lee

+

"By published criteria, he's unsalvageable," I said, looking at 2185's brain scan with Tim. We'd been working nonstop for three days, since the enemy was doing everything he could to discourage the citizens of Iraq from getting out the vote for their first democratic elections, scheduled for tomorrow. Now Tim and I were faced with a fresh batch of IED victims, and we had some tough choices to make.

We were almost out of ICU beds, and we had several Iraqi patients on ventilators who had such terrible brain injuries that we knew they weren't going anywhere soon. The enemy didn't seem to care that the hospital was full — he just kept blowing things up every day. In America, we would have simply let the trauma system know that we had no beds available, and they would have notified all the ambulance crews in the city to divert patients to another trauma center. That wasn't possible in Iraq, since we were the only hospital other than Ibn Sina in Baghdad, and Ibn Sina was full too.

So here we stood, looking at the scan of yet another numbered Iraqi, trying to decide what to do with him. We didn't have his story, didn't know whether he was a terrorist, a merchant, or an Iraqi National Guardsman. We did know he was dying.

"We can keep him alive with a big decompressive craniectomy," Tim said.

"Yeah, but he's not going to wake up. Both frontal and both temporal lobes are hit. At best, he's going to be vent-dependent, comatose, and he'll be here forever."

Tim shook his head and dropped into a chair by the CT desk. "I hate this part. Your call, though. I've got to do the American in a minute, if he survives his open heart surgery."

Tim's patient had an open skull fracture, and part of his frontal lobe was exposed. The Army lieutenant had been ambushed with his unit and had taken a bullet to the forehead, along with two that had hit him in the seam of his body armor, both of which had gone through his heart. Todd and Mike were working on him, and if he made it through that, Tim would clean up his brain. The bullet must have hit the lieutenant's helmet first and lost some of its energy, because his brain injury was really pretty minor. My patient's was not.

"I hate it too," I said, while the last few images scrolled across the screen. A sour taste rose in my mouth—the foul taste of chewing on two equally unpleasant choices.

Back home, when I had a patient whose injuries were neurologically devastating, I would leave the choice to the family. We're very good at keeping people alive, I would tell them, but the brain injury itself determines how much of a person we can actually deliver back to them. With aggressive surgery, I can often save someone's life despite the severity of the injury, only to commit the family to many years of breathing machines, feeding tubes, and long-term-care facilities. Usually, families don't want to save their relative if they're going to be "a vegetable." We then follow the family's wishes and humanely withdraw artificial life support and keep the person comfortable until they pass away.

2185 was such a patient. His injuries were technically survivable, but he was never going to be okay. The problem was that I couldn't go out and speak with his family. I had to decide.

Should I try to save him, knowing that we were already in a critical overflow situation in the hospital? Committing to surgery on 2185 would mean using one of our instrument sets, along with precious blood products and two hours of time during which anyone else who needed brain surgery would have to wait. And after surgery, he would tie up one of the ventilators, the resources of the ICU doctors and nurses, and stretch even further the limits of our ability to care for all the patients the enemy had already provided for us in the past few days.

I walked into the scanner and looked down at the young man. He was small, probably five-six or so, and thin. His brown skin and brown hair and brown eyes contrasted sharply with the bright red blood that dripped slowly from dozens of tiny shrapnel wounds all over his head and neck. The whites of his eyes were bloodshot, and his right eye had the milky haze of an intraocular hematoma. I looked into it with my penlight, and saw a little hole in the corner, where a small fragment had entered his eyeball.

Add blind in one eye to his list of problems, assuming he survives and wakes up.

His left pupil was still small but did not constrict. He had not been intubated yet, since he was still breathing when he arrived at our hospital. I looked at his cracked, bleeding lips and noticed the pattern of his respiration. He took several rapid, shallow breaths and then suddenly made a faint gasp. I watched the monitor as 2185 took no breath for about twenty seconds.

"He's Cheyne-Stoking," I said. Cheyne-Stokes breathing indicates a serious brainstem injury, or that the brain is under so much pressure that the respiratory drive is failing.

2185 made a sudden loud, watery gasp. He took several deep, long breaths, the other half of the Cheyne-Stokes pattern.

I put my hand on 2185's chest. He was only the latest victim of this war. For a moment I stopped being a doctor and became just Lee Warren, thirty-five-year-old kid from Broken Bow, Oklahoma. I wondered about 2185's life, his family, his personality. I wondered whether he was married, and what he thought about the war and our involvement in it, and what his last thoughts had been before that bomb had gone off. He gasped again, which shook me out of my few seconds of being just a guy watching something awful happen to another guy. I took a deep breath myself and went into neurosurgeon mode.

There's a place neurosurgeons are trained to reach. A mental refuge in which to hide when the decisions you're forced to make go against some aspect of your moral code, your upbringing, your basic societal impulse to help people. We're supposed to comfort ourselves with our knowledge of the medical literature, our understanding of things like the inner workings of the nervous system, our higher level of insight into the difference between living and being alive. That's why some of us can seem arrogant, cold, or distant at times; we're hiding in a place where you can't see how much it hurts to be the one to decide when someone else has to die.

I looked at the nurse across the table. "Take him to the ICU, give him some morphine. Keep him comfortable. Let the Czar know 2185 is not having surgery."

Flip the switch, write the order, move on to the next patient. That's how we're trained. *If only it were that easy*, I thought.

I watched the nurse wheel him down the hall, then turned to Tim. I needed a minute to be just another person before I had to be the impenetrable military neurosurgeon again. "Hey, since we can't use the phones tomorrow, I'm going to try to call my kids now. I'll come and help you with your case in a few minutes."

"Good. See you in a few," Tim said.

I walked into the surgeons' lounge. The Christmas tree lights were sparkling away, reminding us that somewhere out there someone was probably celebrating something. I smiled at my good luck: no one was on the phone.

I let myself get a little excited at the thought of hearing my kids' voices. I'd only talked to them twice in the month I'd been gone from them, and at that moment I just needed to know they were okay.

The operators took their usual five minutes to make the connections. I heard the clicking and popping of electrons in Iraq, Bahrain, San Antonio, and Alabama, and finally heard the ringing.

My wife picked up the phone, and I heard the difference in her tone instantly.

"Hello."

"It's Lee. Let me talk to the kids, please."

"I told them."

"You told them what?"

"About the divorce."

She went on to say that it was simply too hard to pretend, and she felt it was wrong to keep misleading them. I realize now that I made a huge error by leaving for the war without settling everything between my wife and me and trying to help the kids understand what life would be like after I returned home. My normal need to control everything had given way, this time, to a desire to let them believe, should I die in the war, in the fantasy of a happily married Mom and Dad. I had been wrong. That was wrong, and it made the whole situation harder on all of us.

I heard the rustling of the kids gathering to talk to me and heard the clicking of the speakerphone.

Mitch spoke first. He was crying. His ten-year-old voice trembled when he said, "Daddy, are you and Mom getting a divorce?"

Kimberlyn, the twelve-year-old, was slightly more controlled, but also more angry: "Mom told us, Dad. Why would you do that to us?"

Kalyn, age seven: "Daddy, you can sleep in my room when you get home."

At that moment, my most sincere prayer was that a mortar would land right on top of me. The crater in my heart was already there. An actual explosion would hurt less.

"Guys, it's going to be okay, I promise. We'll get through this together."

I tried to calm them down, but through my tears and the shock of having to do this over the phone, I didn't have the words. Someone behind me tapped my shoulder.

"Doc, fifteen minutes are up. I need the phone."

I started to say "I love you" to the kids, who by this time had stopped crying, but the line went dead.

I moved out of the way and fell onto the couch, crying into my hands. I was shaking, crushed that I wasn't there to comfort my kids, hold them, try to explain it to them. Instead, I was thousands of miles away and impotent to help them.

Suddenly, Tim was sitting next to me. He put his arm around me, and I cried onto his shoulder.

"What's wrong?"

I told him.

He listened quietly, then said, jaw muscles tensed, "Listen, I know you're hurting, and I'm really sorry. But you have to put it aside for now. You can't survive here if your head is in Alabama. There's too much work to do. You'll deal with that when it's time, but right now you have to suck it up. We need you here."

And I knew he was right. No matter how much pain I was in, or how serious the wounds to my kids' little hearts, I couldn't fix it from Iraq. And if I didn't clear my head and fight on, people here would die.

But whatever part of me had left for the war thinking that my wife and I would work on the marriage when I got home died right then, and a sixteen-year-long relationship went into

Cheyne-Stokes breathing. Distant thuds from another mortar attack hit my ears, sounding a little like a hammer nailing the coffin shut on that part of my life. I accept the fact that my marriage failed, and blame was to be shared between both of us. And I know during those sixteen years I wasn't the easiest person to love. I was never home, I was too driven, I didn't know how to fight or directly handle things emotionally. But hearing my kids ask me why when I couldn't see their faces or hold them caught me unawares, and I was totally defeated.

I walked back into the ICU and watched a tech turn off the monitors beside 2185's bed. He was dead. In the next bed, still very much alive, was 2137, the blind and comatose bomber from one of yesterday's attacks.

At that moment, I saw in 2137 everything I hated in the world. Terrorism, war, meanness, hatred, the hatemongers who love to sow discord and pain. Icy rage crawled up my spine, and for a moment I wished I could choke the life out of him, as if that would make everything right. How can someone hate another group, another person so much that they would be willing to blow up a marketplace full of innocent people?

I took a deep breath and loosened my grip on the bedrail. I was still shaking and would have been still crying but I was out of tears.

The monitor showed 2137's heart rate was way too fast. He was probably in pain, I thought.

Therein lies the problem, I told myself. I'd always been the man to take someone else's blows if it meant avoiding conflict or letting the other person feel good, at my own expense. And no matter how much someone else hurt me or the people I cared about, I always seemed to find myself apologizing and trying to make peace. I could never stand to let someone else suffer. But at that moment, I wanted him to suffer. As if watching him hurt would somehow make me feel better about everything, even what was happening with the kids.

"Right now you have to suck it up," Tim had said.

True, 2137 was an enemy, and he had done terrible things. But it wasn't my job to punish him. My job as a doctor was to help him survive so that others could mete out justice. His reckoning would come if he survived. And, I believed, even if he didn't survive.

I made the decision right then: I was not going to lose myself to this war. Not the one in Iraq, and not the one in Alabama. I couldn't fix my kids' pain, or even fight that battle, at least for the moment. But I could still do my job there in the dusty tent hospital with the tachycardic terrorist-turned-patient in front of me.

"Give him some morphine," I said to the nurse. "It's not right to let him suffer."

CHAPTER 18

WE'LL ALL GET THROUGH THIS TOGETHER

Moments later I walked out of the hospital and looked up into the dusky red sky, my eyes still burning from having emptied themselves. A few stars were faintly visible through the dust and the blowing smoke. I coughed and wrapped my scarf around my face and walked across the lot to the bathroom trailers.

In the mirror I saw a man I hardly recognized. For most of my life I'd been somewhat overweight, and my mental image of myself had round cheeks and a double chin. The guy staring me down had a sharp jawline, sunken cheeks, and hollowed temples—I'd lost almost twenty pounds in less than a month.

My eyes were so bloodshot that I could see hardly any white outside the blue iris. I looked awful.

I splashed water on my face and felt the coolness trickle down my neck under my collar. When I'd boarded the plane to leave for the war, I'd told myself that this trip to the desert might provide the clarity I'd been seeking to figure out how to deal with my problems at home. Now I sighed as I realized that not only was I out of answers, but I didn't even know the questions.

I shook my head at the thin, haggard man in the mirror. For so many years I had been all about work and my kids. I had defined who I was by what I did, and I'd worn that Invincible Neurosurgeon persona like a superhero costume. It was impenetrable. No one could find my hidden vulnerability, the Kryptonite that would render me just another guy with a bad marriage and no idea what to do about it. Church had been a place to smile and pretend that I had it all together, because in my church if you didn't have it all together it meant your faith was faulty. And because I was supposed to be a smart, professional, infallible brain surgeon, I couldn't admit to anyone that my faith was in fact faulty. After all, I *knew* that I didn't have it all together.

In that mirror-moment, the whole jumbled, confusing mess of my life seemed impossible to figure out. I wished again for a rocket to just take me out. My dad had sold me a life insurance policy before the war, telling me how important the policy would be for the kids if I died, and as I looked at my ridiculous tri-colored eyes, it occurred to me that I was worth considerably more dead than alive. And right then, my kids might have agreed.

I heard a noise behind me, and I kept washing my face so whoever it was wouldn't see me looking so pathetic. A hand clasped my shoulder, and I looked up to see John, the occupational therapist who had been coming to my trailer for movie nights for the past few days.

"Hey, man, you coming to worship practice? Starts in thirty minutes," John said.

I'd forgotten all about it. Greg, the worship leader, had set up a practice that night with all the new singers and musicians who had arrived to replace the folks who'd recently gone home. Pete had volunteered me for the band, and I had helped a little over my first few weeks. But tonight, Greg planned on helping the new group get itself together, and he'd all but ordered me to become the new leader.

How can I lead a worship band when I'm not even sure what I believe right now?

I wiped my face with a paper towel. I had no excuses. Tim was on call. When I turned around, John's smiling face was the closest thing to a good feeling I'd had in days.

"Sure. I'll run by my trailer and grab my guitar."

+

By the time I reached the chapel, the team was already there. In the dimly lit tent surrounded by a five-foot-high wall of sandbags, nine people sat in a circle on the little stage at the front, talking quietly as I entered.

Greg turned when he heard me. "Hey, Lee! Glad you could make it. Come join us."

I dragged myself down the aisle and sat in the circle between John and a tiny Air Force captain with close-cropped hair and the biggest smile I'd ever seen. She stuck out her hand and said, "Hi, I'm Shauna."

The rest of the circle was made up of people from all over the United States. Three different racial backgrounds, seven different military jobs, and the Army, Marine Corps, and Air Force were all represented. Directly across from me were Israel, a guitar player and singer with an M–16 and a sidearm, and Luther, a six-six giant of a man who looked a little like LeBron James, but he carried a grenade launcher and a huge machine gun. The two of them were very fit, serious men who looked like they could have delivered plenty of shock and awe all by themselves.

I was uncomfortable sitting in this circle of people who, despite their busy schedules, had volunteered to be in the church band and help other people worship. I felt intimidated by their generous spirit and, I assumed, their spiritual depth and maturity. I thought that they would take one look at me and instantly know that I'd failed in my marriage, failed to save my patient that day, and failed to know where I stood with God, or even to know for sure what I believed. *At least I can play and sing pretty well*, I thought. *Maybe we won't have to talk about all that other stuff.*

Greg called the meeting to order, and of course the first thing he said was, "Okay, guys, let's get to know each other. Beginning with John, tell us a little about yourselves and where you are in your life and in your faith, and about how the war's affecting you. Over the next few months, this should be more than a band. You'll become a family, and help each other through whatever's going on."

John began, and by the time we'd worked our way around the circle to me, I knew that I was in a room full of people with problems and struggles as significant and real as my own. There was no pretense, no judgment. Tears fell, hands were held, and people really opened up about their lives.

It was my turn. I had a choice to make. Continue to be Dr. No Problems? Continue to hide my issues? Or tell the truth and let myself be known?

I searched inside. I couldn't find the energy to hide or pretend anymore. I was tired of being unknown, and less afraid of the rejection I'd feared from my church in the States if my problems were known than I was of the hollowness of pretending to have it all together. So I told my story.

When I finished, Greg asked us to stand and hold hands for prayer. Luther, the giant soldier, leaned closer and in a thunderous bass whisper said, "Doc, it's gonna be okay. We're here for you." John and Shauna held my hands, and John said, "We'll all get through this together."

By the time Greg ended the prayer, I realized that the day's horrible events had somehow delivered me to a place where I'd finally stopped trying to survive on my own.

+

As I tried to sleep that night, my mind replayed my children's voices, again and again. I could hear their sobs, their despair. But I could not hold them and comfort them. I was impotent and absent and unable to help them deal with the worst news they'd ever received. That had been taken from me. But on that same day God had provided a group of people whose openness and love made me believe that it would all be okay — somehow.

A mortar landed somewhere close by, and the *thud-boom* sounds shook my trailer a few seconds before the Alarm Red sounded. I pulled the covers over my head, no longer afraid enough to bother hauling myself to the bunker.

My mind played the tape of 2137's hatred, 2185 bleeding out, and my kids' sobbing questions. Life-and-death decision making, damage control. Battles lost, wars still raging. Decisions to be made.

I made one right then.

I'd left for the war with my marriage in critical condition, but at that moment, as I lay in my bed in Iraq listening to a mortar barrage, it died. Last night, I was a man planning on going home to see if my marriage could be healed. Tonight, I was a man with lawyers and judges and custody battles to look forward to. I'd finish my involvement in the war and go home to a divorce. There would be no more pretending.

The enemy was bombing us again, and death hovered as thick as the smoke in the air. But Tim had told me to suck it up, and he was right on. It was my job to take care of the living.

CHAPTER 19

PURPLE INK: THE MARK OF FREEDOM

I crawled out of bed on Sunday morning, Election Day, after a night of fitful sleep. Dreams of patients bleeding out, my kids demanding answers to questions they shouldn't have needed to ask, and enemies plotting my demise kept me from really resting, and I dressed that morning uneasy about the day.

Our commanders had told us that Election Day would almost certainly be one of the busiest days of the war, with insurgents plotting violence to disrupt the budding democracy and centuries-old battles between Sunnis, Shiites, and Kurds playing out in blood even among those glad to have a new government. No one would really be safe, neither the voters standing in lines to grasp at freedom, the workers in the polling places, or the candidates who would win the races.

That night, the news told us that at least forty-two people across Iraq had died from attacks on voters.

+

EMAIL HOME
Monday, January 31, 2005

Hello, everyone, from the world's newest democracy!

By all accounts here, the election was far more successful than anyone had hoped. We were steadily busy but never overwhelmed. And while the insurgents were trying unsuccessfully to stop the election, they couldn't stop the stork. A very pregnant woman came to the gate in labor, and the first baby ever born in an Air Force theater hospital arrived shortly after.

A man came in severely shot up and had many hours of heroic surgery. General surgeon Brett saved his leg, and vascular surgeon Todd repaired his damaged carotid artery. Joe (ENT) did a tracheotomy and repaired his face, tying off a bleeding facial artery that nearly caused the patient to bleed to death, and Tim and I took out his frontal lobe, removed bullet and bone fragments from his brain, and repaired a huge hole in his orbit that his brain was falling through. He's awake and moving his arms and legs now, and we think he will make it.

A sniper shot a young lady after she voted. The bullet entered through her eye, went through her mouth and through two of her vertebrae. Somehow it didn't tear up her spinal cord; she's moving her arms and legs. She did lose her eye, but she'll walk again.

Yesterday, for the first time in my life, I operated while armed. That was weird. Fortunately, no situation arose in which we felt compelled to load our weapons. If the fate of the war depended on the doctors and nurses shooting anyone, we'd have all been in trouble.

Today, you should thank God that you can vote in the

assurance that no one will try to kill you. Doesn't it make you sad that in America we think it's successful if we have 50 percent voter turnout? We're hearing that the Iraqis managed around 60 percent, despite more than twenty suicide bombings, snipers, mortars, and rockets. People here are willing to die in order to exercise their political freedom.

I love you all.

Lee

+

Rounds on Monday morning took a long time, since we'd performed so many surgeries over the past three days. I was alone to take care of all the neurosurgery patients, because Tim had to ride on the C–17 to Landstuhl with an American soldier who'd been shot by a sniper. Tim thought the soldier was too unstable to travel without a surgeon on the plane with him, and the commander signed off on the plan.

The bomber, 2137, was still on a ventilator and tying up a crucial ICU bed. He was under guard twenty-four hours a day, because we were afraid that Jafar or one of the interpreters might try to kill him. I made a few notes on his chart and watched for a moment as the nurses changed his bandages. The nurses were professional, but there was a subtle difference in how they spoke to him, how they touched him, compared with patients they knew to be his victims. It was as if they feared that some of his evil might rub off on them.

I stopped at the bedside of 2203, an Iraqi woman who'd been hit in the head by shrapnel from a car bomb after she voted. Her ICP was very high, and her pupils were dilated. Tim had operated on her while I was taking care of someone else.

Despite Tim's aggressive care, her brain injury was severe, and she was in serious trouble.

"When was her last dose of Mannitol?" I asked the nurse.

"Six hours ago," he said, "but her sodium level is one-sixty, and she's dumping a lot of urine."

I looked at the collection bag, and saw that 2203's urine was completely colorless, like water.

"Check a specific gravity, and take her to CT stat," I said. The urine specific gravity would tell me whether her hypothalamus was shutting down in response to the high ICP. Her sodium level was too high for me to consider giving her any more Mannitol, because at that level her kidneys might be damaged.

A few minutes later, I looked at her scan and shook my head. She'd had a massive, unsurvivable stroke, probably from clotting off one of her damaged cerebral draining veins. Despite Tim's best efforts, her brain swelling had closed the vein and choked the brain's blood supply so severely that it had killed the hypothalamus, as evidenced by the high sodium and urine output.

The nurse ran into the CT room with 2203's lab results.

"Spec-grav is ten-oh-three," she said.

I closed my eyes for a second, wanting to erase the image of the nightmare playing out on the CT scan. A urine specific gravity of 1.003, or ten-oh-three as we called it, meant that her kidneys couldn't concentrate her urine at all. She was dumping all the fluid that came into her body because her hypothalamus and pituitary gland were failing to produce a hormone called vasopressin, one of the drugs no one thought we might need to take with us to the war.

Ten-oh-three for 2203, who would a few minutes later become Election Day victim number forty-three.

I opened my eyes again. She was probably in her early twenties. Medics had told us that she was a schoolteacher. Yesterday morning, she'd been standing in a group after exercising her newly granted right to vote. Today she was dying of the combined effects of terrorism and intracranial physiology. I thought, *I hope whoever she voted for won.*

"She's going to die. Just keep her comfortable," I said. I walked away from the ICU, unable to stand there and watch another innocent victim of the war take her last breath. I felt impotent and frustrated and angry, and I wanted to go home, hold my kids, and have somebody tell me it would be okay. But at that moment, I didn't believe it ever would.

A few minutes later, I was standing in the surgeons' lounge watching election coverage on CNN when I heard a voice behind me: "Doctor, if you please."

I turned. Saeed (pronounced Sigh-eed) stood in the hallway, his head slightly bowed. He held a piece of paper toward me with his right hand; his left was held over his heart. Saeed had proven to be a reliable and accurate interpreter for us when we needed to communicate with patients.

"Please, sir, take it." He pushed the paper toward me. When Saeed said *sir*, it sounded like *sear*. I tried to think of another time when he had spoken to me outside of taking care of patients — or for that matter, a time when I had spoken to him. Since I had arrived, I had interacted with the local nationals who worked on base only when I had to. Was it because I didn't trust them? Or had I just been so wrapped up in myself that I hadn't been willing to extend myself to them? But here was Saeed, speaking to me, and I suddenly saw him not as a tool to be used, but as a young man with some type of need.

"What is it?"

Saeed lifted his head, his chocolate eyes peering out from behind a permanent squint brought about by all the things they'd seen over the years. I thought, though, that behind the hardened face I recognized something close to a happy spirit.

"It is a letter, for you."

I took the letter, handwritten in blue ink. It took a moment for me to realize that I was reading a note from an Iraqi physician.

Jassem, Age: 7 years

Dear Dr.

Can I refer to you this child who's suffer from head injury (shell) at 9:30 AM 1/30/2005. The patient had disturbed consciousness, also he vomitize for one time. The pupils asymmetrical but reacted to light.

The wound is about 5 cm length in his right side of his head behind the right ear. There is mild hemorrhage also there is big hematoma under the scalp and piece of brain out of his wound...

Dr. Ali 1/30/2005

I couldn't believe what I was reading—a detailed medical report handwritten in English by someone outside the wire— obviously a bright, well-trained physician. Saeed told me the rest of the story. Somehow after a bombing at a polling place, medics had left behind an injured seven-year-old boy. He'd been taken to one of the very few Iraqi doctors still out there working, and that doctor had kept the boy alive for over twenty-four hours.

"Saeed, where is the child?"

"He is right here in Balad, sir. Dr. Ali is my cousin. He have the boy in his home."

We showed the letter to Colonel H, who then radioed the story to his commanders. After a few minutes, they gave orders to scramble a team. Saeed put on body armor and a helmet and accompanied a small convoy of soldiers and medics outside of the wire, putting their lives on the line to go get the boy.

Two hours later I met Jassem, a crying little boy with a blood-soaked head bandage and a filthy teddy bear. He had wavy brown hair sticking out from under the bandage and a face that looked like it had been borrowed from someone older, someone who had needed to worry a lot more than Jassem should have had to at seven. He moved both arms and both legs, squirming like my seven-year-old daughter did whenever she was at the pediatrician's office. Except that my Kalyn had never had mortar fragments in her brain because some Muslim terrorist was trying to keep me from voting.

At the child's bedside a man stood, wringing his hands as I approached. He had the same face as the boy, only older and more wrinkled. Probably my age, I thought, but with a difference. I'd grown up in a country where every twenty years or so we send our sons overseas to fight for certain causes. He'd grown up here, where in his teens he'd seen the Iran-Iraq War, in his twenties Desert Storm, and in his thirties American troops invade. Every day in between he'd lived under the cold reality of Saddam Hussein's brutal tyranny. No wonder he looked older than me.

"I'm Dr. Warren," I said, then listened to Saeed interpret.

Saeed turned to me. "This man is Hikmat. He is Jassem's father. He say they were leaving the voting station when mortars hit. Hikmat woke up and could not find Jassem, then someone tell him that Jassem is with Dr. Ali."

"Tell him I need to examine the boy."

After Saeed spoke, Hikmat held both hands in front as if he were praying, then gestured toward his son and bowed his head to me. He said something quietly to Saeed.

"He say to thank you, and to please save Jassem."

As Saeed and I had spoken to the father, the nurse had given Jassem some morphine to ease his pain. I removed Jassem's bandage. He had an open skull fracture behind his right ear.

Ali was a very good doctor. The wound had been expertly cleaned, and the dirt and debris I'd expected to find was all gone. His scalp had several perfectly squared sutures around arteries that would probably have caused Jassem to bleed to death. I could see the boy's brain pulsing gently through the open wound. Ali had made the wise decision to not close the scalp laceration. Undoubtedly, he had known that closing it would increase the pressure inside Jassem's head. The mortar had basically done a decompressive craniectomy for Jassem, and Ali had been wise enough not to close it back up. I thought, *This guy could teach our field medics a few things.*

I told Saeed I'd have to take Jassem to surgery, and a moment later Saeed gave me Hikmat's answer: "God be with you, sir."

We got a CT scan: Jassem had several metal fragments in his brain, one of which had penetrated all the way across to the left side. The path of that piece of mortar was dangerously close to several major arteries, but somehow it had missed everything important. Jassem had survived a very close call, thanks to a lucky trajectory and the intelligence of a poorly equipped Iraqi physician who had operated on him in a house and then helped get him to me.

An hour later, I walked out of the operating room confident that Jassem would survive and probably make an excellent recovery—if no infection occurred. In the waiting room were Saeed and Hikmat, who sat in a chair praying with his eyes closed.

Hikmat looked up when he heard me enter. His eyes, which were a pale gray color I'd never seen before, were filled with tears. His shirt and pants were splotched with blood. The look on his face was familiar; I'd seen it in other waiting rooms in other hospitals. Fear, anxiety, dread of what I would say, and in the case of parents waiting for news about their kids after an accident, usually some guilt mixed in.

He stood as I approached.

I spoke and Saeed translated. "Your son is alive, and I think he's going to be okay."

Saeed didn't really have to translate Hikmat's answer, because relief and joy are universally recognizable when they wash over someone.

We sat and talked through Saeed for a few minutes. I told Hikmat all about the injury and the surgery and what would happen next for Jassem. After I'd answered all his questions, I told him about Kalyn, my seven-year-old, and for a bit we were just two dads taking a load off, sitting and chatting about our kids, although I'd never swapped kid stories through an interpreter before.

We found one of those natural pauses in conversation, where no one is exactly sure what to say next. I decided that would be a good moment for me to go make rounds and let Hikmat see Jassem. But before I could rise, he leaned forward and buried his face in his hands. For the first time, I noticed the purple ink all over his right hand, and I remembered the commander telling us that the Iraqis were required to dip their hands in ink after they voted, to make sure no one voted twice. I thought about the now-brain-dead schoolteacher, 2203, and remembered that as I'd walked away from her bedside I'd seen the ink on her hand as well, the mark of freedom.

I put my hand on Hikmat's shoulder and said, "I'm sorry for all you've been through, and for what happened to Jassem."

Hikmat sat up and wiped his tears, but when he turned toward me, rather than the heartsick face I'd expected, he bore a huge smile. He hugged me, and I smelled smoke, sweat, and the unique smell of clotted blood. Apparently, he realized how tightly he was hugging me, because he composed himself and spoke.

I looked over Hikmat's shoulder at Saeed. Saeed was smiling too.

"Hikmat say no, you do not apologize for anything. He say has been best two days, because Jassem alive, and because Hikmat was able to vote."

CHAPTER 20

FREEZING TO DEATH IN A MUDDY HOLE

"That's twelve," I said.

Tim and I had been walking back to the hospital from DFAC II, where we'd gone to eat lunch—neither of us had eaten breakfast, or dinner the night before either—when a mortar landed and detonated close enough to us that we saw the smoke and heard the sound at the same time. We'd scurried into the bunker for safety. Since Election Day eleven days ago, the enemy had been pummeling us with mortars and rockets, and the flow of patients into the hospital was higher than ever.

During the thirty minutes since the first explosion, as we'd huddled in the bunker, we'd heard eleven more, all pretty close, and all answered by return fire from our guys. Whoever was shooting at us was close enough that we could hear both the launch—a sound closest to *booof*—and the detonation of the rounds our guys were shooting back.

So for the past half-hour, we'd felt and heard incoming projectiles with their *thud-booms*, and friendly fire with its *booof-booms*. Mixed in with the explosions were the terrifying noise of the Alarm Red sirens, gate gunners letting off fifty-caliber machine-gun rounds, and the steady beeping of our pagers informing us that there were casualties who awaited our arrival and didn't care about our personal safety.

It had been raining for days, and the temperature at night was dipping into the twenties. The entire base was a swamp, and this bunker was two inches deep in mud. Earlier that day I'd done an operation while standing in ankle-high water after the hospital had flooded. At the time, I'd been barely aware of it, concentrating on my case, but when I stepped away from the surgical table the squishing of my wet socks inside my shoes got my attention. It was a miserable day, a miserable situation, and to top it all off, somebody was trying to kill us.

I was amazed when I realized that I was less afraid of being blown up than angry with whomever was making me sit in this muddy hole freezing to death.

"We've got to get to the ER," Tim said. "That's the fourth time they've paged us."

Should we just make a break for it? From here to the hospital was all open sidewalk with no other bunkers on the way. I was freezing, still heartsick over my kids, and hadn't slept in almost twenty-four hours. A direct hit now couldn't really make me feel any worse. And, as always, there was work to do.

"Let's do it," I said.

We ran for the hospital, probably both setting personal records for the two-hundred-yard dash.

In the ER, we found one of the worst disasters either of us had ever seen. Fifteen Iraqi policemen had been standing in formation when a suicide bomber pressed his switch. Somehow, almost all the projectiles had hit the policemen above the shoulders. All fifteen of the men had serious eye, neck, or brain injuries.

Augie, the ophthalmologist, was already working his way around the room. He stopped at each bedside to shine his light into the patient's eyes and assess the severity of the ocular injuries. When he saw an eye that would require surgery, he would put a patch over it and write the patient's number, which eye, and what he needed to do. He dispensed eighteen patches among the fifteen men. He would be operating all night.

Joe from ENT was performing a bedside tracheostomy on a man whose entire trachea was exposed by severe face and neck burns. The man was awake, gasping for air, because every time the medic squeezed his oxygen bag, most of the air came out the hole in the man's trachea instead of making it into his lungs. Joe gave up when he realized that the last breath the man had taken during the bombing had caused him to inhale so much smoke and fire that his lungs were irreparably harmed. After a few more seconds of gasping and flailing his arms, the man stopped breathing.

Tim and I went around the room deciding who needed CT scans first. One by one, we rolled the men into the scanner, and over the next hour we saw a radiologic anthology of wartime brain injuries. Of the now fourteen survivors, six had intracranial injuries. Three were completely unsalvageable; bomb fragments and blast injuries had caused so much damage that no surgery would help. Two had minor brain injuries that would not require surgery, and the last man had a brain hemorrhage.

"I'll take care of this one," Tim said. "Why don't you take these guys to the holding area and control their pain?"

"Yes, sir," I said, acknowledging both Tim's rank and the fact that he had chosen the more pleasant of the two jobs.

A few minutes later I was standing with a couple of nurses, giving orders for morphine administration to the dying men. 2240, 2243, and 2251 were all still conscious but fading fast from brain swelling. 2240 had a hole in the side of his head, and brain tissue was oozing out. This is a terrible fact of trauma neurophysiology: when a patient has an injury that is definitely going to be fatal but who also has an open skull fracture, brain pressure can stay normal for a long time because the tissue can escape through the holes in the bone and skin. So one of the things we have to do to keep that patient from lingering in a near-death state for several days is to suture up the holes so tightly that brain tissue cannot swell out. This causes the pressure to rise, ending the patient's suffering more quickly.

"Hand me a suture kit," I said.

I placed several very tight purse-string stitches around the hole. This is the only technique I ever have to employ that is designed to help someone pass instead of trying to save them. It always causes a guilty nausea to rise in my stomach, because it feels as if I'm deliberately ending someone else's life—although we're trained to take the perspective that the injury produced the problem, and we're simply shortening the time line of its effect. No matter what you tell yourself, though, it still feels awful.

As I finished that procedure on 2240, I said a little prayer for him to quickly lose whatever consciousness he had left. What he was going through sickened me. His head probably throbbed with rising pressure from bomb fragments and brain bleeding, and he was unable to see anything because of Augie's eye patches and his lacerated corneas, and the last sounds he would hear in his life were in a language he couldn't understand.

I was liberal with the morphine.

All three men writhed for a while, moaned, moved their arms. Then one by one, starting with 2251, they slid from the conscious world into the solace of stupor and coma, finally ceasing to breathe at last, adding three more victims to the tally of the suicide bomber and the insurgency. Three men who had decided to try to help Iraq reach for freedom had paid the price of doing business against Islamic terrorism.

"Doc, they need you in surgery," a tech called.

Of course they do, I thought. In some ways, this was the hardest part of the war: the incessancy of carnage, suffering, and tragedy, the steady stream of impossible choices. In an average American hospital, a neurosurgeon might have a horrible case with no clear right answer, or some human catastrophe caused by a senseless crime or a random accident, once every few months. In Iraq, you had to suck up whatever the disaster in front of you made you feel, because somewhere down the hall there was something worse waiting for you.

2243 lasted the longest. I signed his chart, wiped my eyes, and went to the OR.

+

EMAIL HOME
Friday, February 11, 2005

Good morning, friends, from Mudville.

Yesterday was a banner day for the bad guys. They blew up another group of INGs, and I spent a couple of hours trying to save one of them. I was up throughout the night last night dealing with his severely swollen brain. He's going to die.

I saw a good example yesterday of how the press only tells you part of a story. I picked up a copy of *Stars and Stripes*, the daily military newspaper. In it was a feature article on a US soldier who is back home after receiving his Purple Heart. He is the guy I told you about a few weeks ago who was bleeding to death from his scalp and leg wounds, and I fixed his scalp while Todd the vascular surgeon tried for several hours to save his leg. Ultimately Todd's heroic effort to save the leg failed, and he had to amputate it. Nevertheless, we no doubt saved his life, and he went to Germany and then home in great shape.

The article talked about this brave soldier's work and family, and what a good person he is. It was very well written. When it got to the part of the story about his war injuries, it said, "He was injured, taken to a hospital in Iraq, and then on to Germany."

The article wasn't about his injuries or us; it was about his life, so they didn't need to go into all the things we did here for him. I just thought as I read it, "Wow. There's so much more to this guy's story that they glossed over." I remember talking to him on the way to the OR and him asking me about the other guys in his unit. I remember him asking me lucidly if he was going to survive. I remember his piercing eyes as he went off to sleep in the OR, and him saying out loud, "I trust you guys."

The next several hours of that man's life were in the hands of surgeons and God. He came very close to bleeding to death from blood loss. My part was very small — he had a major scalp artery bleeding deep in his temporalis muscle that was hard to control, and then I fixed his scalp wound after I got the bleeding controlled. Todd, however, really did miraculous work for this man, saving his life and going the extra mile to try to save his leg when every other surgeon would have just cut it off. He really cared and wanted to try and very nearly saved the leg.

I tell you that story to remind you to tell your friends who are down on the war because of the media that they don't know the half of it.

Pray for all of us here and outside the wire, for my patient fighting for his life right now, and for me to fight off this fever and chill that I have today. I feel like the bottom of a shoe.

I love you all.

Lee

EMAIL HOME
Sunday, February 13, 2005

Hello, friends.

After lunch yesterday, I was paged to the ER to see an Iraqi man who had been the target of an assassination attempt. He had three bullets in his chest and one in his head, and we went off to CT scan. I can't tell you who he is, but I used the word *assassination*, and there were apparently several Iraqi officials and high-ranking military officers hit yesterday.

The scan showed a horrific and non-survivable injury. I had to make the call to not operate on him, and to let him die. A noble man dying in the service of his country, gunned down by cowards in hiding. In my opinion, they are not soldiers.

Several of our interpreters came up to me later and asked if I would talk to them about one of the men we had operated on earlier in the week. It turns out that he's a friend of theirs, a shopkeeper from Balad. Another innocent victim of a car bomb.

We fear that we now have another generation of young men and women in the US military, much like some of their fathers after Vietnam, who will never again feel completely comfortable in a crowd. Their minds will always wonder if that person in the long coat is hiding a bomb, if that car on the corner is about to detonate, if death lies in wait on the other side of this door. If you figure that there are 150,000 or so US troops here thusly affected, imagine for a minute the long-range impact on every citizen of Iraq, Israel, and other places in the world touched by terrorism. You could argue that even Saddam's military was nobler than these insurgents. At least they wore a uniform and fought and died under their flag, identifiable as Enemy. These people blend in with the citizens and cause untold numbers of them to be injured or killed simply because our troops, when they react with force to protect themselves and other people, can't tell the insurgents from the civilians. So if you run a checkpoint, you are going to die. If you get too close to the gate, you will die. There's no other way to prevent the next Mosul DFAC bombing or car-bomb-too-close-to-the-hospital.

Last night at 7:30, nine (yes, nine) people showed up for movie night. A double feature: We had *Band of Brothers*, episode 7, and *Napoleon Dynamite* (repeated because many had not seen it). Afterward, John and Greg and I played guitars and sang through the set for today's worship. It was a great way to end the evening.

I went to sleep at about midnight and was paged to the hospital at 0300. A terrorist was shot trying to assassinate the mayor of Mosul, and they called me to look at the scan to see if he was salvageable, so that he could be transported here, a three-hour trip, for me to operate on him. He was not, and by the time they got his scans over the Internet to me, the weather had gotten too bad to fly him here anyway.

That's a big difference between Americans and these so-called insurgent "soldiers": when we shoot somebody, our guys risk their lives to pick them up, rush them to the hospital in the same helicopters we use for our own fallen soldiers, and treat them with all the resources we have to try to save them. The insurgents will, instead, burn your body and drag you through the street and film it for the media to play over and over to say terrible things about America.

I understand the sensitivities of church and state and all that, I really do. But don't you think that our Founding Fathers' ethics and belief systems have something to do with the fact that 230 years later we are still the kindest and most compassionate nation on earth, even to people who are trying to kill us?

When I started this letter, it was dry outside. Now it's raining cats and dogs (camels and jackals?) again. So much for no more mud!

I'll talk to you all tomorrow. Thanks for listening, and for the prayers. I love you all.

Lee

CHAPTER 21

THE AMERICAN SOLDIER, THE TERRORIST, AND THE BLOOD DRIVE

And finally, some news about supplies," Colonel H said as he wrapped up the staff meeting he'd called this morning. He sighed and pushed his reading glasses up his nose with his long index finger. I'd seen his hands do some very elegant work back in San Antonio during cases we'd done together. I respected him as a surgeon and had come to see him as a capable leader in the war. But meetings were meetings, and I was hungry and irritable and bored out of my skull.

"The rainstorms have grounded incoming flights. We won't get our weekly resupply for a few more days. That means you surgeons have to conserve everything: make every suture, bandage, and catheter count. We can't afford any waste."

I cast a sideways glance at Tim, who was already mouthing the words "We're nearly out of ICP monitors and drill bits" to me. I was flooded with a feeling I'd never experienced in the States: fear of needing a surgical supply I couldn't get.

Colonel H continued. "The only good news is that the

weather is so bad today that the Black Hawks can't fly either. So maybe we'll have a slow day or two."

In my mind I tried to channel a seething, hate-filled Islamic insurgent. I saw him: six feet tall, five percent body fat; a bearded, black-hearted bomb maker with Russian-made artillery shells wired together around a canister filled with fecal-smeared batteries and rocks and pieces of barbed wire. I could just see him waking up this morning, planning how he would plant his IED and hide in the bushes for Americans to wander by so he could kill them using his cell-phone switch to detonate the IED. But when he woke up, giddy after dreaming all night of the mayhem he would cause, he looked out the window and saw the weather. His smile faded, and his warm mattress called out to him. *Is raining outside,* he'd think, *maybe I hit snooze button and take day off.*

I was jolted out of my daydream by a nurse crashing into the conference room. "Casualties in the ER, sir," she said.

I guess the enemy didn't sleep in after all.

Four Humvee-ambulance crews arrived bearing the victims of a series of early morning car bombings in a nearby town. Over twenty Iraqi civilians and some American Marines were among the first casualties to arrive. We reached the ER and began our now-routine process of sorting them out.

"Three open head injuries," the Czar shouted across the room.

I ran over with Tim, and we chose the two who seemed the worst. "Heading to CT, sir," said Tim, as we pushed our patients to radiology.

My patient turned out to have a tennis-ball-sized metal fragment in his frontal lobe and a large blood clot in his brain to go along with it. I was still operating on him when Tim stuck his head into my room.

"My guy had a skull fracture and a little bleeding. Didn't

take long. I'm going to take the third guy to surgery now. He's deteriorating quickly. When you finish, head back to the ER. There's another ambulance coming in a few minutes."

"Sir," I said.

Tim left and I tried to speed up my case. Once I had the fragment out and I'd stopped all the bleeding, I put the man's bone flap in his abdomen and was about to start closing his scalp when I saw the Australian general surgeon Mitch walk in.

"Lee, the other patients are here. The Czar wants you in the ER. I'll close this guy for you."

Mitch scrubbed in and I showed him how to place the ICP monitor. "Thanks for your help," I said.

"No worries. I'll do a triumphant job."

I'd noticed that Mitch had a habit of declaring all of his operations to be triumphs. Good to be confident, I thought, but as I walked out of the operating room a cold dread hit me in the gut. If I was right, what I was about to find in the ER would not end triumphantly.

Tim had just started his case, meaning he'd opened the third of our four sets of craniotomy instruments. I passed the scrub tech Nate in the hall on my way to the ER and grabbed his arm. "Nate, go find McDonald and tell him to rush the crani sets. We've only got one left sterile, and there are more casualties in the ER."

"Roger," Nate said as he turned toward instrument processing.

I entered the ER. The Czar was talking to two medics. They turned to me when I approached. "This was one nasty attack," the Czar said.

"Yes, sir," said a medic. "They hit one of our convoys with IEDs, and then shot everyone when they tried to get out of the burning vehicles. Our guys returned fire and by the time we got there" — he motioned to the stretchers behind him — "there were bodies everywhere."

"Over here, Doc," a nurse called.

I walked to her, and she pointed to two beds next to each other. An American and a brown-skinned man with 2280 written on his chest. A Marine lance corporal stood next to the American's bed, his hands on the stricken man's chest, his eyes closed, his mouth moving silently in what I presumed was prayer. The nurse touched his shoulder gently. "Corporal, you need to go to the waiting room now. Let the doctors do their work."

The young man looked up at her, his green eyes showing an amalgam of rage and fear. "Yes, ma'am," he said. "Please save Louis. He's my best friend."

"We'll do everything we can," she said, tears welling in her eyes.

The corporal stepped toward the surgeons' lounge, then turned and pointed at 2280. "This guy shot Louis when we crawled out of the Humvee," he said. He looked down for a moment before he continued, "Then I shot him."

As the corporal walked away, I looked down at Louis, a strong, tall young private of maybe twenty. He had a bandage on his forehead, and when I removed it I saw a perfectly round bullet hole in the middle of his forehead. There was no exit wound. His pupils were dilated and did not react. His chances were not good.

"Take him to CT, stat," I said.

While the medics rolled Louis to the scanner, I turned to 2280's bed. He also had blown pupils, no exit wound, and a hole in his forehead. The corporal was a good shot.

"He needs a scan too," I said.

Ten minutes later, I was faced with the most difficult decision — personal or professional — I'd ever had to make.

Tim was still tied up with his surgery, and it would be about three hours before we would have another set of instruments available. Neither of these two patients would survive long enough for McDonald's people to sterilize more instruments. And both Louis's and 2280's scans showed injuries that could be survived with immediate surgery, but that would be fatal if I didn't hurry.

I am trained to make medical decisions, not political ones. These two patients were about the same age, had similar injuries, and the medical issues surrounding my decision as to which of them should be operated on first were decidedly undecidable. There was no medical answer to this problem, and no military training we'd received prepared me for it. Triage was usually more straightforward, and the Americans naturally received priority in non-life-threatening situations, but this was literally a case where 2280 was going to die a preventable death if I said so.

"Lee, come on — room four is open. But we've got more casualties coming in. What do you want to do?" The Czar wasn't interested in my private thoughts.

"Both beds in room four are open?" I asked.

"Yes, both beds," the Czar said.

"Then get me one of the general surgeons, and take both of these guys to the OR."

Five minutes later, I was shaving the Marine Louis's head, and Chris was doing the same to the terrorist. I still didn't know exactly what I was going to do, but I wasn't willing to let 2280 die just because he wasn't an American.

We prepped both men's scalps with iodine solution and draped them for surgery. Nate opened the last craniotomy pack on his table, and a nurse connected our last sterile drill to the foot pedal so I could control it.

"Knife," I said, then felt the pop of the steel scalpel when Nate slapped it into my hand. I held the blade over Louis's head and said a silent prayer, as I always do just before I start an operation.

"Finished my case, I'm here to help," Tim said with his head stuck through the door. "I'm scrubbing in."

That solved the problem of two patients for one brain surgeon, I thought, but we still had only one set of instruments.

"Tim, we've got one drill, and the others won't be ready in time to save either of these guys."

"No problem," he said. "Let's just change drill bits between you drilling your patient and me drilling mine. At least the bit will be sterile."

"Sorry, Colonel," Nate said, "but this is the last bit in the hospital. We were supposed to get more on the resupply flight today."

There was an uneasy pause. "Okay, guys, here's what we're going to do," I said, though I could hardly believe that I was about to propose such a preposterous plan. "I'm going to start my case, and after I've used the drill I'm going to hand it to the nurse. She's going to run sterile saline on it to clean it, rub it down with alcohol, and hand it to Tim. Every time I finish with an instrument, that's what we'll do."

Tim shook his head slowly, his eyes scanning the OR as he tried to think of a better plan. Nate and the others were silent, as if they couldn't believe what we were contemplating. In America, sharing instruments between patients would be considered malpractice. That day in Iraq, it was the only choice I could see.

Tim nodded. "Make it so. Scalpel."

We both made the skin incisions and exposed our patients' skulls, as we'd done so many times before. I used the drill to remove Louis's skull flap, and when I was finished I handed the bloody tool to the nurse. My eyes met Tim's when he took it from her after she'd cleaned it as well as possible.

And so it went. Four or five times during my case, when I was sure I wouldn't need a certain instrument again, I handed it to the nurse to clean for Tim—who improvised during his case until he had what he needed. I passed off the Penfields and the Kerrisons and the Langenbecks and the other tools of our trade, and Tim's operation got easier with each addition to his arsenal.

Louis's brain relaxed nicely after I removed the clot, and by the time I closed his scalp, the ICP monitor read 0. He had a decent chance of surviving, although his brain injury was severe. He would most likely reach Walter Reed alive, and his family would get to see him again. *That's something*, I thought.

Tim's patient, 2280, was having more trouble. The corporal's bullet had torn several arteries, and although Tim handled the bleeding and brain swelling expertly, 2280 lost a lot of blood. And like everything else in the hospital that day, blood was in very short supply.

"Need any help?" I asked when I stepped away from Louis's bed.

"Not with the surgery — I'm done here. But he'll need at least four units of blood. They're checking with the blood bank to see what we have left."

I walked out into the surgeons' lounge and saw the lance corporal sitting on the couch, clutching his helmet to his chest. His eyes had softened. They now held less rage and fear and something more like sorrow or remorse.

He looked up when he heard me, the unspoken question obvious on his face.

"Louis is alive," I said. "He has a chance to recover. That's the best we can do here."

The corporal nodded slowly, then looked me in the eye. "And the other guy?" he asked.

Before I could answer, the overhead speakers crackled and a voice broadcast throughout the hospital.

"Attention: This is the blood bank. We have a critical need for whole blood, type B negative or O negative. If you're willing

to donate, please come to the lab immediately. This is a critical
need."

Every time I'd heard the call for a whole blood drive before,
I'd been in the middle of an operation and thus unable to give.
This time I wasn't a candidate because I'm type B positive.

The corporal stood and stepped past me.

"Where are you going?" I asked.

"I'm B negative," he said. "Sounds like somebody needs my
blood."

I reached out and grabbed his shoulder. He stopped and
turned to me.

"Corporal, there's something you need to know," I said.

"Sir?"

"The blood drive is for the man you shot. The terrorist who
shot your friend."

The corporal stiffened. His eyes filled with tears. He clenched
his jaw tightly and looked at his boots for a few seconds.

Then he pushed my hand off his shoulder. "Sir," he said, "lots
of people have done things for me that I didn't deserve. I shot
that man in battle, but letting him bleed to death when I have
the power to save him—that wouldn't be right. Excuse me."

He walked toward the lab, leaving me standing in the
lounge with my mouth open, wondering if I would have done
the same thing.

I never saw the corporal again. A few days later, we received
news that Louis had survived the trip to Walter Reed and was
improving. 2280 eventually woke up, saved by Army medics
and Tim's skill and ultimately by the corporal's sacrifice. Even
though some of the instruments used during his surgery were
not properly sterilized, he never became infected.

The morning we transferred 2280 to Abu Ghraib, I checked
his labs and saw that his blood counts were normal, even
though he'd lost eighty percent of his own B negative blood

in the operating room. I knew that most of the cells contributing to those normal lab values came from the kindness of an American Marine corporal.

Over the course of the Iraq war, American soldiers were guilty of inhumane treatment of prisoners at places like Abu Ghraib, murdering civilians and children, and committing other war crimes. Those things showed up on the news, and rightfully so. I was fortunate to work in a place where most of what I saw held up to the light of inspection, but I knew some of the soldiers I cared for were not righteous or heroic in every moment of their individual wars. Even in the hospital, signs warned the women not to walk around alone at night because there had been rapes on the base. I will not pretend that everything I saw or heard about regarding our troops' behavior was good, but most of it was. And since most of those stories don't make the news, because human nature usually requires something scandalous to sell papers, it is my hope that the story of the corporal's blood flowing into 2280 will resonate with anyone who's ever benefitted from someone else's sacrifice, especially when it was undeserved.

Show me another army in the world full of soldiers willing to sacrifice their own blood for their enemies.

CHAPTER 22

ROSE IS MY DAUGHTER'S AGE

After six weeks of seemingly nonstop trauma surgery, I was locked into a mind-set of moving fast and trying not to let the tragedy get to me. Every day someone else would come in with his or her face blown off, a spinal cord shot in half, or with some part of the skull missing.

While the war raged on around me, I tried as hard as I could to resist the emotional black hole I was being pulled toward. Every time I called my kids and heard their mother's voice on the answering machine, and with each day that passed without an email, letter, or card from them, I felt less hopeful that I would be able to put my relationship with them back together when I got home.

I passed the downtime playing in the worship band, finding a measure of peace in helping others seek the healing presence of God. Inside, I felt like God was using me to lead others before him while keeping me at arm's length.

Movies in my room helped us relax and forget the war for a few hours. So many people started showing up that we had to move the movies to a large tent next to the hospital. A big-screen TV and several sofas were set up, and my email network's care packages started to include microwave popcorn and movie candy. Movie Night was now routinely attended by twenty or more people.

My daily email journal was being read by several thousand people in twenty or more states, and I was receiving three to six care packages a day, most of them from strangers. I gave away almost everything they contained. The surgeons' lounge looked like a flea market during mail call, with folks from all over the base wandering through, picking out what they wanted, and relishing the generosity of people they would never meet.

I felt numb, my senses dulled. I was robotic in my job as a neurosurgeon and felt as if I were just going through the motions in my roles as worship leader and entertainment coordinator too. When I closed my eyes at night, I was alone in the world, so tired I could barely breathe but so afraid of the dreams I knew were coming that I tried hard not to sleep.

By week seven I wasn't sure about anything.

I spent all of one night in the hospital trying to save an Iraqi who'd wrecked his motorcycle. After surviving thirty years in a totalitarian society and avoiding the perils of war, this man bounced his head off a highway when he hit a pothole. The road did a lot of damage, and on a day when I'd managed to save three other people from their war wounds, I lost him to a stupid motorcycle wreck that could have happened anywhere else in the world.

I walked out of the operating room at around 8:00 a.m., slammed my fist into my locker, and went to check my email. The usual hundred or so messages filled my inbox, but none of them were from the three people I most needed to hear from — my kids. I wasn't sure how I was going to get through the coming day. I pressed my face into my hands and squeezed my eyes shut as tightly as I could, hoping to keep tears from flowing. After all, I was supposed to be Dr. Cool-and-Unaffected.

"Doc, Rose is in the clinic."

I heard Nate's voice and opened my eyes. He loomed over me, six-foot-one and 240 pounds. I rubbed my eyes hard and yawned.

"What?"

"That kid Rose is here with her parents. I guess the commander approved your request to operate on her."

I walked down the hall to the clinic, then stopped just outside the door, collecting my thoughts. A few weeks before, an Iraqi couple had brought their thirteen-year-old daughter to the gate. They were related to one of our translators, Raul, and he'd told them that we might be able to help the girl. The commander gave permission for her and her mother to come in, but on that particular day the girl's dad didn't have some of his identification papers, and he wasn't allowed to enter the base.

I had just said goodbye to baby Mohamed and his sister Vania, and when I came back into the hospital that day a nurse told me to go to the clinic to see Raul's cousin. At the clinic I found a middle-aged Iraqi woman, wearing a head covering and long brown robe. She and Raul were standing next to an exam table, and when I stepped past them I saw a young girl in a purple velour dress, her dark, curly hair pulled back with little pins with red flowers on them. Raul said, "Doctor, this is my cousin Hasim's wife and their daughter Rose. Rose began to have seizures when she was four, and Iraqi doctors have told Hasim she will die because her disease is untreatable. I told Hasim I have seen American doctors save many lives, and he asked me if you could help Rose."

+

EMAIL HOME
Wednesday, February 16, 2005

Good morning, friends.

The highlight of yesterday was seeing Rose, the little Iraqi girl that I've told you about before. She has been having seizures most of her life and has a brain tumor that I am going to remove today. Please pray for her and her mom and dad. They are grateful for the care, but of course very nervous.

I want to tell you a little about this from their perspective, so you can see how scary and exciting this whole thing must be to them. I apologize for the creative license.

Rose was born in 1992, just as the first Gulf War began. Her life has been spent surrounded by armed conflict. She has heard horrible things said about America, the Great Satan, populated by infidels. She developed a seizure disorder at age four and lived in a culture where if you don't have money your disease is untreatable. She became more and more developmentally delayed as the years of seizures went on, and the child whose parents say she was the brightest and fastest learner in her family became slow.

In 2003, Americans showed up in person to deliver the death blows to Saddam's reign of terror, and the little girl again saw war, this time with tanks and soldiers instead of only bombs and missiles.

The seizures continued, and the medicine she was given to treat it seemed to cause her additional problems. Her doctors said they'd done all they could.

Rose's parents heard that the Americans had taken over the hospital at Saddam's old air base. From time to time, one of their friends or relatives would be injured in a bombing and receive care there. Rumors started to spread that the Americans were actually kind and compassionate.

Rose's family had a relative who began to work as an interpreter for the Americans. One day he told them that he met a doctor who might be able to help them. They managed to get copies of her CT scans and sent them to the hospital with their cousin Raul.

When Raul showed me the scans, I asked for and received permission to invite Rose and her parents to the hospital.

Imagine how scary it must have been for them. First, on the way to the base, every time they walked past a crowd, they must have feared a car or suicide bomber. Then, walking up to the gate of an American military base during wartime, any violation of security procedures, any threatening move, could result in death.

While the guard processed the papers, they were searched and questioned, and finally only the child and her mother were allowed in. The father's papers were not in order.

Stepping out of Iraq and into a completely unfamiliar world, accompanied everywhere they went inside the base by armed guards, the brave mother brought her child into the hospital.

It was three weeks ago that Rose and her mom walked into the clinic and Raul introduced them to me, a blonde Oklahoman who could neither speak their language nor understand their culture, dressed in the uniform of the United States Air Force.

I asked Rose's mom if she minded if I examined her girl, and she consented. It must have seemed like forever to her before I finally told her that I thought we could help the little girl, as long as Colonel H approved.

I went to his office. Colonel H said we could probably help Rose, but he would have to ask his higher-ups, and that we definitely had to wait until after the elections.

Through Raul, I delivered the news to Rose's mom: Raul would let them know when and if they could come back for Rose to have surgery.

And so for three weeks, they've been waiting, wondering, worrying. Two days ago, Colonel H gave me the verdict: Surgery approved. Raul went outside the wire to deliver the news to Rose's parents.

Yesterday Rose returned, this time with both of her parents.

Rose's father is a tall man in a turban and robe. He has a grandfather's eyes and a soft smile. Although he carries himself in a stately, reserved manner, he cannot hide his concern or his love for his little girl; that language crosses cultures.

They listened to all I had to say, then politely asked me if I would please remember that God would take care of her. They said they did not need any more information, that they trusted me completely, and that they were grateful to be here.

The surgery starts in two hours.

For these people, this whole war boils down to someone being sent here to try to save their daughter.

Let's all pray today that this operation proves to be more than simply a medical procedure. In a real sense, these people will judge our culture, our religion, our hearts, and our nation by the way Rose is treated here. Please pray that no one, neither the doctors nor the youngest airman, will "have a bad day" in front of them. Pray that the surgery will be successful, that her seizures will stop, that she will do well, and that the tumor is benign. Please pray that they will go home and tell their friends that Americans are good, that we care about them, that we are not to be feared.

Thank you for your support today. Most of you will see this letter after the surgery is over. Thanks for your continued prayers after the surgery, for her to have no complications, no fevers, no infections.

Thank you all for participating in this important day. I will let you know how it goes.

I love you all.

Lee

CHAPTER 23

HIS GRIP LOOSENED AND HIS HAND DROPPED OUT OF MINE

"How long will it take you?"

I looked at Rose's new scan, evaluating how stuck the tumor would be to her right temporal lobe, locating the important arteries nearby, and the nerves she would need in order to see and to move her eyes. I could visualize the tumor, the surrounding structures, and all the ways I could maim or kill Rose if the surgery didn't go perfectly.

Colonel H's question hung in the air, and he is not a patient man.

"Lee, how long?"

"Maybe two hours, if her brain doesn't swell and if there's not too much bleeding," I said. "Could be longer, four or five hours if it's really stuck."

Colonel H shook his head. "That's a long time to have both my neurosurgeons tied up. Plus an OR, an anesthesiologist, techs, and nurses." He tapped his finger on the monitor. "And how long will she need an ICU bed?"

"Three or four days, if she doesn't have any seizures afterward," I said. I realized the depth of what I was asking the boss to commit to on behalf of this little girl. He had given me permission to do the case, but when I told him that I would need Tim's help, Colonel H began to have second thoughts. I didn't think I should do a case that serious without someone to back me up, and Tim agreed. So now, an hour before I planned to start the surgery, Colonel H sounded as if he might rescind his blessing.

He pinched the bridge of his nose and closed his eyes for a moment. "Okay, here's the deal," he said at last. "You can do the case. But if casualties come in, Tim breaks out and does his job. If soldiers need you, or if the other operating rooms fill up, you will close and get her out of there as quickly as possible. If it's complicated or it's going to take you too long, just abort and tell the family you did all you could in this environment. Understand?"

I nodded, looked back at her scan, and wondered what I was getting myself—and Rose—into.

Colonel H started to walk away, then turned back. "Lee, one more thing. Are you sure you can do this here? Because the time to bail out is before you start. No one will fault you for saying no, but if you mess this up, it's not going to be good."

Without giving me time to answer, he walked out of the room, leaving me alone to examine Rose's scan—and myself. The colonel's question summed up the situation perfectly. The issue wasn't whether I had the skills to remove Rose's tumor. The question was whether I could, or rather *should*, try to do it *here*.

What would my mentors do in this situation? Would they think I was crazy for even considering such an operation in a tent hospital with only the most basic equipment? But here I was, and in a room just down the hall a real little girl waited for the only person in her country willing to help her.

I made my decision.

I walked into the holding area where Raul and Rose's parents were talking together at Rose's bedside. "Raul, tell them we're going to surgery in a few minutes," I said.

In the operating room, I looked at the unconscious Rose for a second before we put the drapes over her, praying silently that her case would go well and that there would be no emergency arrival of soldiers needing my attention. I knew that if I had to stop Rose's surgery early, I would not be allowed a second chance.

"Knife," I said.

The surgery took about two hours. It turned out to be fairly straightforward and as easy as it would have been anywhere else, except for a couple of explosions nearby. The tumor wasn't attached to anything important, and it came out with no difficulty.

When I placed the last stitch in Rose's scalp, I put a bandage on her wound and took the drapes off. She was just as precious and pretty as she'd been two hours before, but I wouldn't be able to relax until she woke up and moved her arms and legs. Even after thousands of successful surgeries, it still seems a little magical to me that we can actually go inside someone's head and then, afterward, have them wake up and be okay. But until that moment, I remain very nervous.

After a few minutes that felt more like an eternity, Rose opened her eyes and began to breathe on her own. The anesthetist removed the breathing tube from Rose's throat, and she coughed a little. We took her to the recovery room, and I went out to talk to her family. Although I have performed surgery in three countries and several states, this scene is the same everywhere. Though the setting was very different here, and the sights and sounds and smells were unlike any waiting room I had ever experienced before coming here, the cast was identical:

a mom and a dad, scared to death. I smiled as I entered the room, and said through Raul, "She's all right."

I led them into the ICU, where Rose had just arrived. She was awake but still groggy from anesthesia, but when she saw her mom and dad she smiled broadly and opened wider her still-cloudy eyes. I looked on as her parents lovingly held her hands and spoke to her in comforting tones using words I did not know but completely understood. I smiled as I turned to walk away, looking back when Rose's father called out, in English, "God bless you, Doctor."

Unfortunately, the emotional high of pulling off a successful brain tumor removal in such an unlikely environment didn't last long. By the end of the day, I understood what Dickens meant by "It was the best of times, it was the worst of times" — because the war was not over.

+

EMAIL HOME
Thursday, February 17, 2005

Good morning, everyone.

I need to thank all of you for praying for Rose yesterday.

The surgery could not have gone better. It was beautiful. The tumor is completely gone, and she is fine. Her parents are so grateful. As we speak, the tumor is on its way to Germany to be looked at by the pathologists so that we can know if she requires any additional treatment. Keep praying — she hasn't had any seizures since her surgery — she normally has four or five per day. Sometimes surgery makes the seizures worse for a while, sometimes it doesn't affect them, and sometimes it cures them. Let's pray for a cure.

The entire hospital got on board with taking care of Rose.

The anesthesia folks were arguing about who got to do her case. Practically every tech lobbied me to be the one to scrub, and all the ICU nurses wanted to take care of her.

After the great peak of joy that all of us were experiencing with the success of Rose's surgery, we took another huge fall. Two Americans ran into two Iraqis in a head-on car crash, and one of the Americans was dead on arrival. Shortly afterward, a teenaged Army private came in with a gunshot wound to the head, and I had to pronounce him brain dead in the ER.

The elation we felt about Rose snapped us out of weeks of being emotionally numbed by the constant tragedy of the war. Seeing the young soldier die jerked us back to reality. The contrast was almost unbearable.

Tim and I put the bone back into the last patient I operated on in January with Pete. He's made a remarkable recovery and came back to the gate to ask if we could put his skull back together!

Feeling content after seeing that case to a satisfying conclusion, I rested for the rest of the day and was planning on going to the movie at nine with a bunch of folks, but as I was getting ready to go, I was called in to help Tim in the OR.

The patient had been shot in the base of his skull, and the bullet had lacerated the major vein that drains blood out of the brain and into the jugular vein. Then it had gone on to lacerate the vein in the middle that connects to the other side, meaning that this man now had no way to drain blood out of one half of his brain, except through his wound.

He was bleeding faster than we could replace it, and he bled to death in front of us. I held his hand as the anesthesia doctors tried to give him more blood. A whole-blood drive was initiated, then stopped within minutes, as we all reluctantly concluded that he couldn't be saved.

I watched as his pupils dilated, signaling the end of his young life. His grip loosened and his hand dropped out of mine.

We all stared at each other. It was, for us, a moment of ultimate futility—when all our equipment and our cumulative skills and experience cannot help one dying man.

The chaplain was there. He put his arm around my shoulders and asked if I was okay. He told me he would pray for me. It felt good that in this moment of tragedy, having lost one battle, he was already looking at how he could help someone else. The rest of us were focused on the battle we'd just lost; he was looking to win a different one—the battle for my morale. I can't tell you how much that helped me right then.

I checked on Rose—she was doing great. I changed her bandage and told her mother good night (I think she understood me). Then I went for a walk in the cold Iraqi moonlight. I thanked God for the day, for the hundred-plus thousand American soldiers this day who did not die. I prayed for the three families who will learn today about their lost son or daughter. They will know by the time you read this. I can't give you their names, of course, but all you need to know is that three families in America have received the call they've dreaded since the day their loved one left for Iraq. Your prayers will help them.

I went to sleep around midnight and dreamt of the young soldier's eyes, dilating in the last moments, his grip going slack in my hand. Over and over I saw it.

A new day dawns azure blue and bright outside my window right now. New patients, hope for Rose, heartbroken families, and more bad food await me this day. I pray for all of you that today you will feel the humbling awareness that three more Americans gave their lives yesterday in the pursuit of freedom for the Iraqi people—freedoms you consider a God-given right. Never forget it. Don't forget it when you vote, when you teach your kids history, when you talk to your friends who vote with their wallets, when you pray, when you go to the store, or when you choose where and when and if you wish to worship. Someone died for you to have that God-given right that you take so much for granted that most days you don't think about it at all. I will never again take being an American for granted.

A strange thought flashed through my mind in the OR last night: it's at moments like this that someone inevitably says something profound that later becomes a cliché to those not directly involved. I kept thinking of the T-shirt/bumper-sticker slogan: "All gave some, some gave all."

It's true. Some gave all. Three more yesterday from the US, as well as a few more Iraqis dying in their desperation to have what you already have.

I love you all.

Lee

CHAPTER 24

OUR NEXT STOP WAS ABU GHRAIB

I stood in the ICU, watching Rose sleep. I gently touched her head. One of the nurses had cut a little hole in the back of the head dressing to pull Rose's ponytail out. A pink ribbon tied her hair up, bright against the stark white gauze. I removed her bandages, saw the small area of pale skin where I'd shaved some of her hair, and checked her wound. "Looks great," I said to the nurse.

The labs and the monitors and the post-operative scan were all perfect. In the eighteen hours since surgery, she'd had no seizures. I turned to reach for her chart and accidentally dropped my pen. When I knelt to retrieve it, I noticed how dirty the floor was, and I thought, *Wow, an ICU floor that dirty in America would be considered an infection risk.* I reached for the pen, which caused my holster to shift. My handgun slid around and almost knocked the chart out of my hand.

It occurred to me that the biggest threats to Rose now were those two things: bullets and bacteria. She'd survived years of seizures from her slowly growing brain tumor, and she had come through her surgery better than I'd hoped. But infection and the realities of living in Iraq still lurked both inside and out of our canvas-walled hospital. Like all kids, though, Rose seemed content to let the adults worry about those things; she slept with a sweet smile on her face.

A master sergeant, hair in a tight bun on top of her head, walked in carrying a clipboard. "Major, Colonel H asked me to give you this. Your chopper leaves in thirty minutes." She handed me an envelope, made a crisp turn, and walked away.

I opened the envelope and took out a folded letter. It was an order directing me to travel to Baghdad via helicopter for a meeting with the hospital commander and both Army neurosurgeons there. Pete had told me about the meeting over a month ago, and I knew that the Army was thinking of sending their neurosurgeons home, since Balad had become the primary trauma hospital in Iraq. The order stated that I was authorized to fly to Ibn Sina Hospital and return "space available" the following day. I wasn't sure what that meant.

I ran to my room and quickly threw a clean uniform and toiletries into a duffel. I had on DCUs, body armor, and a helmet, plus I was carrying a pistol and two knives. *Pretty different from how I usually go through airports*, I thought.

Back at the hospital, I found Tim in the surgeons' lounge. He looked up from the computer. "Heading out?"

"Yep. Should be back tomorrow," I said. "Take good care of Rose for me."

Tim stood and shook my hand. "Of course. You be careful." He patted the Beretta in my holster. "Will you be able to use that if you need to?"

I looked down at the black pistol, then at my hands. "I hope so," I said.

A helicopter medic walked out of the ER, wearing his flight helmet and carrying two ice chests with red crosses on them. He stopped next to us. "Are you Major Warren?"

"That's me," I said.

The medic set his ice chests down. "I need to see your orders."

I reached into my pocket and produced Colonel H's letter. The medic scanned the page and handed it back to me. "Okay, sir, let's go."

I followed the medic outside and down the sidewalk to the helipad. I had come this way often, running out to find our next patients coming off the Black Hawks and Chinooks, but it felt funny knowing I was about to leave the base on one of them.

While we walked, I nudged the medic. "What's in the coolers?"

"Blood. We have to drop it off at a couple of field aid stations. There's been a lot of fighting around some of the FOBs lately."

I knew that most of the patients we treated at Balad had stopped at one of these forward operating base aid stations before they got to us. Family practice doctors, allergists, pediatricians, and general surgeons were working at those stations in far more extreme environments than I was, called out of their typical practices to work in battlefield hospitals less well equipped than your average urgent care clinic in America. And they were saving lives.

The helicopter was a medevac Black Hawk. The two pilots were doing their walk-around, checking the machine for our flight. I shook hands with them, and then the medic told me to climb in and sit in the back.

"Should be thirty minutes or so, not counting a few stops," the pilot said as I crawled back to the narrow bench seat. Most of the interior behind the cockpit was set up for transporting patients. I saw oxygen bottles, bags full of IV fluids, and a portable defibrillator. How many injured soldiers had this same crew brought to us before? I thought of all the heroic things this medic must have done on board this Black Hawk.

I slid around a metal partition and found a narrow canvas jump seat, barely wide enough for me to fit into. The seat faced forward, and there were small windows to my left and right so that I could see out both sides. I fastened the seat belt and leaned around the partition in front of me, so that I could see forward. I gave the medic a thumbs-up, and he reached forward into the cockpit and patted the pilot on the shoulder. Then he crawled back toward me and leaned over the partition. "Put in your earplugs. It's going to be pretty loud. Don't try to talk to me during the flight, because I'll have my headphones on. Just strap in and hold on."

The pilots flipped a few switches, and the rotors began to turn. By the time the medic buckled himself into his small seat behind the cockpit, the engine was roaring. I felt the whole machine shudder and then begin to rise into the air. I smelled the smoke and dirt from the air outside, mixed with aircraft fuel.

I saw the hospital from a new perspective as we gained altitude. The pilot hovered for about thirty seconds, and during that time I counted about thirty spots where the dirt was lighter in color than the surrounding areas — places where mortars had recently landed. The distance between the hospital and the outside of the base also seemed very close from the air, and I realized how very dangerous a place I had been in. Flying away from the base, I couldn't decide if I felt more safe — or less.

Moments later, we were flying over the valley between the Tigris and Euphrates Rivers. I could see the shadow of the helicopter projected onto the ground, and the beauty we had been so close to in our uniformly brown world inside the base surprised me. There were lush green fields, trees, and two lovely rivers. It wasn't hard to imagine the garden of Eden being there, as described in the second chapter of Genesis. Watching the sun set over the birthplace of humanity, seeing the end of another day from a perspective high above the ground, I became acutely embarrassed for all of us, sickened at the fractured mess we humans have made after such an ideal start. Somewhere down there, I thought, Cain killed Abel, 2137 killed Yeager, and we're still killing each other.

I thought again of the soldier whose hand I had held the night before as he bled to death. The most frustrating part of his death to me was the irony of him dying as a result of wearing gear designed to make him safer.

The body armor systems US troops wear include a small collar of material in the back, providing some protection for the neck in the exposed area between the top of the vest and the bottom of the helmet. This type of collar created a problem for soldiers when they dropped to the ground in a firing position. The collar hit the bottom of the helmet, forcing the front of the helmet down over the soldier's eyes. Obviously, not being able to see what you are shooting at would be a major problem in combat, so it's no wonder that soldiers complained. The Army made a simple, logical change: raise the back of the helmet high enough to avoid hitting the armor.

While this seemed like a great solution, and it has probably saved many lives, exposing the back of the head created opportunities for snipers and disasters for neurosurgeons and their patients. The back third of the skull contains huge veins, through which all the blood in the brain passes on its way back to the heart. Gunshots there are routinely fatal. The only way to prevent death from such a wound is to prevent the wound from happening in the first place.

The sniper's bullet had found the exposed spot, and we had been powerless to save that young soldier last night. I could still see his lifeless eyes and feel his failing grip as his hand slid away from mine, the memories as vivid and palpable as the vibrations from the helicopter. I had seen many people die before that moment, but the worst part of last night was that I had been powerless to do anything to help that soldier, and I believe he was awake enough to know it.

My thoughts were interrupted—an Apache helicopter gunship appeared outside the left window. A second Apache appeared on the right, and for a moment I felt comforted that we had an escort. My comfort was short-lived.

Suddenly, the pilot made a hard turn to the right. Our helicopter went through a complete 360-degree circle, and then made another spin to the left, this time dropping a lot of altitude. My stomach flipped, and I felt a little nauseated.

I could see the highway and the Iraqi countryside below us, but I had no idea what was going on. The pilot flared to land, and I snapped a few photos out of the window. On the ground below us, I saw pink and orange smoke from a flare, a car on fire, and a few Humvees. Then I saw soldiers and Iraqis, the GIs fanned out in a circle with weapons at the ready. I felt sweat pop out on my forehead. My hands were shaking.

We landed on the highway, and the medic jumped out of the helicopter with his M4 carbine in his hands. He turned and pointed at my holster, then yelled over the noise: "Make sure your weapon's ready, Major. Don't know how long we'll be here."

My heart was beating so hard I could hear my pulse in my ear. I had no idea why we'd landed in the middle of what looked to be a very dangerous situation. I pulled my pistol from its holster and slid the rack to chamber a round, but left the safety on.

For several minutes, I saw nothing, and heard nothing other than the noise of the engine. I played through many scenarios in my mind, most of them ending with a large group of terrorists overrunning the helicopter and me having to fight my way out. I knew how that would end.

Even though I could clearly see US soldiers guarding the helicopter, I had seen many patients who had been hit with

RPGs and mortars, and I knew that my fears were not irrational. I told myself that if anyone who wasn't wearing a US military uniform approached the helicopter, I would shoot them.

I had never before had to contemplate actually shooting another person. My job is to fix people others have shot. But sitting there in that very real situation, I knew that if it came down to me pulling the trigger or dying in the back of that helicopter, I would do my duty.

I remembered my frequent habit on the firing range of missing high and right due to failure to control both my breathing and how hard I squeezed the trigger, so I reminded myself to aim a little low and to the left.

It may sound crazy, but I actually planned what I was going to say if I was captured and became the subject of one of those videos we all saw of the captured pilots during the first Gulf War. I prayed and thought of home. My little field trip had seemed a great way to break up the monotony of daily life at Balad, but this wasn't what I'd had in mind.

After what seemed like hours, two soldiers rushed to the helicopter carrying a stretcher with a man on it. Four other soldiers guarded them as they placed the stretcher into the helicopter's cargo bay. I had to stretch around the partition to see the man, but the first thing I noticed was how bad he smelled. Then I saw that he was covered in blood and that his eyes were open. He wore a black shirt and khaki pants, and he wasn't wearing shoes. He had a beard. He was moaning and writhing. He looked right at me, but I was too far away to touch him. I started to unfasten my seat belt to see if I could help, but the medic held his arm out, signaling for me to stay in my seat. He climbed closer and yelled in my ear, "Don't try to help him! We're not equipped to do anything for him on this flight, because we were just supposed to be making a run to drop off blood and then take you to Baghdad. We'll go straight back to Balad with him."

"Who is he?" I yelled back.

"Terrorist. The pilot will tell you more when we land. Hold on tight—we're going to go fast."

The medic shut the door and gave me a thumbs-up. With great relief, I holstered my handgun. Then I remembered that there was a bullet in the chamber, but I decided to wait to eject it. Visions of accidentally shooting the engine and crashing the helicopter made me keep my hands off the live weapon.

I looked at the patient again. Both of his hands were gone. I could see the stark white of his right radius and ulna bones protruding through the skin where his hand had been. I didn't yet know his story, but I knew that he was suffering terribly. He looked terrified and smelled like sulfur. I prayed for him, glad that I could not hear his moans. Sometimes I dream about him.

We lifted off, made a very fast turn, and flew extremely low to the ground all the way back to the hospital. The helicopter shook with the speed, and my guts were churning with every dip and turn. I could feel the wind rushing through the windows, which brought the terrorist's smoky, burned smell even more strongly into my nostrils.

It was fascinating, as we landed, to see the team running out with the stretchers. I was usually on their side, running toward the helicopter. I watched their faces, determined and intent, showing a strong desire to help whomever it was that they were about to rush into the hospital. I imagined being a patient and seeing their faces as they wheeled me across the helipad and into the emergency department.

Before they had the terrorist around the corner, we were airborne again.

We flew to the other side of Balad Air Base to refuel for our trip to Baghdad. The pilot asked me to get out with him. Once the rotors stopped spinning, I took advantage of the quiet to ask him, "What was that all about?"

"We heard a distress call," he said. "Medics on the ground needed a medevac for a terrorist who blew himself up trying to set up a car bomb. We had a convoy going by, and the man accidentally detonated his bomb before he could get away."

A worker called out to the pilot, "She's ready, sir." The man patted the side of the helicopter before he rolled up the fuel hose and walked away into the twilight.

"Saddle up, Major," the pilot said. "Hopefully that will be all of the excitement for this trip."

We lifted off. I watched the base fade in the distance. I thought about the terrorist, about his agony-filled eyes. He was about my own age, but our lives had been vastly different. Our paths had crossed in the back of a helicopter, but I wasn't a doctor to him, and at that moment he wasn't a terrorist to me; I was just a man, watching another man who was suffering terribly, who probably just wanted to go home. In the hospital, such men were patients to be saved regardless of the uniform they wore or the cause they defended. In the helicopter, he was a ravaged human being in need of help, and I had felt completely powerless.

I prayed for him—for all of us.

We flew to a Marine outpost called "TQ," and the medic delivered his ice chests full of blood to the small hospital there. I knew that whoever received that blood would end up at our hospital eventually. The Marines at TQ were at "the tip of the spear," the guys kicking in doors in Fallujah, clearing out insurgents from Iraqi towns and villages. I had cared for many of these Marines when their missions went awry.

The next stop was the prison at Abu Ghraib. Infamous for a few soldiers who had videoed themselves abusing prisoners, this place felt like pure evil. I could see prisoners standing just inside a barbed-wire fence. These were hard men, men who would not think twice about taking another person's life. I could imagine that guarding them was no easy feat. And yet, once someone is under your care, he or she deserves to be treated with dignity.

Was 2137 standing with the men I could see, recovered now from his wounds and facing his punishment?

Being at war changes people in ways that cannot easily be understood by those who have not experienced it. The line between interrogation, torture, and horrible abuse of another human being had been crossed by a handful of young and undertrained guards, leading to at least two US soldiers going to prison. I felt a chill looking across the wire and into the eyes of the prisoners, partly because I knew what they were capable of, and partly because I wondered what would happen to them. I was glad when we lifted off, the altitude making me feel safer, but my emotions were still stirred as we flew away from Abu Ghraib.

Eventually we landed on the helipad at Ibn Sina Hospital as darkness fell on Baghdad. I could make out mosques and palaces mixed into the skyline, but there were no streetlights or skyscrapers as in an American city. Many of the buildings had huge holes in them or their top stories missing, and I realized that many people had died when all those missiles and bombs fell. Somewhere down there, a man had once tried to build an empire, and the conflict between his ego and my president had caused the damage spread out before my eyes. I couldn't imagine the lives of the people who lived in this beautiful, bloody city.

The medic motioned for me to unbuckle and exit. I patted him on the back and yelled, "Thanks for the wild ride."

He yelled back, "No problem. Hope your return trip is less exciting."

"Roger that," I said. I waved at the pilots and shouted thanks but knew they couldn't hear me. I stooped under the still-spinning rotors and ran to the edge of the helipad, where an armed guard held a door open for me. The Black Hawk was airborne again by the time I reached the door.

I looked back, surprised to feel a little apprehension. I wasn't sure whether it was because of what I'd just been through or because they were leaving me here.

The guard led me to a reception desk in a lobby that looked like a movie-set version of a 1950s-era American hospital. A pimply Army private sat at the desk, and he looked up from his computer when I approached.

"May I help you, sir?"

I showed him my orders and asked where I could find the neurosurgeons.

"We've been waiting for you, Major. I'm supposed to call the hospital commander when you arrive."

A few minutes later, I met a colonel who was in charge of the facility. As we talked, I heard a voice behind me: "Lee! Welcome to Baghdad."

I turned and saw Jeff, an Army neurosurgeon from San Antonio I'd known for a few years. It was good to see a familiar face. Jeff showed me to my room—a hospital room with two beds and its own bathroom and shower. Comparing it to my quarters back at Balad, I felt like I'd just checked into a five-star hotel.

Then Jeff led me down the hall. We passed a small office, and Jeff waved at a kind-faced man sitting at the desk. "Evening, Chaplain."

Then he led me into another office. "This is our computer room. You can use the Internet and check your email." He pointed to a telephone on the desk. "That phone dials directly to the US. Just dial the number you want to call as if you were in the States."

He took me back to my room and said, "I'll let you get some rest. I'm glad you're here. See you in the morning."

Jeff walked away, and I went back down the hall to call

home. I dialed the number, and after four or five rings I heard my son Mitchell's voice. I was so surprised Mitch had answered that I almost couldn't speak. "Mitch, it's Daddy," I said finally.

"Dad! Kimber, Kalyn, Dad's on the phone! Come to the phone!"

I heard commotion, heavy breathing, and then two other voices. "Daddy!"

We talked for a few minutes. The kids explained that their mom was in the shower. Mitch asked if I still loved them.

"Mitch, I'll love you forever," I said. "Nothing will ever change that."

Kimber asked if their mom and I were still getting a divorce.

"Yes, honey, we are," I said.

She was quiet for a moment, and then said, "Will we ever get to see you again, Dad?"

I explained that when I got home I would live very close to them, and we would spend even more time together than we had during all the years I'd been in school and in training. I promised over and over that everything would be okay. Finally, Kimber said, "I can't wait to see you, Dad. I'm proud of you."

Kalyn said, "Daddy, when you finish saving all the soldiers, will you come play with me?"

By the end of our conversation, it felt as if the kids and I had formed a new bridge, one that would take us across whatever happened when I got home and into a new reality. Maybe it really would be okay. Maybe our relationship would survive the war—all of the wars—and come out stronger.

We said our goodbyes and I-love-yous, and then the line clicked and they were gone. My tears fell, but this time most of them were happy ones. I knew that I'd answered some of the kids' questions, and they'd answered some of mine.

I leaned back in the chair and closed my eyes for a few seconds. Then I heard a voice.

"Sir, how long will it be before I can use the computer?"

I looked up and saw a soldier of about twenty-five in full combat gear. He looked as if he'd just stepped off the battle-field. He leaned heavily on the doorpost and slid his Kevlar armor off, letting it hit the floor with a heavy thud.

"I'm done, Corporal. You look pretty tired," I said.

Looking dazed, he took off his helmet and gloves and said, "I need to email my wife because she thinks I'm dead."

"What?"

I got up and he sat down in the desk chair while he told me the story. He said that his vehicle had run over a mine earlier that day, and the medics had used his satellite phone to call his wife to tell her that he was okay. However, when she answered, the medics started the conversation with, "Your husband's truck hit a land mine" — and then they were cut off. They'd been unable to get her back on the line. That had been several hours before.

I put my hand on his shoulder and asked if any of his buddies were hurt. Suddenly the tears began, and he said, "A bunch of them didn't make it out."

He tried unsuccessfully to get into his email, then asked me if I knew how he could make a phone call. I showed him the phone and explained how to dial out. He called his wife. I heard her scream through the phone in relief. He assured her that he was okay and that he loved her. Right before he hung up, she too asked him about his friends. He broke down again and, weeping, he told her their names and what happened to each of them.

How strange it seemed to me that, just before I met this young man, I had been shown the phone and had walked past the chaplain's office. I knew nothing about this place other than where that phone and the chaplains were — and here was a guy who needed that information whom I'd known only for the past half hour. After he hung up, I took him to the chaplain's office, told the chaplain the story, and left the soldier in his care. The corporal gave me a hug and thanked me for my help. He asked me to pray for him.

I found my way back to my room and tried to sleep.

The soldier and his friends stayed heavily on my mind. I was thankful to have been able to help him, even in such a small way. It was as if, because God knew the soldier would need some friendly help, he had armed me with the two pieces of information the young man needed. I felt almost as if I'd been merely an observer of God's provision, simply watching it unfold, so perfectly had God orchestrated the scene.

For the first time since arriving in Iraq, I had good dreams that night. I kept hearing my kids' voices and woke up with a smile. In the morning, I took advantage of the amazing availability of indoor plumbing and showered in my own bathroom. It felt luxurious after many weeks of walking so far to the showers each day that I was inevitably sweaty again by the time I got back to my trailer. My shower lasted longer than three minutes.

Outside the window, I saw dawn breaking over Baghdad. A new day in the ancient city awaited me, and I was excited about the change in fortune with my kids and what that meant for our relationship.

Before I set out to find Jeff, I checked myself in the mirror. I saw something in my weary, pale blue eyes I hadn't seen in a long time. It took a second for me to recognize it, but there it was: hope.

CHAPTER 25

BAGHDAD: A BEAUTIFUL, BROKEN PLACE

I met Jeff for morning rounds with the surgical team, all Army doctors and all looking better than any of us at Balad. Their uniforms were clean, their boots weren't muddy, and none of them were wearing body armor. Every patient was in a real hospital room, the ICUs and ORs were not made from tents, and everybody had indoor plumbing and no shortage of hot water. I was not looking forward to going back to my ten-foot metal cube and the long walk to the bathroom.

After rounds, Jeff took me to a dining hall for breakfast. The large room felt like a five-star restaurant, and I had scrambled eggs and sausage, the first hot breakfast I'd had in Iraq.

Jeff took a sip of coffee and let out a long sigh. "Well, I guess I better tell you now," he said.

"Tell me what?" I asked between bites of what I thought was probably the finest sausage patty ever made in the history of breakfasts.

"Command has decided that no matter what we think, they're going to keep four neurosurgeons in theater."

I held up my hands in confusion. "Why?" But what I really

wanted to say was, "Then why did they make me risk my life flying down here?"

Jeff shrugged. "Good question. I suspect it's political. Imagine what the press would say if a soldier or a diplomat were injured in Baghdad and died before we could get them to Balad."

"But you and your partner have been here over a year," I said. "If the trauma patient flow is really directing more and more people to Balad, couldn't you drop down to one neurosurgeon here, or have shorter deployments?"

Jeff pointed at the bronze oak leaf on my helmet, sitting on the table next to me. "That question is above our pay grades, buddy."

"Then why did they have me come down here?"

He laughed. "My boss just told me this last night. You were already on your way. But look on the bright side. I'm going to take you on a tour of Baghdad."

As we walked back to Jeff's room to get our body armor, I wondered how much the pointless flight I'd taken the day before had cost the Air Force. My trip outside the wire, the danger I'd been exposed to—all for nothing. Then I remembered the young soldier from last night, the one who'd needed to know where the phone was and how to find the chaplain. I smiled inside, knowing that I'd been in the right place at the right time to help him.

Jeff pulled his pistol out of its holster and chambered a round. He motioned toward mine. "Better load that thing. You never know what you're going to find outside."

We donned our armor and helmets to head outside. On our way out, Jeff reached behind his bedroom door, pulled out an AK–47 machine gun, and slung it over his shoulder.

"Where did you get that?" I asked.

Jeff smiled. "Traded someone for it. Can't say more than that."

He walked down the hall. After a second or two of considering the wisdom of going into a city where we needed a machine gun, I followed. With our official business concluded, I figured seeing Baghdad was a nice alternative to a day spent hashing out policies the bureaucrats were going to disregard anyway.

+

We stepped into a beautiful, cloudless day and made a left turn onto a sidewalk. I had to step around a group of Iraqis loitering under the awning at the hospital entrance, smoking cigarettes. We took pictures in front of a statue of Hammurabi, and then we reached the edge of the Green Zone. Inside, where we were, only Coalition forces and "approved" Iraqis can enter. The checkpoint was a beautiful arched monument called the Assassin's Gate.

I expected our tour to stop there, but Jeff waved me forward. "Come on, the really interesting stuff is out here."

He led me through the gate and onto a sidewalk. I could see businesses and homes and people milling around in the early morning sunshine. It was like any other city you might visit, except that most of the buildings had been bombed to rubble, there were bullet and missile holes in almost every wall, and razor wire guarded the entrances to many buildings. War and daily life were juxtaposed in a way that was foreign to me but a fact of life for these people. Other than the interpreters and the few family members of patients I had met inside the complex of Balad Air Base, these were the first non-injured Iraqis I had seen. They all looked tired.

I watched a man lead two small children down the street. He led them as far away from every parked car as he could, and he positioned himself between the cars and his kids.

Everywhere we went, I saw reminders of Saddam Hussein's narcissism. Opulent palaces and monuments stood next to housing areas where people lived in poverty. While most of the population lived with barely enough clean water to survive,

Saddam had ordered many elaborate fountains built as monuments to himself. It was easy to understand why the people pulled Saddam's statue down when Baghdad fell; the city that had thrived since it was founded in AD 762 had been turned into a celebration of the fact that Saddam had everything and his people had nothing.

We passed a government building that had been hit by cruise missiles, and it occurred to me that I was looking at the result of the "shock and awe" attacks that heralded the start of the war in 2003. I tried to imagine what it must have sounded and looked like from the ground. While most Americans had seen those attacks on the news, flashes of light from far away, the citizens of this ancient city had heard and felt those bombs destroying their hometown. From the couch in San Antonio, it had been pretty cool to watch. It did not seem so cool now.

There was a sudden burst of gunfire, and concrete flew off the wall behind my head.

"Get down!" Jeff shouted. He pulled me down behind a low wall, and I drew my pistol. A few more shots rang out, and then there was a short burst of machine-gun fire from the American soldiers in a guard tower at the corner of the street we were on. Silence fell on the street.

Everyone I could see was either on the ground or hiding behind something. After a few seconds, it seemed likely that whoever had done the shooting was either gone or dead. People started moving again as if nothing had happened.

Jeff stood and said, "Why don't we go a different direction now?"

When my heart started beating again, I realized that in this place, I was not a doctor. To the unknown shooter who had fired in my direction, I was an American soldier, bearing arms and occupying his country. I wanted to find a way to tell him that I was just a tourist, looking at this lovely but war-torn city, and that I just wanted to get back to Balad safely. I had a new respect for my little tent hospital. What we lacked in variety we made up for in only having mortars and rockets to worry about; in Baghdad people actually tried to shoot you.

A few minutes later, I heard a loud explosion from not very far away, close enough that I could see smoke rising soon thereafter. Several more explosions occurred throughout the day. I found out later that it was one of the bloodiest days in Baghdad that year, with more than thirty-five people dying from multiple car bombings throughout the city. Of course, I didn't know that at the time, or I probably would not have continued my little tour.

We had lunch in Saddam Hussein's former main presidential palace. Inside the building, in addition to cafeterias, were offices housing government agencies and intelligence units, as well as a dungeonlike room previously used as a torture chamber for people deemed enemies of the state. Jeff told me there was an Army Bible study group meeting daily in the former dungeon.

During our tour, I saw the crossed swords monument, two giant hands holding swords that arch over a street. It represents Iraq's victory over Iran in the 1980s war. Tied to each hand is a large net bag filled with Iranian army helmets, most of which have bullet holes in them.

We climbed a spiral staircase to the top of an observation tower, where I cut my hand on a hole in the metal. I wrapped a bandana around my hand, glad the Air Force had made me have a tetanus shot before I deployed. Jeff pointed at the hole in the metal railing.

"Look up and down the staircase. See all those holes? Iraqi snipers used this tower during the Battle of Baghdad. None of them survived."

From the top of the tower, I could see, among the palm trees and general lushness of the Tigris River Valley, many buildings with evidence of missile damage.

Jeff pointed to a bridge in the distance. "Imagine what it must have been like for those guys to sit up here and watch the Army's Third Infantry Division cross that bridge, knowing they were coming here."

A drop of my blood dripped off my hand and onto the staircase, the only blood I shed during the war.

We visited some former Iraqi government offices, one of which had a ceiling mural painted all the way across the building. Following the details from left to right, you see a story depicted of the Iraqi army's overwhelming victory over the Americans in the first Gulf War. The American soldiers are shown cowering and surrendering, utterly defeated, as the Iraqis hold their flag high and press the battle.

I imagined the children who were raised in Hussein's Iraq in the early 1990s. They saw the bombs fall, knew that their country's army had been sent off to Kuwait to fight the United States, and expected to eventually see American ground troops fighting in their backyards. But the soldiers never came.

One of the soldiers who worked in the building told me that the Iraqi government taught their children that they had crushed the Americans in Kuwait. The reason US troops never reached Baghdad, they said, was that the Americans surrendered in the desert. An entire generation of Iraqi schoolchildren learned that history, and they believed it.

The problem with this is, of course, that it is untrue. As everyone else in the world knows, the Iraqi army was overwhelmingly defeated, but the American government decided not to move ahead with a military assault on the Iraqi government.

When I saw this mural, it struck me that there must also be things I've been taught that simply are not true. I started thinking about political and religious beliefs I was taught as a child and how many of them I accepted as true or right simply because I was taught them. How much of the world's history is simply decided on by those in power, based not on the truth but on their agenda, and taught by governments and their supporting media?

Then I thought, *Don't we all do that in our own lives?* We have our versions of our stories, our marriages, and our way of seeing the world. Those versions may be only partly derived from empirical truth. I made a decision that day to try to see things, and tell things, as they are.

We returned to Ibn Sina Hospital. As we walked under the awning where the crowd had been gathered earlier, Jeff stopped and pointed at the sunset over the palace in the distance. "Beautiful, isn't it?"

"It is," I said. "A beautiful, broken place. Maybe someday people will stop fighting and rebuild it."

Jeff shook his head. "Maybe."

My day in Baghdad provided me with many memorable moments, but as the long day and the ten-mile walk in a helmet and body armor wound down, my prevailing emotion was sadness. This great city and its proud people had such a long and fascinating history, yet it was in shambles because of the savagery and arrogance of one man.

Jeff walked me to the waiting area outside the helipad and asked to see my orders. "Oh, you're flying space-A," he said. "You might be here a while."

I remembered that I'd intended to ask the Master Sergeant back at Balad what that meant. I asked Jeff.

"It means that getting you back to Balad isn't a priority," he said. "You have to wait until a chopper going there has room on board for you."

Four hours later, I was still sitting there, watching CNN describe the carnage throughout Baghdad that day. The odds of me getting "home" that night seemed slim, and I was exhausted and starving.

Just then I saw a flight crew walking toward the door to the helipad and noticed parallel silver bars on one of their helmets. It occurred to me that I outranked the captain.

I hoped I was a good enough actor to pull this off.

"Excuse me, Captain," I said. "Are you flying anywhere near Balad Air Base tonight?"

The pilot stopped walking and squinted at me. "Pretty close, Major," he said. "Why?"

"I'm a brain surgeon stationed there. I have to get back tonight. If any casualties come in and I'm not there, somebody might die."

I handed him my orders, and his squint narrowed even more. "Sir, this says you're space-A. We don't have any space, and these orders mean you're not a priority."

I stepped closer. He was about my height, but looked like he could easily drop me in a fight. But he didn't need to know I thought that.

"Captain, I'm telling you that I need to get to Balad tonight. If any of your guys are shot up, believe me—you want me there."

He looked at his copilot, a first lieutenant, who shrugged and said, "We could move those ammo boxes and he could sit in the back, if he holds his stuff in his lap."

A few minutes later I crawled into the tight space the combat Black Hawk crew had made for me. They requested permission to fly me to the hospital at Balad and spun up the engine.

I hoped they wouldn't tell Colonel H I'd bossed them into giving me a ride.

Looking at the sporadic lights scattered across Baghdad as we climbed, I thought about my day there: the explosions, the gunfire aimed at me, the man and his kids who would grow up knowing more about car bombs and terrorists than homework and playgrounds.

After we landed at Balad, I walked into the hospital and

checked my email. I was surprised to see that my colleague Jeff had already written me.

A chill crept through me as I read his report. An unexploded IED had been discovered at the front entrance of the hospital. He said it had probably been planted by one of the Iraqis who had been standing in the entryway as we'd left the hospital to explore the city.

I shook my head. It appeared that I'd found the answer to my previous question of where I felt safest. I was now sure that I felt safer in my little tent hospital, if only because we were largely ignorant of the dangers most of the time. But *safety* was a relative term, as the ringing gunshots, IEDs, mortars, and rockets reminded me that many people out there didn't appreciate our presence.

Before I gave in to the fatigue and mental exhaustion from the previous two days, I went to check on Rose. Her mother was at her bedside, and they both smiled at me. Rose motioned for me to kiss the teddy bear I'd given her. Her mother said through the interpreter that she'd been praying for my safe return. The insurgents may not have been particularly happy to see me in Baghdad, but I realized that at least two people in Balad were glad I was there.

On my way out of the hospital, I passed through the conference room, where someone had hung a huge, vintage picture of a very young, suit-wearing Saddam Hussein. He'd been quite handsome in his youth, I thought. Whoever had taken that photograph had probably had no idea of the monster Saddam would become. People in the conference room were lining up to have their picture taken with the now-deposed and imprisoned dictator, and I decided to as well. When it was my turn, I smiled for the camera, thinking that being on Saddam's old air base and posing with his picture was as close as I would ever come to him.

I was wrong.

✚

CHAPTER 26

YOU GOT TO KEEP MOVING OR YOU GET HIT, BRO

The day after I returned from Baghdad, I felt a little like a movie star. Everywhere I went in the hospital, people wanted to know what it was like to be in a Black Hawk, and they wanted to hear all about my experiences outside the wire.

The enemy didn't seem to notice I'd been gone, though. During those twenty-six hours, Tim had had to do four emergency brain surgeries, and the rest of the surgeons were busy with new trauma patients also. From the moment I walked back into the hospital, I was taking care of patients as if I'd never left. Tim gave me the beeper and immediately went to bed.

I was in the ICU taking care of Tim's newest patients when the general surgeon Mike walked in. "How was Baghdad?"

I looked up from the chart I was writing in. "Lovely, other than getting shot at and having to land on a highway to pick up a terrorist," I said.

Mike looked surprised. "Wait a minute. Were you on the chopper that brought in the guy who blew himself up with an IED?"

I nodded. "He looked pretty bad. What happened to him?"

Mike sighed and looked at his boots. "He blew off both his hands and had really terrible burns and intestinal injuries. Todd and I worked on him for several hours. I thought for a while we could save him, but he died this morning. Saeed said he knew the guy, used to be in the Republican Guard. His name was Omar. He had three kids."

I remembered what the commanders had told us: that when the Iraqi military was disbanded, all those former soldiers were suddenly unemployed. Iranian funding had helped the insurgency offer a lot of them new jobs as terrorists. Omar had to feed his kids somehow, and the Americans weren't hiring former Iraqi soldiers. What would I be willing to do to take care of my family if I lost my income and had no ability to earn a living?

I squeezed Mike's shoulder. "Good try, man. You guys have saved a lot of lives here—you know that."

Mike looked up. "Yeah, but every time we pull the plug on somebody, it feels like I haven't done enough."

"Exactly," I said. "I know how you feel."

Mike looked ready to change the subject. "By the way," he said, "Chris is looking for someone to take my place on his dodgeball team tonight. I'm way too tired. You want to play?"

I laughed. "Dodgeball? Like in junior high?"

Mike smiled. "Yep. You'll love it. Gives you a couple of hours away from this place."

I hadn't played dodgeball in years, and I was terrible at it in eighth grade gym class. In those days, I was more of a "mathlete." I shrugged. "Tell Chris I'm in."

Mike said, "Welcome to the Hurling Panthers. Oh, and we're playing an Army team full of infantry guys."

+

If I hadn't seen it coming, I would have thought it was a bullet. The ball hit me so hard that I was pretty sure it broke something, and my face slammed into the floor as I fell.

Then I heard a thundering voice. "You okay, man?"

I shook my head and actually thought I saw stars for a second. My ears were ringing as I lay on the floor of the gym, in more pain than I remembered ever feeling before.

I rolled onto my back and looked up to see who'd knocked me down. We were playing an Army team comprised of players who were mostly huge, chiseled Polynesians from a National Guard unit. I hadn't expected to be hit in the small of my back from five feet away by a six-foot-five, two-hundred-fifty-pound Samoan. We'd both been running toward center court after a loose ball, and once I realized he was going to get there first, I'd turned around to run. But before I had taken a single step, he'd nailed me.

He wore a huge smile as he reached down to offer me his hand. I took it, and he lifted me to my feet. His bicep was bigger than my thigh, and it was covered with a terrifying reptilian tattoo. I was glad he was my opponent in dodgeball and not in battle.

"You got to keep moving or you get hit, bro," he said before he turned away.

Chris yelled across the gym, "Lee, you're out. Get off the court, if you can still walk." I dragged myself off to the corner and decided to retire from my career as a replacement dodgeball player.

When the game was over, we shook hands with the other team. The big Samoan soldier who'd crushed me earlier shook my hand and said, "Good game, bro."

Still hurting, I went by the physical therapy clinic and found some sports cream for my back. I rubbed it into my sore muscles, hoping the menthol would provide a little relief.

It was too early to go to bed, so I decided to check on Rose. She made a funny face when I bent down to see her, and Saeed translated her words: "Dr. Lee, you smell bad."

A few days later, my back was well, I didn't smell like Icy Hot anymore, and Rose was ready to go home. Raul and Saeed and I went to the clinic for me to say goodbye. Rose smiled and gave me a hug. We had been briefed extensively about not touching an Iraqi woman or speaking to them without their husband's permission, so I formally nodded to Rose's mom and shook her dad's hand. Then Rose's mom whispered something to her husband, and he nodded to her.

They said something to Raul, and he turned to me. "Doctor, Rose and her mother would like to take a picture with you."

Rose's mom dropped her veil, stood on Rose's left side, and smiled for the camera. Raul took the photo, and Rose's dad, Hasim, placed his hands over his heart.

After the picture, Rose's mom turned to me and extended her hand. I looked at Raul and he said, "She wants to shake your hand. Hasim says it is okay."

I took her hand. Both of us had tears in our eyes, and she said, in English, "Thank you, sir."

Custom and culture couldn't contain her gratitude, and in that moment I felt like the purpose of the whole war had been to bring me to Balad to help Rose. I put my hands on Rose's head and said to Saeed, "Tell her that she is going to do great things. Tell her that I believe in her."

Saeed translated, and Rose smiled. Hasim stepped close, put his hands on my shoulders, and hugged me. "It is time for us to go," he said through Raul. "But you will stay in our hearts. You will always have friends in Iraq."

+

After Rose left that day, I wondered how long it would be before we had something positive to think about again. February had been brutal; our spirits were sagging, and our bodies had been pushed to their limits by the fatigue and stress of the unspeakable things we had to see and do every day. The team that had arrived in late January now seemed as if they'd been combat medics their whole lives, and I couldn't remember what it was like before they came.

We took care of good guys and bad guys alike and lost a lot fewer than we saved. We knew that Americans and the Coalition soldiers would have deployed with their medical teams to any war their governments sent them to, and we understood that any other country would likewise have sent doctors and nurses with its army to the fight. But we also knew that not every army in the world would have let its medical teams care for the enemy, and we felt lucky to be fighting for the side that would.

But being allowed to take care of civilians and kids created some of the brightest days for us. Those were the saves—like Jassem and Mohamed and Rose—that we knew would never have happened had we not been there.

So when I watched Rose and Hasim and his wife leave, I knew that the happiness I felt at that moment wouldn't last long. I knew it because the only thing consistent about the war was that the enemy was always out there, ready to take your hope and turn it into despair.

I went into the ER, where two of the emergency doctors were walking away from the bedside of someone they'd been working on. There was trash all over the floor, the empty IV bags, syringe wrappers, and cut-off clothing that mark the site of a resuscitation attempt because the team is focused on the life they're trying to save and not on making sure everything gets into the trash can.

A nurse unfolded a sheet and was about to cover the obviously dead soldier when I passed by. I stopped when I saw his bloody arm, because I recognized the tattoo.

"What happened?" I asked the nurse.

"IED. He was DOA, but we tried anyway. Three others were dead on the scene. They stopped their convoy to check on a disabled vehicle, turned out to be a car bomb."

The dead soldier's torn body and lifeless eyes contrasted so starkly with the memory I had of him from the dodgeball game a few days before.

I felt numb, and for a second I thought I was going to be sick. It was the first time I saw a body in the war that I'd known before they died. And I couldn't believe it. Even this strong, smiling warrior with the giant muscles and the terrifying tattoo couldn't withstand the terrorists' bombs.

I thought of how much more pain he must have felt than I did when he hit me with the ball.

"You got to keep moving or you get hit, bro," I said softly.

Someone called my name, and I turned to see a tech running toward me.

"Doc," he panted, "all the other surgeons are in the OR, and Dr. Chris needs some help in the ICU. He told me to find someone. Will you help him?"

"Of course. I'll be right there," I said.

I took one more look at the big Samoan, put my hands on his chest, and said, "Good game, bro."

The nurse pulled the sheet over the Samoan's face as I turned to walk away. I went to find Chris, hoping to clear my head and find a way to keep breathing.

I heard a baby crying before I reached the ICU.

CHAPTER 27

WE HAVE A SPECIAL PATIENT HERE TONIGHT

Need some help?"

Chris was leaning over an ICU bed. One of the Australian nurses was standing across from him, her back to me. I could hear the cries of a small child but couldn't see the child. The nurse was blocking my view.

Chris looked up when he heard my voice. "That would be great. Meet Maria."

I reached the bedside and looked down to see a beautiful two-year-old Iraqi girl. Her eyes were glazed over from the anesthetic and pain relievers dripping into her IV, but she was still whimpering and moving her legs. Her body was wrapped in gauze from the chest down, all the way to the tips of her toes.

"What happened?" I asked.

In the time I'd worked with him in Iraq, Chris seemed to always have a smile. He'd been steady and cool in the worst situations we'd been through together, and all of us looked to him as a leader and a good example of handling the stress of the war. But when I asked him about the baby, darkness crossed his face.

Chris is very thin, and I could see every vein in his shaved scalp. His jaw muscles clenched. "Help me unwrap her legs and you'll see," he said, in a tight, low voice. He looked at the nurse and said, "Belinda, give Maria more Ketamine so maybe she won't remember this. Then please hold her down while we do the dressing change."

Belinda injected a syringe full of the medicine into Maria's IV. After a few seconds, Maria's eyes rolled back and she seemed to relax more. Belinda held both of Maria's shoulders to the bed so that the baby couldn't interfere as we changed her dressing.

Chris took a deep breath and said, "Let's go. Follow my lead and unwrap your side as quickly as you can."

We began to unroll the gauze from Maria's feet, and she whimpered and slightly moved her legs in spite of the Ketamine. As soon as I could see her skin under the bandages, I smelled the unmistakable odor of burned flesh.

Maria's feet were terribly burned, and the skin came off with the bandages. As I worked higher up her leg, the burn seemed to get deeper. She moaned and pulled her little leg away but the drugs had taken most of the fight out of her. By the time we got to her chest, the full display of Maria's injury made me almost retch. Most of her body from the nipple line down was deeply burned, except for the backs of her buttocks and thighs. Somehow, Chris had managed to insert a urinary catheter into Maria, in spite of the horribly blistered, swollen nightmare I saw in her groin.

In America, a baby this badly burned would need dozens of operations, skin grafts, long-term ICU care. And even then, even in America, this injury would be hard to survive.

"How did this happen?" I asked.

"Maria's dad volunteered for the ING," Chris said. "Some terrorists from his village retaliated by throwing firebombs into his house." He wiped his red eyes with the back of his hand. "They knew he wasn't home, so they bombed his house to send a message to him and other men in the village about helping the ING. Maria's mom and her two-month-old sister were also badly burned, but Maria got the worst of it."

Chris opened a jar of silver sulfadiazine cream and scooped a glob onto his fingers. He motioned for me to do the same.

"Rub this into the burns. It will help prevent infection. You've got to really rub it in, though, even though she'll resist."

I rubbed the cream onto Maria's legs. There were spots where her muscles were visible because all three layers of her skin were burned off, along with the underlying fat babies should have. The serum and blood and blistered muscle felt sticky and warm to my fingers. Maria pulled her leg away harder.

Chris put his hand on top of mine, squeezing my fingers onto Maria's leg even more tightly. "Lee, it won't help her unless you work the medicine into the tissue. She needs this. You can do it."

Even during medical school, burns were the hardest things for me to treat, because of the smell, the amount of pain the patients have, the horrible disfigurement that comes as the skin heals and scars. The caregiver's compassion and the patient's courage are as important as the medical care the patients require. In my field of medicine, even though I treat devastating problems and perform delicate and dangerous operations, my patients are asleep, and I never have to look in their faces while I hurt them. But burn patients look you in the eye the whole time you're taking care of them, and you have to hurt them to help them. I hate it.

Still, Chris was right. She did need it. And with me helping him, Maria's dressing change would take only half as long. I swallowed hard and scooped more cream out of the jar. With Chris coaching me, we got the cream applied all over her burns and then wrapped new gauze. By the time we were done, and with one more dose of Ketamine, Maria had fallen asleep.

Belinda covered Maria with a pink blanket and placed a

stuffed animal on the bed next to her. Chris and I tossed our gloves into the trash and he shook my hand.

"Thanks for your help. I'll have to do this for her every day, so come on by whenever you want."

I took one last look at Maria. With her blanket hiding her bandages, she looked like any normal sleeping child. I thought of the terrorists who'd thrown the firebombs into Maria's home. What kind of religion teaches that it's okay to do that? What kind of man could light the fuse and throw that bomb?

My internal ideological debate was interrupted by the arrival of more patients in the ER. Chris and I ran down the hall and back into the war.

+

I helped Chris change Maria's bandages several times over the next few days. Between trauma surgeries, Chris had to manage her burns and perform several operations on Maria to place skin grafts and treat her severe leg swelling. Because the back of her torso, buttocks, and legs wasn't as burned as the front, Chris was able to find enough skin to cover most of the burned areas. His diligent care of the broken child helped her turn a corner, and when Maria became interactive, she proved to have a sweet and playful personality. Like Mohamed before her, Maria became a focus of hope and a source of smiles for the hospital.

Whenever I wasn't busy, I would go by Maria's room, bring her a stuffed animal or a toy, and spend a few minutes just pulling for her to make it.

One evening, after I had been in surgery rescuing an American soldier from a gunshot wound to the head, I went to the ICU and found Maria sitting up, drinking from a Styrofoam cup. She looked so good and full of life. I sat at her bedside for a minute and talked to her. She lay down, her eyes heavy with sleep. I sang "Jesus Loves Me" to her until she was out, breathing heavily and sucking her thumb. She looked like any other two-year-old—apart from the monitors and the gauze wrapped around her body. As I turned to walk away, I glanced up at the screen and saw that her temperature was about one hundred degrees.

"When did she develop a fever?" I asked the nurse.

She came to the bedside and reached up to the IV pole to show me a bag of medicine hanging there. "Earlier today. Dr. Chris already sent labs and changed her antibiotics."

Of course he did, I thought. Chris, as always, was taking care of it. *Come on, Maria*, I thought. *We need you.*

I walked down to the surgeons' lounge, wondering whether world leaders would start wars if they had to change the bandages on babies who were firebombed or hold the hands of teenagers while they bled to death.

In the lounge, the general surgeon Mark was standing by the desk, talking to two Special Forces soldiers.

It was a running joke on base that the best way to tell if a guy was a Special Forces operator was to walk right up and ask him. If he refuses to answer, you know he's an operator. In the field, these two guys standing in the lounge were probably ninja-like, stealthy super soldiers.

When we went to the PX or Pizza Hut on base and saw a group of guys in brown T-shirts and khaki pants, wearing beards and carrying very scary guns, and noticed that their uniforms had no names or symbols on them, we knew who they were.

The two men standing next to Mark looked serious. They both wore earpieces connected to microphones on their body armor, and both had Glock sidearms in shoulder holsters, as well as submachine guns strapped tightly in front of them. When I approached, one of them turned and stepped into my path.

"You can't go past here," he said.

"It's okay, he's one of our surgeons," Mark said.

The soldier relaxed his posture a little but did not move.

"What's going on?" I asked.

Mark stepped closer and motioned for me to look through a door into a small exam room we used for female patients or as an overflow room when we had too many patients for the ER to hold. A man lay inside on a stretcher, with two armed guards flanking him. It was too far away to tell more than that.

"We have a special patient tonight," Mark said. "I'm about to go check on him."

"Who is he?"

Mark smiled and said, "See for yourself."

I followed Mark down the hall with the two soldiers right behind me.

We entered the room. The man on the stretcher, wearing a hospital gown, had a black hood over his head, and his feet and hands were chained to the bedrails. He was writhing from side to side, obviously in a lot of pain.

The guards stepped in front of us, and one of them whispered, "Do not tell him where he is. Do not tell him your names. And you are not to tell anyone he was here. Understood?"

Mark and I slowly nodded. I said, "Who is he?"

The guard's eyes narrowed, and he looked over our shoulders to make sure no one else was nearby. He leaned close enough for me to smell his breath and said, "Ace of Spades."

We stepped toward the bed while I processed what the guard had said. I remembered the deck of cards our soldiers were issued to help them recognize the most-wanted members of the Iraqi government, and I wondered if I'd heard the guard right.

The second guard removed the hood from the moaning patient.

I looked down into the face of Saddam Hussein.

Mark examined Saddam, who looked pale and sweaty and

a little jaundiced. He didn't look like a person who could have killed thousands of people, or who had held a nation in an iron grip for many years, or who had had the guts to provoke a war with George Bush. He looked like he needed some morphine.

When Mark pressed on Saddam's abdomen, the former dictator gasped in pain and pulled against his chains. He'd been captured about fifteen months ago, and from what I knew he had been in a secret prison since then, awaiting his trial and his eventual execution.

"He needs an operation," Mark said. "It's his gallbladder."

I didn't touch Hussein, but he looked into my eyes. My head spun with so many thoughts that I couldn't quite order them. He was an aging man in pain, chained to a bed. But in his eyes I saw death and hatred and a callousness that unnerved me. I actually backed up a step or two when he looked at me.

Mark motioned toward the guards. "When are you guys going to let me take him to the OR?"

The guard shrugged his shoulders. "We have to get permission first. You guys need to step out of the room until we have orders."

Mark straightened. "Look, this man needs an operation or he could die."

Both guards came around the bed and positioned themselves between Hussein and Mark. One of them said, "Doctor, you step out of the room. We'll let you know whether you can proceed when we hear."

Mark deflated a little. I could see the realization wash over him that he couldn't argue with these armed men. We left the room with the tech and walked into the surgeons' lounge. Mark and I dropped onto the couch.

"Unbelievable," Mark said.

"In more ways than one," I said.

"Say that again." Mark looked at the ceiling and let out a

long sigh. We'd both been awake for twenty or so hours, but we were used to that type of fatigue. I think that being in the room with the man responsible for us all being here in the first place took us both to another level of exhaustion. I felt as if I'd just seen some evil being. His evil was palpable, worse than anything I'd experienced from any terrorist or insurgent. I felt cold, almost numb, and nauseated. But Mark had the added burden of having to worry about taking care of Saddam. I knew that Mark was professional and compassionate enough that not being allowed to end Saddam's suffering made him even more sick, and that having nonmedical people make decisions on behalf of his patient made him furious.

A nurse approached the sofa. "Dr. Warren, they need you in the ICU. Your patient from this morning is having trouble."

I squeezed Mark's knee before I got up. We looked at each other, but neither of us had words for the surreal experience we'd just been through together.

In the ICU, the soldier I'd operated on earlier that day was still on a ventilator. I asked the nurse, "What's the problem?"

She pointed at the monitor. His brain pressure was reading 40. It had been less than 10 the last time I'd checked on him. I went through the checklist of reasons his pressure could be so high and ultimately decided that his monitor was malfunctioning. I replaced the sensor, and his monitor showed a normal pressure.

I found Mark standing next to the room where Saddam had been. All four guards and Saddam were gone.

"They said that they were ordered to take Hussein to a more secure facility to have his surgery," Mark said, "because they were afraid the local Iraqis might find out he was here and try to either kill him or help him escape. I told them they'd better hurry, because if his gallbladder ruptures he'll probably die."

I looked at the empty room. It still felt unreal that he'd been here, in this tent hospital.

Mark walked away. "I'm going to bed. Tomorrow tell me this was just a dream."

Maybe it was, I thought.

Someone else was on the computer, so I went to the command office, where at night some of the computers were usually available. A picture of George W. Bush hung on the wall, the official commander-in-chief photo on display as it was in every US government facility in the world.

I suppose the thought had been swirling in my head all along, but on that night it congealed into a crystal-clear idea: These two men, Bush and Hussein, wrestling with each other over power, oil, weapons of mass destruction, old family business, or whatever else they used to justify war, had both made decisions and taken steps that had led directly to my being there in Iraq. I'd been in a small auditorium once in college and heard then-Governor Bush speak from maybe twenty feet away. And tonight I'd stood closer than that to former President Hussein and looked into his cold, deadly eyes. There couldn't be many people in the world who had been so close to both of them. I found myself wishing I could sit them both down and question them: Was it worth it? Would you tell Yeager's family it was worth it? Could you, with your own hands, help Chris take care of the burned-up baby Maria and still think you were right in what you did? In the grand scheme of things, what have you gained from all the palaces and parades, from the bombs and the bullets and the dollars spent and the lives lost?

The problem, I realized, was that I didn't think either of them would be able to answer my questions. I wondered if my kids would look at pictures of their mother and me and ask similar questions, in the wake of our divorce. It hit me then that wars always have different impacts on the populations than they do on the participants. And I'm not sure anybody really ever wins.

I walked down the hall to check on Maria before I went to bed.

+

EMAIL HOME
Friday, March 25, 2005

Good morning, friends.

It's cold here in Iraq. The temperature dropped steadily throughout the day yesterday as the wind blew hard. After the sun went down it got really chilly. They're forecasting a low of 39 degrees for tonight.

Yesterday was a hard day. After rounds were finished, I was working at a computer when Chris came to tell me that Maria was doing very poorly, and he didn't think she would survive. We went together to her bedside, and I put my hands on her little swollen body and asked the Lord why this was happening. Someone had placed a little Beanie Baby skunk at the end of her bed. It was one of those really cute little critters that people love—they take an animal that you would never associate with cuteness or cuddliness, like a snake or a T-Rex, and make a loveable toy out of it. Here was this cute little skunk, lying there on the bed of a dying baby in Iraq. Cuteness aside, the metaphor was compelling: the whole situation stank.

Chris is a fantastic doctor, and an even better human being. He and the nurses and other doctors caring for Maria gave their all for this little girl, going above and beyond and delivering a standard of care for her that absolutely could not have been achieved elsewhere in this country. Maria would have died from her injuries much sooner, and her family would not have had these weeks of her improving, being playful, seeing her smiling face again had it not been for Chris and his team of heroes.

Maria died last night.

Chris and I went to the chapel and cried and prayed for a long time. He looked at me and said, "Did I do everything I could have for her?"

I said, "You did more than anyone else could have. You gave her a chance."

We sat in silence for a while, and then Chris stood and said, "We better try to get some rest. There's still a war going on out there."

Not surprisingly, the sun rose again today, beautiful as always, signaling that the world spins on. Rounds today will be very hard when we pass the empty bed that so recently held an angel who made us soar with hope and then crash with despair. And despite our pain over losing Maria, all of us know that the enemy has more in store for us today. So, we soldier on.

Watching the care and compassion with which Chris cares for his patients, and the incredible job so many of my colleagues here are doing in the midst of such suffering, made me feel a heavy burden to be better.

People like Chris make me want to try harder, to do more, to be more than I am. I hope there's someone like that in your world.

Lee

CHAPTER 28
NOT SO GOOD FRIDAY

March had exceeded the previous two months in its volume of bloodshed, its interesting patients, its poignant and heartbreaking moments — and also in its incessant efforts to break our spirits. As we neared the end of the month, I hoped March would follow the old adage and go out like a lamb.

It kept roaring all the way to the end.

I woke on Friday, March 25, in a bad mood and with a bad headache. I'd tried to call home the night before and heard that machine — again. I wondered: was the hope I'd felt after my short reconnection with the kids while I was in Baghdad just wishful thinking? I rolled over in bed, picked up the picture of the three of them from the bedside table, and told them all about Maria.

"You would have loved her," I said. "I did."

I wrote the daily email on my computer and saved it to my thumb drive to send out when I got to the hospital. Then my beeper rang, summoning me to the ER. *No shower for me today*, I thought while I threw on my DCUs.

On the way to the hospital, I ran into the sergeant who had shown me around when I first got to Iraq. He was walking the same direction as I was, but not in a hurry. "Morning, Major," he said.

"Hey, Sarge," I said, picking up my pace to show that I didn't have time for a chat.

He matched my stride. "You'll be heading home soon, right?" he asked.

I actually stopped dead when he said that. I'd gotten into such a bad mental place I had started to think that I would always be in Iraq, that my life would forever remain the carousel of carnage it had become in Balad.

"Yeah, about five weeks, I guess. You?"

He chuckled and pointed to the front of his DCUs. "Ha! I'm Army. Another six months for me. But at least I only have to drive folks around and work on computers. If I had to be in the hospital every day, I'd lose my mind."

I started walking again, remembering what my squadron commander had said to me the day he told me I was going to Iraq: "The Air Force doesn't think its medics should stay at Balad too long because of the psychological effects of what they'll see every day, and because most of them will be working twenty-four-seven."

At the time I'd felt bad that I was only going to war for four months—as if that wasn't long enough to count. But now I realized that if I could have paid someone to let me leave that very day, I would have. Five more weeks sounded impossible to survive.

At the corner, he said, "Well, Doc, this is my turn. Keep your head down."

As he walked away, I touched the *US Air Force* label over my DCU pocket, glad that I'd decided to talk to that recruiter and not the Army guy next to him at my college's student center that day back in 1989 when I first thought about taking a military scholarship for medical school. How much of me would be left if I had to stay in Iraq for a year? And then, as clearly as if it were written on my soul by God himself, I knew something else, and said it to myself out loud: "Lee, you will always feel like you didn't do enough here."

When I reached the hospital, an Army Chinook helicopter was landing. I ran out to the helipad behind several techs.

The Chinook's rear ramp opened. Inside, an Army flight medic straddled a stretcher, performing CPR on a soldier. Another medic was squeezing a ventilator bag, breathing for the injured man.

The other stretchers in the Chinook contained black body bags. No one was working on those patients.

The techs lifted the stretcher onto their gurney, and I ran behind them into the ER.

"No pulse," one tech said.

One of the nurses connected a heart monitor to the soldier. His face was swollen and blue, and he was wrapped in a space blanket and zipped halfway into a body bag to keep him warm. His eyes were open, a startling hazel color with little green flecks. It struck me that this might be the first patient I'd seen who did not seem to be bleeding anywhere.

The helicopter medics came in behind us, pushing a stretcher that held another body bag, zipped shut.

An ER doctor looked at the hazel-eyed soldier's heart monitor and said, "He's dead. Mark the time."

There are always a few seconds after someone calls the code—when a physician determines and announces that the patient is gone—when everyone stops what they are doing and just stands there. In that silence, we look down at the person who has just died and feel useless. I'm always sad, always wish I could have done more, could have somehow saved the person's life. This time, as usual, I stood looking down at the dead, blue, bloated young man and wondered what happened. I could see no injury, no blood.

I heard a noise behind me and turned to see techs bringing

other stretchers carrying zipped-up body bags. Six more. Techs opened the bags to identify and tag the bodies. All of them were also bloated and blue.

The helicopter medic sat on a chair in the corner, dropped his helmet onto the floor, and put his face in his hands.

A nurse asked him, "What happened to these guys?"

The medic sat up, pinched the bridge of his nose, and said, "Their truck rolled into a ditch full of water and they all drowned. This one still had a pulse when we got there. The rest were already dead."

I walked off into the surgeons' lounge, feeling completely empty. It was such a bizarre, senseless thing—this truck full of highly trained soldiers who'd flown halfway around the world to fight terrorists but ended up drowning in the middle of a desert. I'd grown accustomed to the sounds of trauma: screaming victims, doctors yelling orders, the soundtrack of the chaos in the emergency room. My mind just couldn't adjust to eight silent, swollen soldiers who went off to war but died in the water.

I sat on the couch, feeling that I was drowning too. How much worse could this place get?

Someone had decorated the Christmas tree for Easter. That was the first time all day I'd remembered that this was Good Friday. I sat and stared at the ceiling, feeling numb and cold and exhausted.

Pete had said "We'll see" when I told him I'd never sleep on the terribly uncomfortable couch in the surgeons' lounge. But on that Good Friday morning, my brain and my body gave in to the headache and heartache that were pushing me down into the cushions.

When I woke up a couple of hours later, I found that someone had placed a huge sombrero over my eyes. It took me a few seconds to realize why it was dark, and when I moved the sombrero, it took my brain a few more seconds to realize what it was. I still have no clue why anybody thought they needed a gigantic Mexican hat in Iraq.

My stomach rumbled; I hadn't eaten anything since lunch the day before. I thought about Maria and the drowned soldiers and my inability to reach my kids, and I wondered how in the world I was ever going to last another five weeks. This Friday did not feel so good.

+

EMAIL HOME
Saturday, March 26, 2005

Hello, everyone.

First of all, thanks to all of you who wrote to offer condolences for the loss of Maria. Yesterday, everyone in the hospital was kind of down. There have been many casualties in recent days, and all of us are tired. Some of them I can't tell you about here, but trust me when I say that we've been busy.

I was in my room when I got a "911" page at about 6:00 p.m., just after the alarm had sounded for a mortar attack. I had to put on my battle gear to walk back to the hospital to see where I was needed. Two of the general surgeons had called for me to go into the operating room to look at something they had discovered.

An American had been shot in the back with a very large rifle round. The bullet had torn his abdomen to pieces, and he'd been stabilized at another base before being sent here. The wound was infected, so the surgeons had taken him to the OR, where they'd found the bottom of his spinal cord and all the nerves to his legs floating free from his destroyed spinal column. The nerve sack was in the middle of the infected material, and they wanted to know if there was anything I thought I should do. I looked around in the wound for a while and could find no evidence of spinal fluid leaking out, so I decided that more harm would come from exploring aggressively. He'll be paralyzed permanently, and he'll need spine stabilization surgery after his wounds heal.

After the operation, the All Clear finally sounded, and we watched *The Passion of the Christ* in the tent. What a powerful way to spend Good Friday in the war zone. Here we are, so close to where these events happened. We're seeing daily the terrible things that people can do to one another, and watching them doing those things to Jesus on the big screen was very troubling.

This Easter will be unforgettable for me — in fact, for all believers here in Iraq. Our hope in the resurrected Lord remains strong, but this year seems somehow more important, more real, and more personal. I don't know if that makes sense. I've just seen an innocent baby firebombed because her father's attackers hated his way of working for a better way of life. Then we watched an artistic representation of the innocent Jesus being murdered because people hated the standards he set, the purity he revealed, and the truth of their own sinfulness.

We watched as those hate-filled people killed Christ, and I thought of the hateful murderers who killed the innocent Maria. Hate, pride, fear of change, and sinfulness caused both.

I've only got about five weeks left here, and right now that seems like an awfully long time. But my life has been changed forever by the things I've seen and done here, the people I've touched and been touched by. And God has been good to me here in this desert place.

Tomorrow is Easter, the day Christians celebrate the fact of Jesus' resurrection and his empty tomb. The war's been filling a lot of graves around here lately. It will be good to worship and to remember the hope that Easter gives to us, because hope is in short supply in Iraq.

Lee

+

On Easter morning, two hundred soldiers gathered in the chapel for a worship service. John, Luther, Andre, Shauna, and I began singing a hymn, without our instruments. As our voices combined in harmony, I found myself for the first time in weeks not thinking about the war or my own problems. I played my guitar while Shauna sang the next song, and in the back of the chapel I noticed a tall Special Forces soldier walk in. He carried a tactical shotgun with a grenade launcher under the barrel. He wore body armor, and his helmet had night-vision goggles strapped to it. He wore black knee and elbow pads. This man was one serious soldier.

As the song progressed, I watched him. Shauna sang about Jesus on the cross, and the soldier loosened the straps on his armor. When she got to the line about Christ in the grave, the soldier set his gun on the floor at his feet and took off his armor. Then with her powerful alto growl, Shauna sang about the stone being rolled away and the tomb being empty, and I saw the man slide down the wall and sit on the floor. He buried his face in his hands while the song ended.

Chaplain W came up front and the worship team sat down. I couldn't see the soldier from my seat.

At the end of the sermon, we stood and sang another song, and I saw the soldier again. Now he was standing and singing along, tears running down his face. When the song ended and Chaplain W ended the service with prayer, I watched as the soldier shouldered his armor and weapon and stepped out the back door, looking taller than he had when he came in.

I've thought about him a lot over the years since — about how we come to worship with our lives strapped onto us, and the longer we stay the layers begin to peel off, until ultimately all that's left is just us, standing before something bigger, something more important than ourselves. When we reach the place where we can say, "I am here to say thank you, despite what I'm going through," we're finally really worshiping.

After church, I walked with the team and Chaplain W to DFAC II for lunch. I was dragging after another long night in the hospital, and my spirits were somewhere south of low despite the great worship service.

"You seem pretty down today. Want to talk about it?" Chaplain W said.

No matter what I was feeling when I started talking to him, conversations with Chaplain W were always upbeat. He had a breezy air about him, one of those preachers who seemed to think that you should never let life get you down, and he had a catchy little phrase for every situation, like "You're too blessed to be distressed," or some other bumper-sticker slogan. But somehow he managed to sell it, like his faith was so real that I couldn't help but respect it.

I let out a long sigh. "I'm worried about what's going to happen when I get home. I haven't been able to talk to my kids since I was in Baghdad, and I don't know if they'll want to have anything to do with me."

Chaplain W stopped walking and put his hand on my shoulder. He looked into my eyes and said, "Worry is like paying interest on a debt you don't owe. Pray more, worry less, and let God do the rest."

I know that some people might think his words trite, but I thought about them all afternoon. The hospital was quiet, so that evening I lay down in my room, hoping to get a few extra hours of sleep. Every time I drifted off, though, I saw those drowned soldiers and wondered what it must have been like for them, trapped upside down in the ditch while their vehicle filled with water. Suddenly, the instant death offered by IEDs seemed more humane.

Chaplain W had told me not to worry, to pray more. I really tried to follow his advice, but on that Easter Sunday I felt like I couldn't possibly get any sadder or feel any more alone.

Sleep finally came, but after about an hour the beeper went off again.

By the time I got to the hospital, a full-blown mass casualty was unfolding. Four Black Hawks were on the helipad, and I ran into the ER to find the Czar standing in the vestibule of the trauma area with his hands on his hips. Every bed held a patient, but no one was doing CPR, no one was running to CT or calling for blood.

"Sir," I said, "what's going on?"

The Czar just shook his head. It was the only time I saw him cry, and his tears were silent.

An Army captain I hadn't seen before stood next to the Czar. The unit designation on his DCUs told me he was an unexploded ordinance officer. "These guys are a bunch of Coalition troops from Europe," the captain said. "They found an unexploded IED, and they decided to gather around it and have someone take their picture."

I looked into the trauma bay. Every single one of them, I realized, was dead. Their uniforms were mostly burned off, the blood was baked onto their skin, and they all had open chest and head wounds.

"We think that the radiofrequency signal from the camera flash detonated the bomb," the EOD captain said. "Most of them still had a pulse when the medics arrived, but they all bled out on the way here."

The whole Easter weekend had been wrapped in tragedy. Apropos, I supposed, since Easter memorializes the most tragic event in human history. But unlike the weekend when Jesus died, there would be no resurrection of drowned or blown-up soldiers to replace the sorrow with joy.

CHAPTER 29

IT'S GOING TO TAKE A WHOLE SERIES OF MIRACLES

On Tuesday, March 29, 2005, a few miles outside the wire, a group of Pennsylvania National Guard soldiers were looking at the crater made by an IED that had detonated near them. As they looked at the still-smoking hole, their sergeant pointed at something nearby.

"Guys, hold up," Sergeant Paul Statzer said. "I'm going to go check that out. Stay alert."

Statzer had joined the Navy after high school and was deployed in the first Gulf War. He left the Navy, went to work, and then decided he needed to do more for his country. He joined the Guard and was sent off to his second war. On this Tuesday morning, he was doing what he'd always done: taking the lead, checking things out to try to protect his team.

He walked slowly, his weapon ready, carefully choosing his steps to avoid land mines. Sergeant Statzer was three feet away from the object he'd spotted when it detonated.

+

Inside the wire that morning, I was more exhausted than I'd ever been in my life.

Everyone in the hospital seemed stunned after several days of working nonstop. We had become robotic and lifeless, waiting for the next wave of inevitable horror. I walked through the emergency department with Tim on our way to the operating room to re-implant the bone in an Iraqi shopkeeper from Balad who had survived his injuries and recovered enough to go home. He wanted his head put back together first, and we planned to do it that morning.

Just as we entered the ER, the radio operator called, "Sirs, we just got a call from an incoming Black Hawk. They're about five minutes out, and they say they've got an American with a severe head injury."

Tim went down the hall to tell anesthesia to cancel our case and be ready for an emergency. I told a tech to have radiology prepare for a CT scan, then ran out to the helipad where a team was already waiting to unload the injured soldier when he arrived.

I heard the familiar sound of an approaching Black Hawk, and since there were so many people manning the stretcher, I stood back and took some photographs of the helicopter as it landed and the medics unloaded the soldier. I'd taken thousands of pictures since I'd been in Iraq and always kept my camera in my pocket, since I never knew when something was going to happen I'd want a picture of. I kept taking pictures until they rolled him into the ER. His head was completely wrapped in gauze, but the gauze was soaked in blood.

I stepped up to the bed and saw the soldier's DCU blouse before the medics cut it off. His name tag said "Statzer." He was an Army staff sergeant.

"Pressure's really low, Doc," a nurse said. The anesthesiologist started an IV and began squeezing saline into Statzer's vein.

I unwrapped his head, revealing the worst head injury I'd

ever seen in someone who was still alive. The left side of his face and forehead were gone. His brain swelled out of a fist-sized hole in his skull. Part of his jaw was missing, and his mouth was full of blood. It was a miracle that the helicopter medics had been able to get a breathing tube in him.

He was bleeding from his scalp and his face and had a huge laceration in his neck that gushed the dark, non-pulsatile blood that meant his jugular vein was torn. His scalp was so swollen that he had serum oozing out, and he had several burns across his chest and neck.

"Let's get him to CT," I said, "and somebody go get vascular surgery and ENT. Tell them to meet me in the OR. And get Tim. I'm going to need his help."

Statzer's scan showed that there were several large pieces of shrapnel deep in his brain, along with a lot of blood, air, and fragments of bone. I shook my head and wondered what I would have to do to help this young man. Whatever it was, I had to do it right now, or he would be dead in minutes.

I heard over the speakers: "Attention in the hospital. We need blood immediately. There is a whole blood drive in the lab now."

We put Statzer on the surgical table in the OR. I shaved what was left of the hair on his head while the anesthesiologist hung the first of many bags of blood the sergeant would need to survive.

"Knife," I said to Nate. I held the scalpel over Statzer's head and said a silent prayer that he would survive—and that I could figure out what to do.

Just as I was starting the incision, Tim backed into the room, his arms dripping the yellow iodine soap we scrubbed with before surgery. "I saw the scan," he said. "Can't understand why he's still alive."

Tim and I clipped and cauterized and tied off dozens of

arteries and veins that were torn and bleeding. Vascular surgeon Todd explored Statzer's neck to gain control of the jugular vein. Little by little, as we stopped the bleeding and replaced his blood with new units donated by hospital personnel, Statzer's pressure and vital signs began to improve. Now that he was stabilized, we could start trying to put him back together again.

His skull was shattered so badly that I barely had to use the drill. I removed almost all of the remaining left side of the bone and found that the covering over his brain had been shredded by the many objects driven through it by the bomb blast. As I expected, his left frontal lobe was mostly gone, but the brain he had left began to swell dramatically with his rising blood pressure. Red, bleeding brain rushed out of Statzer's head, and I again heard my old professor Dr. Baghai's voice urging me to maintain control.

"Nate, give me a ventricular catheter," I said. If I could place a catheter into the ventricle of Statzer's brain, the release of spinal fluid would stop the brain from swelling out. The CT scan had shown me that the ventricles had shifted from their normal position, and placing a catheter deep in the brain when the anatomy is so altered by swelling is extremely difficult. But if I failed, Statzer would die.

"Here we go," I said. I chose a trajectory and slid the catheter into Statzer's brain. Normally we use a depth of seven centimeters as the maximum safe depth for the drain, because deeper than that and you risk injuring the brainstem. But because of the brain shift, Statzer's ventricles were a lot farther away, and when the catheter reached seven centimeters, there was no fluid coming out yet.

"I'd go deeper," Tim said.

I pushed it to eight centimeters—still no fluid. The brain was getting more and more tense. I was sweating because I knew that if I couldn't get the catheter in and relieve the pressure, he was done for. But if the catheter went into his brainstem, I'd kill him on the table.

"Your trajectory is good, Lee. Go a little farther," Tim said.

I pushed the catheter a centimeter deeper. I felt the pop, and spinal fluid gushed above my head, under so much pressure that it hit the ceiling and dripped back down onto my neck. Statzer's brain relaxed and settled back into his skull.

I removed the rest of his frontal lobe, finding a walnut-sized metal fragment and Statzer's left eyeball buried in the white matter. Several of his major cerebral arteries were torn and actively bleeding, and I was afraid that once I got them stopped, he'd lost so much blood supply that he would have a stroke. I doubted that he would ever use his right arm and leg again, even if he survived and woke up someday.

Tim placed Statzer's skull fragments into his abdomen, and Joe from ENT performed a tracheostomy while Todd finished repairing the torn veins and arteries in Statzer's neck. I sewed up the hole in the skin where Statzer's eye used to be, and by the time we were done he had several hundred stitches.

Somehow that drain stayed open, and in the ICU after surgery, Statzer's brain pressure was normal. If he could avoid infection, I thought, he just might survive. Recovering would be an entirely different story.

In the surgeons' lounge, I prepared to call Statzer's family. We didn't do death notifications from Iraq, but we did call families when a soldier had been injured badly enough to send them home. We wanted to let the families know their soldier was alive and on the way to Germany and then America, so that they could make travel plans to be there when the soldiers reached Walter Reed.

The operator connected me to the number on Sergeant Statzer's Red Cross form. After a few rings, I heard a man's voice. "Jim Statzer," he said.

"Mr. Statzer, my name is Dr. Lee Warren and I'm a neurosurgeon at the 332nd Air Force Theater Hospital in Balad, Iraq. Your son Paul has been critically injured in battle, but he's alive." I went on to tell him that Paul's injuries were very severe, and that, although he had come through his surgery and was stable, I was unsure if he would survive the trip back to America.

From thousands of miles away, I heard Mr. Statzer suck in a breath, and when he spoke next, his voice shook. "You said he's alive, right, Doctor?"

"Yes, sir," I said.

I heard Mr. Statzer repeating what I'd said to his wife. Then he cleared his throat and said, "Then you send him home. Doctor, by the grace of God, I know my son is going to be okay."

I hung up and walked back to the ICU to check on Statzer. His dad's words hung in my mind, and I thought, *For Paul Statzer to be okay is going to take a miracle. A whole series of them.*

To my great surprise, in the ICU a critical-care transport team was preparing Statzer for his flight to Germany. Normally, we first had to contact the team to let them know we had a patient, and then it would take a day or two before they were able to move that patient. This team had a C–17 ready to leave, and they just came by the hospital to check to see if we happened to have any patients who needed to go.

I watched Paul Statzer roll out of the ICU with a brain pressure of zero, leaving Iraq less than four hours after his surgery. He'd survived an IED blast to the face from three feet away, a combat helicopter ride, and three hours of surgery by four surgeons, and his veins were full of other people's blood. The most injured man I'd ever seen alive had a normal blood pressure, heart rate, and body temperature when he left our tent hospital. I thought, *There have been a few miracles already.*

CHAPTER 30

NO PLACE
TO HIDE

Bloody March finally, thankfully, gave way to April. But any hope we had of the enemy slowing down was quickly dashed, and March's cool temperatures and rain gave way to April's heat and oppressive dust storms. Entering my final month in Iraq, I couldn't remember what a long hot shower or a comfortable bed felt like. I couldn't even remember the last time I slept all the way through the night. As the days crept by, I felt both excited and afraid at the thought of going home, in almost equal measures. I had no idea how my kids were going to react to me. And every time I talked to one of my Army colleagues, I felt guilty that they had to stay so much longer.

I checked my email one morning and found a message from a friend of a friend in West Virginia. "My family has been reading your letters every day. We're praying for all of you. Thanks for your service," it said. I checked the map I kept showing the states my emailed letters had reached, and saw that West Virginia made fifty. I was amazed. The email journal I'd intended for my family and friends was being delivered every day to at least twenty thousand email addresses I knew of. I'd received messages from fifteen other countries as well, and I was getting over one hundred emails a day. I was happy that so many people were benefitting from my stories — but what a frustrating irony: I could reach people in Scotland and South Africa, but not my own kids. It didn't seem possible in this age of instant communication that my children could essentially be quarantined from me, but I was living it.

A few days after Paul Statzer left, I tried to call the kids and got voicemail again. This time I got angry. I decided that I wouldn't just go back to America and meekly try to work my way back into their lives. I went back to my room, sat on the edge of the bed, and started planning. I would control every aspect of my life tighter than ever before, and no one would keep me from succeeding. I would keep it my little secret that I was in fact scared to death and had no clue how to be a single dad.

Armed with a renewed commitment to my "Lee's in Control of Everything" game plan, I decided to walk to the PX to pick up a few things, traveling the nearly two miles by the most direct route.

That route avoided the roads and crossed large swaths of empty desert between developed sections of the base. The weather had gotten a lot warmer, and we hadn't had a mortar attack in a couple of days, so I decided to wear running gear to make the trip faster, rather than strap on my body armor and Kevlar helmet.

I was about halfway to the PX and in the middle of an open field when the Alarm Red sirens began to wail. A few seconds later a mortar landed close enough that I felt the concussion and heard the explosion at the same time. I looked around for the nearest bunker—but in this part of the base, there were none. The only protection for a quarter mile in any direction was a twelve-foot-high concrete T-barrier. I ran to it and sat on the ground with my back to the wall. At least I was protected from one side.

Several more explosions came over the next few minutes, and smoke rose into the air across the base. I sat on the ground in shorts and tennis shoes and hoped that none of the mortars would land within the ten-meter "kill radius" around me. I pressed my back against the concrete wall, tried to shrink myself into the smallest area I could, and waited.

A half hour passed. I thought about running for a bunker. I stood, flattened myself against the wall, and tried to swallow the acid fear burning in my throat. I heard the *fffffppp* of a rocket overhead, then the detonation far enough away that the sound was muffled. I decided I was safer where I was.

"My kids need me," I said out loud. "I will get through this. I've got to get home and fix everything with them."

Another *fffffppp BOOM*, this time much louder and closer.

The sirens wailed on, and black smoke from the exploding mortars mixed in the air with the blowing sand and the usual smell of burning waste and oil. I choked on it. My eyes were burning at least as badly from the hot tears in them. I wiped my nose on the back of my arm.

Another detonation nearby.

I decided to ask God for help.

"Please, please get me out of here alive," I prayed. "I've got so much to do."

Every time something blew up, I pled anew for God to rescue me. And each time the enemy answered with another explosion. I saw vivid mental images of the burned flesh and brokenness that similar shells had caused in people I'd treated as recently as the day before.

After an hour, I stopped pleading with God to get me out of there, because it seemed like every time I did, something else flew over my head and exploded.

By the time the twelfth mortar landed another terrifying hour later, I was shaking and crying, lying on the ground, curled into a ball. I had no place to hide, and never before had I felt so exposed, so powerless. But in the chaos, I found a moment of clarity. My powerlessness demonstrated to me that my plan to control how my kids would react to me was just as irrelevant and ineffective as my wish that the terrorists trying so hard to kill everyone on base that day would just go away.

Dr. Baghai's words to me years before — "You have to maintain control" — had become my mantra not just for surgery, but for my whole life. During that attack, huddled against a concrete wall in nothing but a running outfit, it became laughingly obvious to me that even my own survival was utterly out of my control.

And then, just as unexpected as the Alarm Red siren that had caught me in an open field two hours before, I heard Chaplain W's words: "Pray more, worry less, and let God do the rest."

What happened to me that day is hard to explain. It would be inaccurate to say that I stopped caring, but at that moment, with Chaplain W's words ringing in my mind, I just let go of the fear. The mental clarity that resulted was stunning to me, and the list of things I could not control played across my mind like movie credits rolling up the screen:

There was absolutely nothing that I could do to stop the war.

I could not control where any of those mortars or rockets would land.

I could not control what would happen to my kids if I died on that field.

I could not control what would happen with my kids if I survived.

And then, at the end of the list of all the things I couldn't do, I finally understood the one thing I *could* do: have faith that whatever God intended to do would be best for me and for my kids.

Once I let go of the fear, it felt as if with each breath I drew in peace and let out worry. The relief and sense of calm I felt was beyond any rational understanding. I *knew* I was going to be okay—and not just physically, but emotionally and spiritually and professionally and personally. And I knew, somehow, that the peace would follow me home.

Finally, the All Clear sounded. I picked myself up and walked back to my trailer, because the PX didn't seem so important at the moment. My legs were shaky, my stomach was churning, and my head was pounding.

But my heart was healing.

CHAPTER 31

SAYING GOODBYE

By mid-April I had mixed emotions concerning my fast-approaching departure date. I couldn't wait to hug my kids and start my new life with them, but there were so many unknowns. I knew I was going to Montgomery, Alabama, since my kids and their mother had moved there when I deployed, but I didn't know where I was going to live. I knew I was going to join a practice there, because I'd accepted an offer from two neurosurgeons before I left for the war. But I didn't really know them or what my practice would be like. I had no other family in the area, no church, no friends, and no idea what being a divorced single dad and civilian doctor was going to be like. I could feel my old need to control everything bubbling just under the surface of my newfound peace, and I had a hard time concentrating on anything else.

Perhaps God had been waiting for me to stop worrying, to stop trying to be in charge, because all of a sudden my access to the kids improved greatly. It started with one phone call.

"Hello," I heard Kimber say.

"Kimber, it's Dad."

"Yay! Dad, I miss you so much. Come home!"

From that point on, the kids answered every time I called. There was only one rough spot in those conversations. One day

Mitch asked, "Daddy, are we moving into a new house with you as soon as you get home?"

I realized that I hadn't yet explained to them that I still owed the Air Force some time, and that when I first saw them, we would have only a few days before I would have to leave again to go back to Texas until I was out of the Air Force for good.

Kalyn cried, "No! You can't leave us again."

I said, "Honey, if I don't go back, the Air Force will put me in jail."

"And besides," Mitch said then, like an incurable optimist, "we only have to say goodbye one more time, but we get to say hello twice."

His logic seemed more convincing to Kalyn than mine had been, and the rest of the conversation went well. The hope I'd felt in Baghdad when the kids sounded so eager to reconnect with me grew stronger every day. I grabbed on to it and would never let it go again.

+

April 24 was my last Sunday in Iraq. Two hundred people filled the chapel, and the worship team sang its heart out.

I met with the whole team afterward. "Guys," I said, "this is my last service. I'm heading out soon."

We talked for a while, shed a few tears, and prayed together. Then John grabbed my shoulder and said, "Hey, do you think you'll lead worship in your church back home?"

I slowly shook my head. "I don't think so. I'm about to go through a divorce, and my personal life is going to be a mess for a long time after that. I don't think God would want me up there leading worship."

Chaplain W put his arm around me, pulled me close, and said, "Listen. Worship is not a place where perfect people get dressed up and go tell God how great they are. Real worship happens when broken people tell God how great he is. And that's grace: you tell God how great he is, that he's enough for you in spite of what your life sometimes feels like, and then he gives you forgiveness and peace."

I walked away from the chapel that day with a new feeling simmering in my heart, and I hoped it would work its way into something I could hold on to. Before the war, I'd thought that religion was about keeping rules and acting happy. But after all I'd been through in Iraq, I was starting to believe that maybe it really *was* about praying more, worrying less, and letting God do the rest.

+

On Monday morning of my last week in Iraq, I received an email from the base command section. It contained a departure checklist, along with a schedule of briefings I was required to attend before going home. I shook my head, wondering how the bureaucrats could think I would have enough time to do all of those things unless they had also sent the enemy an email asking him to stop sending us casualties every day until my checklist was complete.

If they did, the enemy didn't listen.

For the next three days, I worked almost nonstop, as usual. Between Black Hawks and Chinooks bringing us more carnage, I stood in lines and filled out forms and answered questionnaires. One of them was titled something like POST-DEPLOYMENT DEBRIEFING. There were only six questions. Two of them were:

HAVE YOU BEEN IN COMBAT, OR BEEN EXPOSED TO SITU-ATIONS IN WHICH YOU FELT YOUR LIFE WAS IN DANGER?

and

Have you seen or been exposed to things you feel
may be difficult for you to forget or which you
feel may be troubling to you in the future?

There were three choices: Yes, No, and N/A.

If I checked Yes, I could explain my answers on three lines.
I checked Yes. I didn't bother to write in the details.

I didn't yet know that those surveys would be the only questions the Air Force would ever ask me about what I had experienced in the war or how I felt about it.

The last thing on my checklist was to appear at a small clinic near the flight line, where a nurse checked my vital signs, drew some lab work, and signed a form that said I was healthy enough to go home.

Whenever I wasn't standing in a line somewhere, Tim and I performed ten craniotomies in one twenty-four-hour period, and I operated every day and night. Those three days felt like a greatest hits compilation of Warren's Wartime Neurosurgery Experience, because every type of case I knew how to perform showed up, one at a time. Subdural, epidural, and intracerebral hematomas, skull fractures, spinal cord injuries. And one more baby arrived, this one with spina bifida.

Chris and I worked on the baby together, and during the operation Tim scrubbed in to help. "Somebody get that cat outta here!" he said. I smiled under my mask and sighed a little when I realized that this would probably be the last time we would ever work together.

Spina bifida is a birth defect caused by part of the spinal column not forming properly before a baby is born. The lower part of the spinal cord sticks out of a hole in the skin, and if it is not repaired the baby usually develops meningitis and dies. Halfway through the complex operation to repair the baby's spine, Chris shook his head and gave a nervous chuckle. "This operation makes me nervous when we do it in a real hospital. I can't believe we're doing it in a tent."

Just as Chris said that, an explosion shook the operating room and the lights went out. The Alarm Red siren wailed, and we stood there in the darkness. I had been placing a stitch in the baby's nerve sack when the darkness came, and I knew that any possibility that this kid would someday be able to walk would be jeopardized if I made the wrong move.

"Hold on, everybody," I said, "stay calm."

A few seconds passed. Then the backup generators kicked in and the lights came back on. We finished the case as quickly as we could and got the baby to the ICU before the All Clear sounded.

We all shook hands and took a picture together, partly because we knew we might never be together again, and partly because we were pretty sure that operation had never been done in a military hospital in Iraq before.

That night, Tim walked into the surgeons' lounge with a goofy grin on his face and handed me a cigar. "I just got off a webcam call with my wife and watched her deliver our little girl."

I gave Tim a hug. But just as he started telling me all about his daughter, a tech ran in from the ER. "Docs, there's a guy in the ER with a huge brain tumor."

Tim and I looked at each other and shook our heads. What else would this war bring us?

"I'm too psyched to sleep," Tim said. "Go get some rest and finish packing. I'll take care of getting him to Germany."

My attempts to sleep that night were interrupted by more mortars and by a dream that was like a slideshow of every dying and dead person I'd seen in Iraq. A singer provided a soundtrack to my dream, a heavy-metal song with only one line: *Lee, you didn't do enough for me. Didn't do enough for me.*

+

The next morning I awoke to a mortar attack not far outside my trailer. After the All Clear sounded, I dressed and walked to the hospital, starting what I expected to be another Groundhog Day in Iraq. But when I entered the surgeons' lounge, there was a message waiting for me from the commander.

I walked down the hall to Colonel H's office, where I found him sitting at his desk. "Sir, you sent for me?" I said.

Colonel H looked up, took off his reading glasses, and asked me to sit. "Lee, you've done a great job here. I know it was hard for you to come early and be part of two different teams, but you handled it well."

"Thank you, sir."

He pushed a couple of sheets of paper across his desk. "Take a look at these," he said.

I looked down at the papers, silently reading them but not believing what they said. They were my orders to go home.

"Just came in," he said. "You're leaving tonight."

I couldn't believe it. After all this time in Iraq, it almost felt as if I'd always been there. And the reality of what I would face in the "real world" struck me cold and hard. Whatever I thought was going to happen, whatever I might have thought I could control or anticipate would be proven to be fact or fiction, starting tomorrow.

I stared at the orders that would spring me from this place of death and pain and screaming and explosions. A simple piece of paper had the power to send me back to the real world, to normal life. Only I wasn't sure it would ever feel normal again.

"You going to say anything?"

I startled out of my thoughts. "I'm sorry, sir. This is great. It's just that I thought I was here for at least a couple more days. My replacement isn't here yet."

"That's okay, Lee. You've done your part. You survived over a hundred rocket and mortar attacks, and you saved a lot of lives. We'll get by for a couple of days without you. You're dismissed."

I shook Colonel H's hand, saluted him, and walked out into the hospital to say my goodbyes.

I stopped by the physical therapy clinic and found John. His musical talents and love of worship had made him an integral part of the team, and we'd spent a lot of time talking and in prayer together. I'd grown to respect his professionalism as a therapist and his advice as a man. It hit me for the first time then that I would probably never see him again, since he was early in his Air Force career and I was at the end of mine.

"I'm leaving in a few hours," I said.

John turned and said what I'd expected he would say: "Well, then, we need to pray."

In the surgeons' lounge, I found Todd, Augie, and Tim watching television. A story was on an American news channel about how US forces had mortared an Iraqi school in Balad.

A soldier sitting on the couch said, "That's terrible, dishonest reporting. We got permission to fire at that schoolhouse, which was abandoned, because the insurgents were mortaring us from the roof for eight days. We even sent scouts out there to verify there were no civilians around, and they faced enemy fire to get that intelligence. And our news media only reports that we shot at a school! I can't believe it." The soldier stood, shouldered his M–16, and stormed out of the room.

The biased and inaccurate reporting reminded me of the mural in Baghdad showing Iraq's fictitious triumph over America in the first Gulf War. I wondered how many people in America bother to verify what they hear on the news. How often do we believe something just because we read it or hear it on the news? Where did the American news media get this story—Al Jazeera? Or worse, was the media biased to report on us as the bad guys?

We watched the soldier leave, and then I extended my hand to Todd. His excellence and determination to save limbs and lives had been inspiring to me, and I hoped that I would see him again someday. Augie's technical expertise was impressive, and he'd saved the eyesight of dozens of people there. His intellect made for fascinating conversations, although he'd destroyed me in chess more times than I could count. And Tim had been a steady partner and friend, even under the strain of missing his first child's birth.

"It's been an honor working with you men. I'm leaving tonight," I said.

We talked for a while, and then Tim borrowed a car from the command section to help me get my things together. We had dinner at DFAC II, where I bumped into some of the chaplains and Shauna and Andre from the worship team. We cried and prayed and hugged, and Chaplain W said a special prayer for my trip home and my future life: "Lord, bless Lee in his travels, in his reconnection with his family, and in the healing of his heart no matter what he has to face in the coming months and years. And let him remember to let go of worry and hold on to you."

After we finished our goodbyes, Tim let me off at the hospital, because there were two things I still had to do. I hadn't said goodbye to Chris, and I had one more email to send.

+

EMAIL HOME
Thursday, April 28, 2005

My dear friends:

Good news: I just received my orders to come home! For security reasons, I can't say exactly when I'm leaving, but it's soon.

Last night we had the final installment of Movie Night with me as the "Morale Officer." We watched *Napoleon Dynamite*, and it was as stupidly entertaining as always. There were two highlights of the night. First, Todd came. We'd begun taking bets on whether Todd or Elvis would show up at Movie Night first, but since he knew it was probably my last one, he came. He's always been too busy or tired before, but tonight he came, and I have pictures to prove it.

The second highlight was that a mortar round actually hit the roof of the tent during the movie, indented the canvas, and bounced off into the air before it landed by the door of the ER. It didn't detonate, but it scared the dickens out of all of us. EOD came and picked it up, but since they wouldn't let us leave the tent, we finished the movie anyway.

When I actually have time to sit and look back on my experiences in Iraq and write the postscript, I'm sure that some of the things I realize will surprise even me. I am already struck by several things that I never thought would be a part of this, or any part of my life:

I am not a soldier, but I've been attacked and I've been afraid.

I am not a diplomat, but I have been asked to represent my nation and its values.

I am not a man of great power or influence, yet I have had

the opportunity to talk to thousands of people daily about whatever is on my heart, via these emails.

I am not a callous man, but I've been asked to face unspeakable horrors and carry on unaffected, and at times to ignore the terrible tragedy of one person's injuries in order to attend to another person who may have a better chance to survive.

I am not a chaplain, but I have held the hands of dying men as they took their last breaths. I've shed tears and prayed with colleagues who felt they could not take another step, and they have done so for me.

I arrived in Iraq unsure if I could handle what would be asked of me. I depart a seasoned combat neurosurgeon.

I arrived almost broken by months of family struggles, wondering if God had given up on me. I depart unsure of what tomorrow holds for me, but with faith that God will make it right.

I arrived needing a clear picture of things to feel safe and leave convinced that Grace is sufficient for me.

I love you all.

Lee

+

After I sent the letter, I went to the ICU to find Chris, and we sat in the hospital chapel for a few minutes together.

"Lee, I need to tell you something," he said. "You really helped me get through losing Maria. Through this whole time, actually. You made it more bearable to be here."

I wiped a tear and said, "I wouldn't have survived here without you either. And I definitely wouldn't have been able to take care of Mohamed or Rose. It's been an honor to serve with you."

Chris hugged me and shook my hand, and then we just sat and looked at the cross on the wall for a minute or so. I can't say what Chris was thinking, but I was remembering Maria and the seemingly countless soldiers we'd lost or saved together.

A sergeant stuck his head into the chapel; it was time to go.

A few minutes later I was in a concrete bunker where Navy customs agents searched my belongings before allowing me to board a bus to the flight line. There I sat in another bunker for several hours, along with the other lucky people whose names were on the "go home" list.

At long last, the order was given, and we walked out onto the runway and boarded another C–130. On the Tarmac, I saw another group exiting their airplane after landing in Iraq to start their deployment. I had no idea who they were or what their jobs entailed, but I felt a kinship with them because I knew some of what they were about to experience.

I looked out the back of the airplane as the ramp lifted, sealing us inside. The last thing I saw in Iraq was a parked Humvee, its headlights illuminating the runway behind the C–130. I was filled with excitement, fear, sadness, and happiness, all at the same time. The engines started, and their roar almost drowned out my racing thoughts.

The faces of those troops I'd just seen made me remember my arrival in Iraq four months before. I'd been so unaware of the dangers I would face, so unsure of whether I was up to the job about to be set before me. Now I had similar questions, but they related to what would happen a few days later in Alabama.

As the ramp closed and sealed me into the blackness of the C–130, I knew that the Lee Warren who had arrived in Iraq was much more innocent and naïve than the version who was about to leave. And I hoped I could live with the person I'd become.

+

When the ramp dropped at Al Udeid Air Base in Qatar four hours or so later, I stepped off the plane and away from the war, but I knew that a part of me would always be in Iraq.

Al Udeid had seemed so primitive only four months before when I'd arrived there from San Antonio. Now its paved streets, swimming pool, and lack of sandbags and portable toilets were strange sights to my eyes, accustomed as I was to the never-changing backdrop of brown camo and bleeding scalp wounds I'd seen every day in Iraq. The only thing familiar was the roar of the jets from the nearby flight line.

I had to wait in Qatar for several days before I was finally cleared to board the airplane that would take me home. As the distance from Iraq increased, I felt bits of several specific stressors peeling away. I knew that it was unlikely anyone would shoot at this airplane, and that when we landed, there would be no terrorists, no mortar attacks, no ER full of brokenness awaiting me. And yet, as the miles passed, different fears began to bubble up. The checklist of my post-war responsibilities played through my mind, and it seemed much more daunting than the one I'd completed before leaving Iraq. The actual process of starting over in my life at thirty-six years old felt as impossibly unmanageable as the first mass casualty in Iraq had four months before. The difference was: this time I somehow knew it was going to be okay. I couldn't see the steps yet, but I knew I had the strength to take them.

We finally landed at BWI in Baltimore. Walking off the plane into the terminal, I felt almost overwhelmed by the number of people, lights, and stores. Everything had been so monotonous in Iraq; in the Baltimore airport that day, it seemed like a million different things were streaming into my brain. I became a little anxious and was unsure why — until I realized that I'd felt the same way in large crowds in Iraq, afraid of a bomber or a mortar. I told myself I was safe, but my heart didn't believe me for a while.

We had a long layover before my flight to San Antonio, so I found a pay phone to call my children. I was surprised by the dial tone and by the lack of an operator telling me how long I was allowed to talk. Nervous, I dialed the number. After a few rings, my eight-year-old daughter Kalyn answered.

"Hello."

"Kalyn, it's Daddy. I'm back in America."

I heard a slight gasp, and then Kalyn whispered, "Hold on, Daddy."

Next there was a loud crash, as if she had dropped the phone, and a thumping sound for several seconds. Finally, Kalyn picked up the phone again.

"Sorry, Daddy. I was jumping up and down."

CHAPTER 32

AND THEN I LOST MY MIND

You're free to go, Major. Seven days of leave is authorized."

I signed the form and handed it back to the chief master sergeant. I'd just turned in my chemical weapons suit and the rest of the three duffel bags full of gear I'd deployed with.

"Thanks, Chief."

I walked out of the processing center at Lackland Air Force Base in San Antonio, blinking hard in the morning sunshine. Clean air filled my lungs, and I could breathe through my mouth without coughing. The notion that I could go anywhere I wanted or do whatever I felt like seemed almost unbelievable.

Despite all that freedom, there was only one place I wanted to go.

It took two days to get there, and it felt like years. I pulled into the driveway of my kids' house in Montgomery, Alabama, and stepped out of the car. My heart was racing, and I felt a little bit like I might pass out. In a moment that still plays like a slow-motion highlight reel in my mind, I saw my children race out the front door and across the yard toward me—Kimber first, followed closely by Mitch and Kalyn, still in her pajamas.

I fell to my knees, and the kids crashed into me. We fell to the ground, all three of them kissing and holding on to me tightly. Mitch kept touching my face and saying, "Dad, you're really home." I stood, and Kalyn clung to my leg.

I heard another voice say, "Welcome home."

With Kalyn still wrapped around my leg, I turned and saw my wife. "Hello," I said.

I had anticipated this moment and wondered how it would feel, what we would say. She stepped closer, and we awkwardly hugged for a few seconds. Sixteen years of marriage had produced in me a lot of patterned behaviors toward her, and one of them was showing affection in front of the kids. Especially when she was upset, I had tried to show my kids that a husband should be tender and loving to his wife. But that wasn't my role anymore. I had to be consistent and truthful with the kids. We backed apart, and when our eyes met I think we both knew.

+

The kids and I spent a few days together there in Montgomery, building the initial bridges of our new life together as a different family than we'd previously known.

We stayed in a hotel with two queen-sized beds in the room, and every night the kids argued about who got to sleep with me. It didn't really matter, because by morning they were all three in my bed anyway.

"Where are we going to live, Dad?" Kimber asked one evening while I was tucking them into bed.

"I'm not sure yet, honey. Tell you what — tomorrow we'll go look around."

"What about furniture?" she said.

I hadn't thought about that. I didn't have even a folding chair to my name, I didn't know a futon from a fireplace, and I wasn't about to make my kids live in two half-furnished homes. This was going to be harder than I'd thought.

Kalyn said, "Don't worry, Daddy. We can make tents and sleep on the floor."

"Or maybe a fort!" Mitch said.

I laughed. "Okay, tents and forts. It will be fun. Now go to sleep."

That night in bed, I woke to Mitch shaking me. "Wake up, Daddy, wake up!"

I sat up, and for a minute I couldn't tell where I was. I looked for my body armor and didn't find it. The sheets were soaked with my sweat.

"What's wrong, Dad?" Kimber said from the next bed.

I wiped my eyes and pulled Mitch into a tight hug. His hair smelled like fresh air, rather than clotted blood and smoke. He was about the same size as 1954, the Iraqi boy who had died from the car bomb terrorists had tried to drive onto our base a few days after I arrived in Iraq. But Mitch's heart was beating strongly, and his brown eyes looked up at me full of life—and also full of fear at whatever I'd done and said before waking.

"Just a bad dream, honey," I said.

"About the war?" she said.

I nodded. "Yeah, Kimber, it was about the war."

We all tried to go back to sleep. Kimber crawled into bed with us, and she and Mitch never let go of me that night. Kalyn never woke up.

Too soon, it was time for me to leave them again. I drove them to their mom's house, and we hugged and cried and held each other tight.

"I won't let you go, Daddy," Kalyn said while wrapped around my leg like a koala.

"The sooner you let him go, the sooner he'll be back," Kimber told her.

Kalyn's grip loosened a little. She looked up at me and

blinked hard. "And then you'll take us to our new house?" she said with a quavering voice.

I smiled. "Yes, honey, I promise."

Kalyn let me go and stood up. We all hugged again, and I got into the car for the long drive back to San Antonio. I took one last look over my shoulder and saw my past, and my future, standing on the porch together.

As I drove toward Texas, the road stretched before me like the empty canvas of what my life would become. I felt a peace that everything would be okay eventually, but little data with which to answer my millions of questions about how I was going to get there.

In Mississippi, a highway patrolman stopped me for speeding. When I looked in the side-view mirror to watch him walk up, I saw his handgun and for a second I was sure that he would draw the gun and shoot at me like the insurgent in Baghdad. I held my breath as he approached the window of my car.

"License and registration, please," he said.

I opened my wallet and was about to pull out my driver's license, which was behind my military ID. He reached for my wallet and pulled it closer to his face. Then he handed me back my wallet.

"Your hair's awfully short, sir. You been deployed?"

"Just got home from Iraq a few days ago," I said.

Squinting in the sunlight, the trooper stood tall and said, "I'm Sergeant Vaughan, Army National Guard. My unit's going over there soon." Vaughan gave me a crisp salute and made a right face. Just as he stepped away he said, "Thanks for your service, Major. You be safe."

I drove away, happy to have not received a speeding ticket but also worried and sad, because I knew that Sergeant Vaughan was about to see some things I wished I had not. His war was about to start, and mine was almost over.

I still owed the Air Force six weeks.

+

In San Antonio, I stayed in the home of Dennis McDonald, the minister I'd turned to the previous year when I'd first realized how much trouble my marriage was in. Dennis and his wife, Patty, had become like extra parents to me before the war and had sent numerous care packages to me in Iraq. In one of those, they had sent a note that invited me to stay with them if I ever needed to. Now I took them up on it.

Wandering the halls of Wilford Hall Medical Center, where I had worked for four years, I felt unknown. I was the first of my group to return from the war, and nobody else had ever been deployed. There was no one to talk to, and since my date of separation from the Air Force was so close, my squadron commander wouldn't let me work. He placed me on terminal leave and ordered me to spend my days finalizing my out-processing paperwork. Every day I would scratch a few items off the list, while also searching for a new place to live and working on credentialing paperwork for my new hospital in Alabama.

The last thing I had to do before I left Texas was to finalize my divorce. We'd both hired lawyers and worked out the details, and all that remained was for me to appear before a judge to sign the final paperwork.

The night before the hearing, my usual Iraq nightmares were also populated with images of my kids blaming all of their future problems on their parents' divorce, and of every member of my old church lining up on both sides of a street marked "Road to Hell," along which I was walking alone.

The next morning I went to the courthouse and stood before a judge.

Looking down from his bench, a white-haired judge said,

"This divorce is uncontested. The other party has already signed and waived their appearance here today, so all you have to do is sign these papers. Are you sure about this?"

He handed the papers to the bailiff, who handed them to me. I looked down at the form and saw my soon-to-be-ex-wife's signature, and then I picked up the pen. "Yes, sir."

It felt very much like the hundreds of times I'd seen families decide to withdraw life support from an unsalvageable loved one they'd been keeping alive until all the relatives arrived. The decisions had been made long before and the emotions had all been experienced and expressed. Now it was time to flip the switch, pull the tube, and declare it legally dead. In the ICU, these moments are never celebrations, but neither are they usually especially tearful. The tears have been shed, and as the monitors show the heart's last few beats before it flatlines, the prevailing emotion is relief.

I signed the form.

+

On the final day of my fourteen years in the United States Air Force, I was handed a folder by a master sergeant, who shook my hand. "Thank you for your service, sir," he said.

There was no ceremony, no one lining up at the door to say goodbye. I felt anonymous, simply a part of a big machine, a part that had been replaced and discarded. I felt as if I was losing my community, and in a strange way I almost wished I could go back to Iraq. As Lackland Air Force Base's gates closed behind my car, I realized that the rest of my life would be spent outside the wire.

The highway to Alabama felt different this time. Six weeks ago I was married; now I was single. Then I'd been Major Warren the combat neurosurgeon; now I was Dr. Warren the civilian.

I joined a practice in Montgomery, with two good neuro-surgeons who were kind to me. I had an office and a private parking space and a clean white lab coat with my name stitched on the front. It seemed perfect.

The kids and I spent a lot of time together, and every other weekend they stayed with me. They seemed happy and were doing well in school, and I felt like our new little family was coming along just fine. As far as anyone could tell from the outside, it looked like I was back on my feet.

The workdays felt manageable. As long as I was busy, I was fine. But nighttime was a different story. I slept in short spurts of fifteen or twenty minutes. Rarely did I manage more than two or three hours of sleep a night, and every night I startled awake at 2:00 a.m., expecting to hear the fighters on their take-off rolls nearby. When sleep finally arrived, it came with night-mares of terrorists and dying babies and soldiers I couldn't save.

One morning, as I shaved, I realized that the man in the mirror was a man I didn't recognize. My temples were hollowed out, like people in those concentration camp pictures, and my blue eyes had a pale hollowness to them. When I dressed that morning, I cinched up my belt and found that even on the last hole it would not hold up my pants.

I went to the office early and stepped on the patient scale. I weighed 157 pounds, forty-eight pounds below my deploy-ment weight of 205. The last time I had weighed less than 160 pounds, I was in the eighth grade.

That day in the operating room, I picked up a pair of deli-cate scissors used for cutting tissue away from nerves. They didn't feel quite right to me, and I used the microscope to zoom in on them. I saw the problem immediately. "Blades are bent," I said. "That's why they feel funny."

The scrub nurse handed me a different pair. "No problem," he said. "We've got ten more of these in the back room."

I finished my case, thinking the whole time how extravagant it was to have ten copies of the same instrument. I wished I could send some of them to Balad, where I knew the surgeons would use them to save lives. I felt guilty that I was hoarding them all in Alabama to treat somebody's low-back pain.

When I walked past the front desk of the operating room, I heard a heart surgeon cussing out the charge nurse. "How do you expect me to work under these conditions?" he hissed. "I can't do my work if you incompetent people can't give me what I need."

I kept walking, thinking that Todd and his partners in Iraq could do five cases in half the time this guy could do one, with five percent as much equipment, in a tent—and not complain about it once.

I tried to eat lunch in the doctors' lounge that day, but my stomach hurt and everyone at the table was complaining that the food, served on a white-cloth-covered table, was a little too salty or cold or wasn't as good as yesterday's. A group of doctors was arguing about whether Gettysburg really was the turning point in the Civil War, and what they would have done differently at Little Round Top.

I got up from the table to leave, and my partner Bob grabbed my arm. "Hey, why don't you tell those guys what a real war is like?" he said.

"Some other time," I said. "I have patients to see." I walked away, feeling overwhelmed by the excess of food and equipment and opinions. I wanted nothing more than to go to sleep. Except that sleep wouldn't be much safer for me.

That weekend, I had to travel to another state for the wedding of a relative. Most of the people at the wedding had been receiving my emails each day during the deployment, so they seemed to feel as if they already knew me. My sister sat me at a table full of strangers and said, "Everyone, this is Lee. You all read his emails from Iraq. I'm sure you have questions for him." And she walked away to talk to someone, leaving me alone with her friends.

I was taking a bite of wedding cake when a woman said, "What was your worst case?"

I thought, *Lady, you do not want me to answer that.*

As I took a sip of champagne, a man asked, "What does it feel like to watch a soldier bleed to death?"

I thought, *It feels like you're dying too. And like it's your fault. And it's worse than you can imagine.*

+

On the plane home, I tried to make sense of why I'd felt so upset at the wedding and why I was so irritable and reclusive at work. I felt ridiculous, and I told myself that I shouldn't be any different than I was before my deployment. I hadn't even been in combat, after all. Regardless of whether I *should* have those feelings, though, I *did* have them, and they were ruining my life. Since I didn't know what to do, I did what came naturally to me: I pretended that I was fine, stuffed all the memories of the war deep inside, and refused to think about them.

Over the next few months, I worked hard at acting more normal at work. But between patients and operations, I mostly sat in my office alone and stared at the walls.

The kids were happy in their new life with me, and I was happy when they were with me. But at night, between the nightmares and the brief intervals of sleep, I felt alone in the world.

One weekend I had to go to San Antonio for a professional meeting. Dennis and Patty invited me to dinner at their house after my meeting. When Dennis opened the door, he wrapped his arms around me and gave me a huge hug. Patty cried and told me how much she'd missed me. And then their daughter

Lisa stepped around the corner. I knew Lisa before the war, when we sang together on the worship team at our church in San Antonio, and we had a few mutual friends. She is also a professional interior designer, and at Patty's suggestion a few months before I had hired her to furnish my new house in Alabama. But I hadn't known she was coming to dinner that night.

All four of us sat down at the table. Dennis said grace, and we all held hands during his prayer. When Lisa took my hand, I was startled—I felt something in her touch I hadn't anticipated, though I'd been with her in social or professional situations several times before. I didn't really know what it was that I was feeling, but I regretted Dennis's "Amen."

When it was time to leave that night, Lisa walked me to the door. Her hazel eyes caught the light just so, her soft voice had just the right tone, and her gentle spirit had just the right feel. I surprised myself when I said, "Would you like to have dinner with me sometime?"

She cocked her head a little and her eyes narrowed slightly. Her smile didn't fade, but it relaxed just enough that I could have predicted her answer: "I don't think that's a good idea right now."

When I turned to walk to the car, Lisa called, "But you could email me."

After a few months of our emailing back and forth, I realized that I'd never before been in a relationship based purely on communication. We really got to know each other over those weeks because all we had was our words. I found her combination of intelligence, humor, and kindness to be beguiling. And she had her own story of how her faith had rescued her from trouble.

I called her one day and said, "So, since we've been talking for a while now, I wonder if you would reconsider letting me take you to dinner?"

The pause was shorter this time. "Yes. I would like that," she said.

I flew to San Antonio the next weekend and picked up Lisa at her parents' house. She was wearing a pink dress and had her hair pulled back. The last time I had gone on a first date with someone, I was nineteen and felt all the combinations of chemical and societal things that young people confuse with love. Now I had months of deep communication with someone a thousand miles away to make me believe I really knew who she was, and once I looked into her eyes across the dinner table that night in San Antonio, I knew exactly what it was that I felt, and I knew it was for all the right reasons.

I was in love.

I made a few more trips to San Antonio, and eventually we decided to introduce our children to each other. Lisa had Josh and Caity, twenty and eighteen at the time, and they fit in with my three like they'd all grown up together. After a while, my Kalyn and her Caity suggested that Lisa and I should get married.

One night after dinner we danced. When the song ended, I got on one knee and said, "Lisa, will you marry me?"

And so, one Saturday in May, at a little church in San Antonio, I looked up and saw Lisa standing in the back in a wedding gown. I looked into her eyes and smiled as I heard the echo of Chaplain W's words from over a year ago: *Pray more, worry less, let God do the rest.*

We had written our own vows. One line said, "I will love your children not as step-anything, but as my own flesh and blood."

When Lisa said, "I do," I felt a fresh infusion of the peace God had first shown me on the mortared field in Iraq that day when I finally let go of the compulsion to control and worry that I'd held on to so tightly.

I kissed the bride.

The next four years of my life felt as if they lasted only a day. Lisa closed her interior design firm in San Antonio, and with her business experience and my medical expertise, we started a new practice together in Auburn, Alabama. We loved and nurtured each other's hearts, and over time I found myself sleeping all night, with the war's memories only rarely waking me. Each time, Lisa's soothing words would help me push the war away again until it seemed like it might be gone forever. The kids were happy, and it felt very much as if my story was going to have a happy, almost fairy-tale ending.

And then I lost my mind.

✛

CHAPTER 33

UNPACKING
THE BAGS

One night in 2010, Lisa and I were sitting on the couch, flipping through channels on television.

Lisa had clicked through several shows when I suddenly shouted, "Stop! Go back."

I was back in Iraq. On an HBO show called *Generation Kill*, American soldiers in their Humvees had just hit an IED, and Black Hawks were swooping in to rescue them. It was chaotic and noisy and my heart raced as we watched.

One of the actors portrayed a helicopter medic who bravely ran into the fight to help a fallen soldier. "We've got to get him to the hospital," the medic yelled over the cacophony of battle.

"They're taking him to my Balad, to my hospital," I said to Lisa. "Those are the guys I took care of."

For several weeks after we watched *Generation Kill*, I once again had nightmares about Iraq. Yeager bled to death over and over again, despite my efforts to save him, just as he had in real life. I could smell Maria's burned flesh from the firebomb meant for her father. I could hear the screams and the explosions and feel the fear.

One night, I woke up crying. In a cold sweat, I kept trying to find my kids' picture on the bedside table.

"Honey, it's okay," Lisa said. "Lie down. You had another nightmare."

When I realized that I was actually at home, I put my head back on the pillow and rolled over.

"You want to tell me about it?" Lisa said.

"It's nothing," I said. "Just a bad dream. I'm going back to sleep."

I felt as if I were going crazy. Here I was, safe and sound — things were good, in both my practice and family life. I was happy, healthy, and out of the military. I had never shot anyone or been in combat. Why was I still tormented?

While treating real patients, I would daydream about patients I'd treated in Iraq. I became moody and irritable, and the lack of sleep began to affect me on every level.

One day as I was driving somewhere with Lisa, I stopped at a red light. A helicopter crossed the road above us.

The next thing I remember is Lisa saying, "Honey, are you all right?"

I turned to her. My heart was racing, and the driver of the car behind us was honking his horn. "What happened?" I said.

"You stared at that helicopter all the way through a green light," she said.

When we got home, Lisa grabbed my arm and spun me around. "Lee, you have to talk to me. You're having nightmares and zoning out, and you're not acting like yourself. What's wrong?"

I looked into Lisa's eyes and knew she was right. Ashamed, I swallowed hard and said, "I can't stop thinking about Iraq. When I saw that helicopter, I kept waiting for it to turn and land on the highway so I could operate on whoever was inside."

I told her about the nightmares and the daydreams.

She said, "I think you need to start writing down some of the things that happened. It might help you get past it."

I didn't listen.

I continued to have dreams, sleepless nights, and depressed days.

One day at the hospital I bumped into a friend, a psychiatrist. "Steve," I said, "do you have a minute?"

We grabbed a cup of coffee and sat down in the doctors' lounge.

I fidgeted nervously, having trouble getting started, then gave him a thumbnail sketch of what I'd been through and what had been happening lately.

"So," I said at the end of my confession, "do you think I'm nuts?"

Steve gave a gentle smile and squeezed my arm. Then he said, "You have symptoms of PTSD. You should try writing down specific memories you have. It can help you move on."

I nearly choked on the coffee I was trying to swallow. "Come on — you've been talking to Lisa, haven't you?"

He held up his hands. "Not me," he said. "We're not conspiring against you. Writing it down would help you get a handle on everything your mind is trying so hard not to remember."

I shook my head. "How can I have PTSD? I wasn't even in combat."

"No," Steve said, "but you were mortared and rocketed, and you had to sit there every day and wonder when and where the next one was going to land."

I nodded and took a sip of coffee.

"And almost twenty-four hours a day," he said, "you had to see and do things that were horrifying."

"Yes," I said.

"And when you got home from the war, what type of counseling or support did the Air Force offer you?"

I looked down. "None," I said, nodding again.

Steve quietly said, "Lee, I'm surprised it's taken so long for this to come out. What you're feeling is perfectly normal. How long has it been since you looked at the things you brought home from the war?"

"I haven't," I said.

Steve leaned closer. "You mean you haven't even pulled out those things to tell your wife about your experiences?"

"No. They're all still in some trunks in my garage."

Steve smiled. "Then here's my prescription. Go home, get Lisa, and unpack your Iraq bags. Today. Tell her everything you went through, and then write it down."

+

Lisa held my hand when we stepped into our garage that evening after having backed our cars out into the driveway. From the shelves against the wall, we pulled four black plastic trunks down onto the floor. Five years ago I had taped them shut to mail home. There they sat, still taped—I had never opened them. We got on our knees and opened them one at a time.

"What's this?" Lisa asked as she examined the contents of the first trunk.

I took it from her hand. It was a Coke-can-sized plastic jar full of metal objects. I opened it up, dumped the objects in my hand, and stared at them for a few seconds.

"This one is an AK–47 bullet I took out of a little Iraqi boy's head," I said. I could envision the boy, whom we'd called "Lucky," while I told Lisa his story. Lucky had been at a soccer game, and someone had fired the rifle into the air to celebrate the winning goal. The bullet struck Lucky's head but did little damage. Tim and I removed it, and Lucky was able to go home in three days with no long-term damage. Lisa's eyes widened, and she rolled the bullet back and forth between her fingers.

"And this is a piece of shrapnel I removed from a Marine's neck, but I couldn't save him."

As I put the memories back into the jar, Lisa reached for one: a semi-circular piece of metal with grooves on the inside of the curve, and a sharp, jagged edge. "What's this one?" she said.

"That's a piece of a rocket. I was walking to the PX one day and got caught out in the open. I had to hide by a concrete barrier during the mortar and rocket attack. The rocket blew up about two hundred feet away, but I saw this piece land about thirty feet away and decided to bring it home."

Lisa was holding her breath. She slowly put the rocket fragment onto the floor of the garage, then put her hands on my leg. She started breathing again, and tears filled her eyes.

As I rummaged through the contents of those trunks, I found myself reliving the emotions I'd had when I first held them. Unpacking the uniforms and photographs and bits of metal that had been sitting in my garage for years made me feel that I was finally putting the war in its proper place—my past. But it felt like an odd trade—I had hauled a lot of emotional baggage *to* Iraq, and the war taught me to leave it there. Now, here I was physically unloading my trunks in an attempt to work through the mental luggage I'd brought home in exchange.

At the bottom of the last trunk was a USB flash drive. We took it into the house and used our Mac computer to open the files on the drive. It contained several thousand pictures I'd taken in Iraq, along with digital CT scans from many of the patients I'd taken care of there, all organized into file folders.

Lisa double-clicked a file folder labeled "American Surgical Cases," and the little Mac pinwheel spun for a moment on the screen while the folder opened and displayed its contents. She pointed to the screen. "That's odd," she said. "All of these folders are labeled only with their creation date, except for one. Why did you keep this person's name?"

I looked where she was pointing. For reasons I couldn't remember, I had labeled one folder "Statzer, Paul." I clicked on the folder, and Lisa watched as I played her a slideshow of the worst case I'd ever seen.

"How did he do?" Lisa asked.

"I have no idea. The odds were against him. He probably died before he got home."

Lisa typed Statzer's name into her Internet search engine.

I watched, disbelieving, as a video came up of a reporter interviewing Paul Statzer, very much alive.

I was shocked. There he was, missing half his skull, talking about the upcoming operation to rebuild his head. The reporter mentioned that Paul Statzer grew up in and still lives in a suburb of Pittsburgh, where I'd learned how to be a brain surgeon.

The news story explained that Sergeant Statzer had been three feet away from an IED when it detonated and blew off half of his head. He was transported to a hospital in Iraq, where doctors removed parts of his skull and brain and repaired the holes in his neck and face. An unidentified doctor called Sergeant Statzer's family to tell them that he was unlikely to survive long enough to reach Walter Reed.

Lisa took my hand. "Breathe, honey. It's okay."

"Lisa, I was the doctor who called Statzer's parents. Three other surgeons and I operated on him, but none of us really thought he would survive."

"Here's another link," Lisa said. It led to the website of a teenager in Indiana named Alison Mansfield. Alison had started an organization called "Operation US Troop Support" after a fifth-grade assignment led her to discover the story of Sergeant Statzer. I read the story and saw again how the fog of war and the stretch of time can cloud facts. For example, she wrote that a nurse had called the Statzers that night, but I knew it had been me. Probably, the phone call from the nurse came to the Statzers when Paul was in Landstuhl, Germany, before the final flight to Walter Reed.

Lisa and I kept clicking through Ms. Mansfield's website, and we saw pictures of Paul playing golf, meeting congressmen, living his life. I shook my head.

"I can't believe it," I said.

"I think you should email Alison and see if she can arrange for you to talk to Paul," Lisa said.

After a very long few days, we received a reply from Alison Mansfield. She wrote that Paul's father, Jim, would like to speak with me.

So on a Tuesday afternoon at my office, Lisa held my hand while I timidly dialed Mr. Statzer's phone number. After several rings, a man's voice answered: "Jim Statzer."

"Mr. Statzer, this is Dr. Lee Warren. I was the neurosurgeon who operated on your son in Iraq."

"Are you the one who called me that night also?" he said.

"Yes, sir, I am."

After a long pause, Mr. Statzer cleared his throat. "I don't mean disrespect, Doctor," he said, "but before I tell Paul about this I have to be sure this is real. Would you please tell me what I said to you after you told me Paul was alive?"

"I can," I said. "Your exact words were, 'Doctor, by the grace of God, I know my son is going to be okay.'"

Another pause, and Mr. Statzer said in a shaky, hushed tone, "Thank you for saving my son's life."

Over the next several minutes, he filled me in on what had happened to Paul after leaving Iraq. The doctors who treated him at Walter Reed Medical Center believed that his case was hopeless. Mr. and Mrs. Statzer, however, believed that Paul had survived this long for a reason and that his survival should be in God's hands. They fought bravely to get the doctors to try harder, and miraculously, over time, Paul started to show signs of waking up.

Once it was clear that Paul's neurological injuries would not necessarily end his life, neurosurgeons and plastic surgeons began to think about how to reconstruct his horrific skeletal injuries. Through a series of surgeries, Paul eventually had a new skull flap created out of plastic; he had skin grafts and bone grafts to rebuild the area around his missing left eye. After months at Walter Reed, Paul was able to transfer to a rehabilitation facility, where he eventually regained most of his memory and learned how to walk again.

Finally able to go back with his parents to Pennsylvania, Paul was home from the war at long last. He was missing a huge portion of the left side of his brain, as well as his left eye. He had pieces of shrapnel still lodged in his neck.

"As hard as it is to believe that he survived," I said, "I'm truly astounded that he woke up."

Mr. Statzer laughed. "Oh, he woke up all right and started talking, and before very long we knew that this swollen, blown-up man was still our son. Doctor, he's still Paul. He is absolutely still Paul."

And something inside of me said: *Lee, you and your colleagues did make a difference.*

Then Mr. Statzer said, "Doctor, would you like to speak to Paul?"

After several seconds, Lisa nudged me—I was simply staring at the speakerphone. My head was spinning, but I said, "Yes, sir, I would love to."

A few seconds later, I heard a voice I'd never expected to hear in my life say the words that made me understand why I'd been sent to Iraq: "Dr. Warren, this is Paul Statzer. Thanks for being there when I needed you."

Five years after I met him in his most desperate hour, I was on the phone with the most injured, yet still living man I'd ever met. And I found that I didn't know what to say.

"Sergeant Statzer, thank you for your service," I said at last. "It was an honor to take care of you, but I'm even more grateful to be speaking with you."

After we all stopped crying, Paul's mom, Cathy, said, "Would you and Lisa be willing to come to Pittsburgh to meet Paul?"

In April of 2010, Lisa and I boarded a plane in Atlanta, bound for Pittsburgh. I was seven thousand miles and five years away from the 332nd Air Force Theater Hospital in Iraq, but as the plane began to roll I felt like I was going to that dusty ICU to check on a post-operative patient.

I needed to see Paul Statzer, make sure he was okay, make sure I'd done my best. And then, maybe, I could really come home from the war.

✚

CHAPTER 34

LONG JOURNEY HOME

Lisa and I arrived in Pittsburgh at about 1:00 a.m., and I suffered through a few hours of fitful sleep. That night's dreams contained virtually every horrible thing I saw in Iraq.

At noon, Lisa took my hand and we walked into the restaurant lobby. As we rounded the corner, I saw a man wearing a patch over his left eye, carrying a plastic helmet, and standing with an older couple. The left side of his head was caved in, and he held on to his dad's arm for balance.

I felt as if I was running down the sidewalk toward the helipad in Balad, the first place I'd met this man. Only this time, there was no prop wash from the Black Hawk, no bloody gauze around his head, and he wasn't half-zipped into a body bag.

I extended my hand and said, "I'm Lee Warren. It's good to see you again."

He said, "I'm Sergeant Paul Statzer. Thank you for saving my life."

We embraced, all of us teary-eyed.

We sat in the back of the restaurant, and I watched Paul handle a fork and knife while he ate lunch. I had removed more than half of his frontal lobe in Iraq, but here he was, with no discernible weakness or speech difficulties.

Mr. and Mrs. Statzer told us the entire story of Paul's

recovery, with Paul filling in the pieces of his time in Iraq before the IED went off and picking up after he began remembering things again a few months later.

When they were finished, I reached into my bag and pulled out my computer. "Would you like to see what you looked like in Balad?" I said.

Paul looked at Jim and Cathy and then back at me. He slowly nodded. "Yes, sir."

I came around the table, sat between Paul and his parents, and opened my Mac. Lisa stood behind me as I clicked on the first picture. Suddenly, all of us were in Iraq on March 29, 2005.

"This is you coming off the Black Hawk," I said.

Cathy squeezed Jim's hand. Paul's right eye focused on the screen, and I saw the intensity he must have brought to soldiering.

"And this is you as they unwrapped your head." The picture showed a very bloody and swollen man that no one could have identified as the same person sitting next to me. "Let me know if this is too much to look at."

Paul said, "We want to see all of it, Doc."

The next photo showed Paul and me in the operating room, me with a scalpel in my hand and the wounds that earned him his Purple Heart medal very much in evidence.

Cathy's fingertips were just touching her lips, which were moving without making a sound. She shuddered, then reached around me to touch Paul and said, "How did you survive that? How could anyone survive that?"

"Because of the medics," Paul said. "The docs, like Doc Warren here, Mom. Everybody worked hard, and I made it home."

Lisa squeezed my shoulders.

I shook my head. "Paul's recovery is the most amazing thing I've ever seen," I said. "We did our best for a lot of people who weren't hurt as badly as Paul was. Not all of them made it."

Jim said, "Doctor, it's all by the grace of God."

The last slide was a picture of Paul being wheeled out of the ICU, on his way to Germany. "That's all of them," I said. I closed my computer.

With her eyes wet and makeup running down her face, Cathy said, "Doc, you'll never know how much this means to us. We've always known that God had faithful people in place where Paul needed them, and now we've met one of them."

It was time to go. Paul hugged me, and we both cried. He smelled like a regular person, with none of the char and blood and antiseptic he'd smelled of the last time I'd touched him. I touched his collapsed head and the scars from stitches I knew I'd placed in March of 2005. He was so alive, so happy, and so normal after all he'd been through, even though anyone who looked at him could see the external effects of the war. But both of us, I knew, carried wounds in our lives from the events we'd lived through in Iraq that were less visible, yet every bit as real.

"Goodbye, Paul," I said. "God bless you."

"He did, Doctor, by making sure you were there when I needed you."

Lisa and I got on the plane, and as the miles between Paul Statzer and me increased, I felt as though I was getting farther and farther away from the war also. I'd gone to Pittsburgh not knowing how it would feel to meet someone I'd taken care of there and hoping it would answer some of my questions. I got more out of it than that. After months of nightmares, daydreams, and an inability to escape the war's memories, seeing Paul Statzer alive changed my perspective.

Listening to the jet's radio station, I heard one of those cheesy country songs about the red, white, and blue. I wondered if the singer had ever been in the military. I thought about how we live in a country where a song about the war can make somebody millions of dollars, but our injured soldiers struggle to make ends meet. There are people who lost limbs and eyes and private parts for the cause of Iraqi freedom. What type of accounting can make a soldier who has lost his ability to walk with, see, or make love to his wife feel like the country has repaid him adequately for his service?

I thought about Paul. For the rest of his life, he will bear the scars given him by a bomb in Iraq and a bunch of surgeons trying to save him. And despite his faith and his positive attitude, some of his scars resemble some of mine. You can't ever really leave the war behind, but you can come home stronger for having lived through it.

I asked myself a question: *Did I do my best?*

I did for him, I answered.

We were probably over Virginia or North Carolina by the time I got around to understanding why, after all that time, my one hundred twenty-five days in Iraq continued to have such a profound effect on my life. After all, in the final telling of the history of the war, my small role will likely go unmentioned. And yet the war had changed me—the bombs and bloodshed had pushed me to the point of surrendering to the truth that I was a control freak hopelessly unable to control anything at all. Perhaps I was so hardheaded that God had needed to radically alter my environment to get my attention. Or maybe he just saw an opportunity to fix me while providing someone to take care of a few hundred soldiers, dozens of terrorists, and a few Iraqi children who needed a chance.

I had come home from Iraq with no idea what I was going to face but believing in my heart that it would all work out. Of course, it hasn't always been easy—our family has had to deal with the realities of life like any other has. But like the biblical Job, I've been given back more than I ever lost. It's unlikely that Job's renewal erased all the memories or pain from his mind, but it did teach him that as long as you're breathing, you can survive.

I was startled from my thoughts when the wheels hit the runway in Atlanta. We drove back to Auburn, and the next day I started writing.

It has taken me a long time to find the right words to tell my story, but it took George W. Bush and God sending me to the desert for me to understand it. I had to go off to war, experience horrible things, and be bombed almost into oblivion to learn the simple truth of what Chaplain W said: *Pray more, worry less, and let God handle the rest.* It would have been simpler if I had just believed it when Jesus said it in the gospel of Luke: *If you cling to your life, you will lose it, and if you let your life go, you will save it.*

Despite our promises to keep up with each other, those of us who fought our war together really haven't. Pete and Chris came to my wedding, and I hear from John and Shauna and a few others from time to time, but all of us have moved on into our "normal" lives now. I still think about them frequently, and I am proud to have served with all of them. I fly the flag outside my home, carry the VFW card in my wallet, and still cry on Memorial and Veterans Days or when I see the red poppies bloom in the spring that remind me of those who fell for my freedom and those who died in front of me. War is never really in your past; it just stays with you.

The last American combat troops left Iraq in 2012. That war is over, officially. But it still rages in the minds of the thousands of soldiers with PTSD, and in the bodies of the amputees and injured on both sides. And part of it will always be with me.

As I write this in 2012, it has been seven years since I set foot on Iraqi soil. The seven thousand actual miles I traveled to get back here took only a few days. But it took every moment of those seven years, plus telling you this story, for me to finally be able to say I'm home from the war.

AFTERWORD BY PHILIP YANCEY

Like schoolteachers or police officers, doctors slip into the
role society assigns them, and we can hardly imagine their
lives apart from that role. Do they yell at their teenagers? Fall in
love or out of love? Do they ever think about their patients after
hours or perhaps discuss us over coffee with their colleagues?
Do they laugh at us behind our backs? Cry when treatments
fail and we die? Do they feel anything? What goes on behind
that professional mask?

Soldiers are more transparent. Scores of memoirs reveal
in chilling detail what it's like to kill an enemy, lose a comrade, order a drone attack, interrogate a suspected terrorist. We
learn the lingo of abbreviations used ubiquitously in the armed
forces. We listen in on soldiers talking casually about everyday
encounters, any one of which would be the most dramatic event
of our lives.

I have read accounts of war, and I have read (and even written) accounts of medicine from the doctor's perspective. But
when I saw an early draft of *No Place to Hide*, I got a new set of
eyes, the raw vantage of a brain surgeon working in the midst
of hellish combat conditions in Iraq. Outfitted in body armor
and a battle helmet, operating in a tent with minimal surgical
equipment, Major Warren pieced together fragments of skull
and brain from Allied soldiers and terrorists alike, sometimes

with rocket fire whistling overhead and mortars thumping around him. In one day of mass casualties he treated injuries that would have kept him busy for a month in a calm, sterile hospital back home. He was going about the daily business of reassembling human beings.

War is hell, especially this war. Few Iraqis greeted their American "liberators" with flowers. They were more likely to fire at them or bury IEDs in hopes of killing them. Historians will debate the merits of an invasion that spilled so much blood and treasure. Warren's account leaves those issues to others and instead gives the view from the ground up, by a specialist who, devoted to healing, found himself plunked down in the vortex of destruction. Iraqis as well as GIs come to life, their lives intertwined in the terrible dance of war. As another soldier explained, "We treat everybody. We're Americans."

I came across Lee Warren quite by accident. He had read books I had written with the good and great doctor Paul Brand and rather sheepishly sent me a collection he had self-published, a loose compilation of emails, articles, and miscellaneous reflections on his time in Iraq. A lot of self-published books come my way, few of which merit attention and investment from an established publisher. As I read Warren's, I knew it was different. Like Dr. Brand, he treated persons, not bodies — a trait rare in neurosurgeons, who specialize in sifting through data and then barking orders to their assistants. Through Warren's eyes we observe not only the delicate mechanics of brain surgery but also its lifelong effects on real people and their families, both when the surgery succeeds and when it fails.

With some coaxing, in subsequent drafts Warren shed the military doctor's normal reserve and turned the spotlight on himself. He tells of the toll of war on his family. On return to the US he faced the ordeal of reentry. He had to learn not to duck every time a helicopter flew overhead and not to cower at a state patrolman wearing a weapon. Battle-hardened, after daily enduring experiences no one should have to live through, he gradually slid back into the routine of a high-tech hospital with picky surgeons working to address patients' lower-back pain.

Thank you, Lee Warren, for letting us see the world through your own unique vantage point. Thank you for the lives you saved, for the compassion you showed, for the faith you rediscovered, for reminding us of the precious gift of life. May you find the second chance at life that you gave so courageously to others.

ACKNOWLEDGMENTS

That you are holding this book in your hands or reading it on your screen reflects the kindness and extraordinary help I received from many people. For me to simply say "Thank you" would be wholly inadequate. And yet I must try.

God has been so faithful to me, and so patient with my many misguided efforts that got in the way of this story getting out. His grace and mercy have led me safely along the long road home from the war. I pray that reading about my journey will help you with yours.

Several groups and individuals deserve recognition for their roles in bringing this story to the world:

The professors who trained me in neurosurgery each had a hand in saving every life I was a part of saving, and even the people we lost had a better chance because of them. I am so very grateful to have been given such a great education.

To the hundreds of American troops I treated in Iraq — those who survived, those who perished, those who came home whole, and those for whom the war still rages: May these stories help people know what you've done for all of us, and impart a little of what you went through.

To the Iraqi civilians and children I cared for: I pray that my impact on your life was more than the stitches and staples and prescriptions I provided.

To the insurgents, the terrorists, the enemy I treated: I hope that at least some of you have thought, "Those Americans treated me better than I would have treated them." You see, we fight only when we have to, but we would rather reach out, help you up, and befriend you.

To my colleagues at the 332nd Air Force Theater Hospital in Iraq: Your service to our country and to the patients we treated together was inspiring. We went to war together, and all of us came home. I pray that all of you know how much your service means, to everyone.

And to Lisa Warren: When I couldn't sleep, you said, "I'm here." When the nightmares came, you sang to me. When the tears flowed, you shed yours with me. And when it was time to write this down, you demanded that I tell the story of my war. You did it with an iron hand in a velvet glove, and I needed both. Thank you for not letting me quit, not quitting on me, and for loving me through it all.

When I first saw the sunlight flickering in Lisa's hazel eyes, my war-wounded, fibrillating heart began to beat more steadily. For seven years now, I've found something else to love about her every single day, making me excited about spending the rest of my life discovering all the treasures of knowing this one person so completely. I never thought, when I stepped off that plane on American soil, coming home from the war, that I would some-day be able to say, "I am so happy." But I am. Loving me back hasn't been easy, I know, but I'm alive and mentally healthy today because Lisa keeps doing it.

Poets and songwriters have been writing about love since God gave us language. Lisa, I will be writing about ours until I take my last breath. Your love is everything to me. Everything.

Lisa is also the primary reason this book exists, because until she demanded that I start typing, these stories were trapped in my head, coming out only in the nightmares and daydreams of post-traumatic stress disorder. And so what began as therapy for me is now hopefully helpful or at least interesting to you. Thank you, Lisa, for everything.

Keith Leslie, editor of the *San Antonio Christian Beacon*, gave me the first outlet for my Iraq stories, which ultimately led to the decision to turn them into a book.

The actor and peerless artist Darren LeGallo, whose encouraging feedback made me believe that someone other than my wife would want to read my story, extended himself and passed it along to his fiancée, Amy Adams. Darren and Amy, your friendship to us is invaluable, and your belief in this work means more than any business transaction ever could.

Philip Yancey, my favorite writer and spiritual mentor, showed me again what is so amazing about grace. Lisa and I still cannot believe and could never repay you for your kindness.

Dan Raines took a chance on an unknown neurosurgeon with a story to tell and put the weight of his agency behind me.

Meredith Smith suffered through several hundred thousands of my words and patiently coached me into becoming a better writer. The words in this book are much better for her having done so.

Kathy Helmers came all the way to Auburn, Alabama, to decide whether this story had the makings of a book and whether I could write it myself or needed a co-writer.

I said, "Do you think I can do this?"

She said, "I don't know yet. Write me a first draft and we'll see."

Kathy, I'm sorry it took a year.

Kathy also introduced me to Dave Lambert. What a perfect editor for me! Dave took that first draft and led me through the process of producing this book. You're right, Dave: Writing is like opening a vein. But it's worth it.

Sandy Vander Zicht and the entire Zondervan team have

been amazing. Thank you for believing in this work, and for giving it to the world.

To Josh, Caity, Kimber, Mitch, and Kalyn, my wonderful kids: Thank you for your patience and tolerance during all the times I said, "I've got to write today."

As I said, "Thank you" is inadequate. You've all done more for me than I deserved.